MEMORIES

Thomas Johnston

MEMORIES

By

THOMAS JOHNSTON

COLLINS
ST JAMES'S PLACE, LONDON

FIRST IMPRESSION   OCTOBER, 1952
SECOND IMPRESSION   DECEMBER, 1952

Acknowledgment

The portrait of Mr. Johnston which
appears as a frontispiece is a Scottish
Tourist Board photograph. The lines
taken from *The Exiles* by Neil Munro
are reprinted by kind permission of
the author's trustees.

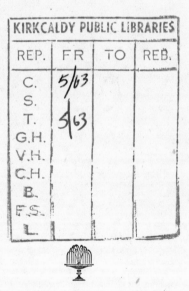
PRINTED IN GREAT BRITAIN
COLLINS CLEAR-TYPE PRESS: LONDON AND GLASGOW

CONTENTS

Contents

PART THREE

PROLEGOMENA

WHEN ANDREW MELVILLE with two companions visited George Buchanan at Edinburgh in the autumn of 1581, the year before the great scholar's death, they found him teaching his servant the alphabet. After salutation, said Andrew Melville to Buchanan:

> "*I sie, Sir, yie are nocht ydle.*"
> "*Better this,*" quoth he, "*nor stelling scheipe
> or sitting ydle quhilk is as ill.*"

Now (though scheipe stelling is not phonetic middle Scots for sheep stealing) I am afraid I can offer no such gambit as excuse for filling up my few leisure hours in collecting and selecting reminiscences of a long and not inactive life in public affairs. The pages which follow have been compacted solely for my own amusement and entertainment. They are coloured no doubt with some propaganda for my personal convictions or—perhaps—prejudices, and they are now published in the hope, however ill founded the hope may prove, that through them an audience not only of my generation may be intrigued, encouraged or amused.

This volume is not an autobiography. An autobiography is usually, if not always, a vanity; episodes and incidents, perhaps unimportant to everyone but the chronicler, are paraded, the more especially should they flatter his self-esteem, while struggles in which he was worsted or played a more or less humiliating part, are trimmed in the telling, if told they be at all.

Nevertheless in any collection of reminiscences the narrator must be announced and have his background explained. He must have a *compère*, or be a *compère* for himself.

Whatever therefore of Scottishness and the pride of it obtrudes in these pages, may be linked with and traced back to the warrior reivers who for centuries kept the Scottish Border, bore the brunt of every English invasion, and preserved Scotland's integrity. William Camden, the Englishman, and George Buchanan, the Scot, were in their day—the sixteenth century—

7

rated as considerable historians and men of learning; and Camden, who tells us that he browsed over original rolls and records so that, as he said, " the honour of verite might in no wise be impeached," averred of all the Border clans that the Johnstouns were the " most noted," while both Camden and Buchanan described the Johnstouns as the most important of the clans of the west—the great obstacle to English conquest—and that the King of Scots could always depend upon them for prompt service, loyalty and patriotism.

There is of course another angle of vision on the matter. Originally the family motto on the crest of the Johnstons of Annandale was the somewhat dubious one of " *Light Thieves All*," but this was later changed to the more appropriate, or at least more polite wording: " *Nunquam Non Paratus* " —" Never Unprepared! " Nevertheless it was of the early seventeenth century that Aikman, who added some volumes to Buchanan's History of Scotland, could write:

> " The debateable lands which had hitherto afforded the freebooters an asylum were divided and appropriated to each kingdom. Yet many years elapsed ere they were brought under a proper subjection to the laws; and the thieves of Annandale, till the labours of the persecuted ministers after the Restoration introduced among them a knowledge of religion and morality, continued to harass and rob the western borders."

Such then was the reputation and police record of the Johnston clan until the seventeenth century—they and the Elliots, Maxwells, Jardines, and their like.

Colonel Walter Elliot tells a story of how upon one occasion an English army crossed the Border into Scotland, the Scots adopting an early version of the scorched earth policy, hurriedly evacuating themselves, their live stock and all their belongings to remote fastnesses in the hills. But by some mischance a small child had been left behind. That child—a girl—was the invaders' only capture. The soldiers plied her with questions, but all in vain. At last they produced their chief ecclesiastic, a bishop—he being of benign appearance it was thought was more likely to extract information from the child—yet still without result. At last the Bishop in despair asked:

" Are there no Christians here? "

To which came unexpectedly the answer:

" Nae, Sir. There's nane hereaboots. Only Johnstons and Elliots."

But if the Johnstons were not civilised, or if they had not had vouch-safed to them a knowledge of religion and morality until a century after the Reformation, well anyhow they shared the blackout in a goodly com-

8

pany. Also they kept the Border, and in the fullness of time, and with their newly acquired knowledge of religion and morality some of the Border clansmen birsed north into Lanarkshire and Stirlingshire and took to upland sheep farming, becoming as civilised as their neighbours.

But the narrator has another main stock pedigree, Ulster-Irish Alexanders. Immigrants via Wigton and Glenluce: " Sma' folk," but respectable, and at least so far as is known, always strong for the orthodoxies, sometimes moving about among the Men of the Covenant, throwing up now and again a kirk elder or an innkeeper. The Alexanders too had marched north and from them would come my earliest memory of a bogeyman in politics —a man called Gladstone, who was in cahoots if not with the Devil at least with the Pope.

And now, borrowing from the switch-over jargon of the B.B.C. sporting commentators: Over to the little burgh of Kirkintilloch on the Stirling-Dunbarton border in the closing years of last century.

T. J.

*If we interlace merriness with earnest matters, pardon us, good reader;
for the fact is so notable that it deserveth long memory.*
— John Knox. *The History of the Reformation in Scotland*

*All ye that are present, if you will be liberal towards me, I will tell
you what follows.*
— *The Adventures of Hajii Baba of Ispahan*

*What is to be done for thee? wouldest thou be spoken for to the king,
or to the captain of the host? And she answered, I dwell among mine
own people.*
— *The story of the Shunammite woman, 2 Kings iv, 13*

PART ONE

CHAPTER I

BY THE WALL OF LOLLIUS URBICUS

This is my country
The land that begat me
These windy spaces are surely my own,
And those who here toil
In the sweat of their faces
Are flesh of my flesh
And bone of my bone.

—'*Scotland*,' *Professor Alexander Gray*

258 92

THE EARLIEST preferment or honour ever conferred upon me was when a wheezy, half-ragged negro in charge of two elephants, at a circus which visited our town, graciously permitted me to carry pails of water for him. A later circus visitation, I remember, had an outside boxing tent where village boys who could stand up for two rounds with the proprietor's son got threepence and a burst of applause. I got neither the threepence nor the burst, only a bloody nose, and the tale of my exploit carried home by some busybody, where a rather dim view was taken of the episode.

There were occasions too when we had a visit from strolling players. The late Will Fyffe's father was business organiser for a touring team who came with 'The Dumb Man of Manchester,' 'Reddy's Bonny Dochter,' and such-like thrillers, and, especially on a Friday night when our colliers got their wages, a lachrymose piece which never failed: 'The Collier's Dying Child.' He staged, too, for the class which my friend David Kirkwood would have called the intelligentsia—'Hamlet,' 'Rob Roy' ("in which a local townsman will positively appear in the leading characterisation"), and 'The Escape from Siberia.' The 'Escape' was a great favourite, especially the discomfiture of the secret police and the last act declamation by the Tsar that henceforth he would, God willing, model his life upon the precepts and example of the good Queen Victoria! On one occasion though, the 'Escape' was rather spoiled when a local banker's son, badly stage struck, was rowing across a Siberian lake, howled at by wolves in

13

the wings, and with snow (white confetti) falling all around him; the escapee's was an easy part; what he had to do was to pretend to row, and as he rowed to cry in a loud voice: " I will escape them yet "; but suddenly the boy in the rafters who was spraying the snow fell, confetti bag and all, plumb upon the top of the rower, and the curtain had to be dropped for first aid repairs to the escapee from Siberia!

One other incident about Fyffe's travelling ' Gaggie,' and which many years later, to his great amusement, I recalled to Will Fyffe. The gaggie shed or theatre was built of wooden partitions and while a glaring oil lamp illuminated the entrance door and pay box, the rear of the structure was in Cimmerian darkness. It was a dark winter's night; the play was ' Hamlet '; a venturesome but impecunious pioneer called Bryce had prised open a board at the rear of the hut and crawled in to a free seat; he was followed one after another by a hundred or more equally impecunious but anxious patrons of the drama; the play started; the hall was filled; everything was going well until the graveyard scene when Fyffe *père* stamped angrily on to the stage shouting: " Put up them lights! " When the lights went up the proprietor delivered himself in expostulation thus: " Ladies and gentlemen—and others. This hall tonight is filled to capacity, yet my total drawings are eighteen and sevenpence. How the hell is it done? " Nobody ventured with the answer!

As was proper and fitting in an old burgh built upon the wall of Lollius Urbicus, and with Roman coins and altars continually being thrown up around us, we were subject to much lecturing upon local antiquities, and I remember being specially thrilled by speculations that the Syrian bowmen who left their tablets on the nearby Bar Hill were the first cohort of the Hamii who mayhap had in their ranks men whose fathers, uncles, or grandfathers, were soldiers present at the trial and execution of Christ.

But sometimes we appeared not to be so highly rated and esteemed in the world as we had flattered ourselves we were; and once during the second world war I was taking a train from Baker Street to Harrow on the outskirts of London, when there entered my compartment a young navyman; he appeared to be in some perplexity over a map of London; I volunteered to assist: " Can I help you, Jack? " He looked up and smiled almost incredulously: " Gees, are you frae Scotland? "

Quite pleased that my accent still held good I replied: " Aye, and what part of Scotland do you come from? "

" Oh! A come frae Glesca; and whaur, Sur, dae you come frae? "

And I, with pardonable pride in the antiquity of my burgh, which was a St. Ninian Settlement when Glasgow was a swamp, replied " Kirkintilloch "—and just left it at that.

"Kirkintilloch," speculated the navyman. "Noo whaur hiv a heard that name? Oh, aye, I mind; it's on the road tae Campsie Glen whaur Benny Lynch was trainin'."[1]

There was at least one occasion in my youth when it was decided to add surreptitiously to our antiquities. A church hall was being built; the leading elder was a well-known enthusiast in all good causes, and the convener of the hall building committee, another elder who was well qualified to fall for an ingeniously contrived hoax. So James Slimman, the poet (whose "Burns Centenary in the Poorshouse" later attracted wide attention), a hosiery manufacturing uncle of mine, and two or three *farceurs* decided to plant a Roman slab in the soil which was to be turned up for the church hall foundations. A stone slab was got; I was sent into the Hunterian Museum in Glasgow to collect an appropriate inscription or two of the reign of Antoninus Pius. When these were cut upon the slab it was boiled in copper in an iron boiler to give it the appropriate colouring, and then at dead of night the slab was buried in the church hall site. The builder, who was in the plot, arrived on the scene next morning and appropriately guided his navvies to a timely excavation. Great was the subsequent excitement. There were interviews with learned F.S.A.'s from Edinburgh, and a Glasgow newspaper gave the discovery a great view-halloo with drawings. As treasure trove, I suppose it could have been claimed by the Crown, but somehow that claim was submerged in a ding-dong battle between the local authorities and elders for ownership, and in the midst of the turmoil the venerable relic of antiquity unaccountably disappeared, *spurlos versenkst*!

Many years afterwards it turned up at a local bazaar in a glass case with an inscription that it was kindly lent by the then proprietrix. And for aught I know to the contrary it may now be in some American millionaire's collection awaiting either a new cataloguing or a hydrogen bomb from Muscovy.

It was, as I recollect, a cruel generation of boyhood, that one which flourished in the late eighties and the early nineties of the last century: a time before the naturals and simples and half-wits were all certified off to institutions, and a time when rude, cruel, thoughtless boys were free to make frolic and sport of them. We had, as I am sure all Scots burghs had, quite a collection of these misfits and freaks. One old man who wore a petticoat, and who shovelled coals into domestic cellars for a living, achieved more than a local notoriety. Petticoat Dan, as he was called, for some unknown reason always reacted angrily to shouts of 'Skeedlar!' accompanied by rude windy noises; and he threw coals at and chased tormentors with uplifted shovel. There was Woodilee Mick too, who could always be

---

[1] Benny Lynch, lightweight boxing champion.

15

incited to cry: "Some day I'll go away and never come back," and a whole horde of characters with opprobrious nicknames like "Oafie Tam" (a rhymster) and "Midden Wull."

Religious revivals swept us periodically. There was, of course, the annual Orange turn-out on 12th July, when Swanky Semple would put on his pit buits "to fight for an unchained bible," and a band would march through the town playing "Kick the Pope" and "Boyne Water," while the local priest strove manfully to shepherd his fighting men into bye-ways.

But the real emotional frenzies with their penitent forms and testimonies and hot gospelings were exciting while they lasted. Once a woman called Maggie McPhee was converted and an announcement made that she would, at a succeeding séance, give her emotional experiences. Maggie, whose cross, borne with more or less fortitude during her wedded life, had been a rather shiftless husband, drew a crowded attendance for her testimony; and it was a sheer if unexpected delight to the more irresponsible elements in her audience when she began clasping her hands in prayer and looking skywards in the most approved petitionary fashion, and in a shrill voice crying: "Oh Lord, but it's hard hard tae be a Christian and merrit tae Sanny McPhee!"

Those too were the days when the detestable habit of chewing tobacco was prevalent (one good thing about the cigarette is that it has killed the 'chow') and the streets were often bespittled almost like Bombay with its *Pan Supari* juice expectorations. And once, when Dick Letford the poacher was converted, he too drew a crowded house for his testimony. As I recollect the gravamen of his effort, it was that: "praise the Lord he had now stopped swearing for a week, and whenever the wee bit thin black twist he had left was finished he would stop the chowing too."

In this delayed moral amendment action Dick had some good precedent. Did not honest old John Bunyan in his Pilgrim's Progress preface say: "Another thing was my dancing. I was a full year before I could quite leave that."

Years afterwards I once, as a magistrate, had Dick before me on a charge of stealing a duck belonging to an Englishman called Jonathan Beck. Jonathan's evidence, entirely unsupported, was that Dick had been seen among his 'jeuks,' and that thereafter one was missing. But Dick swore an oath that he had not touched a 'jeuk.' The only possible verdict was 'not proven,' yet after the trial when Dick, discharged with only previous stains upon his character, was asked by a young clerk of court: "Did you really steal Jonathan's duck, Dick?" "Aff coorse," retorted Dick with scorn, "A' have his 'jeuk' in ma guts!"

By the Wall of Lollius Urbicus

One great institution of our childhood was the Band of Hope. It met on Friday evenings and provided an occasion for the appearance of old gentlemen with magic lanterns showing entrancing pictures of mice being poisoned in beer, and of dipsomaniacs, wife and child beaters, being ultimately buried in paupers' graves, or hanged for murder committed while under the influence of the demon Rum. Once or twice there arrived an old fellow with a board upon which were stuck a dozen candles, and after a discourse upon "let your light so shine," one candle at the end of the board was lit, and from it the light was dexterously passed to the other candles. The process was simple enough but was rather spoiled when two bad boys, of whom I was one, surreptitiously wet the wicks so that they refused to light. The other bad boy was one George Whitelaw who later became an eminent press cartoonist in London.

Of the Sunday school I have no great memories but that we maintained, or at any rate were supposed to maintain, a coloured brother at an African Mission School. The coloured brother went by some such name as Tababeer, and it was a sore point to many that this dusky child of Africa should be steeped in the luxury of our pennies while Cheuch Jean at her little shop in the West High Street, should have splendid sticky balls for sale, and we go without.

CHAPTER II

STRIFE AND SCHISM

He shall be an exile from everyplace where habitations are built,
where the waves mount with the wind, and where the karle sows corn.
He shall be driven far from the church and christian men, and far from
every abiding place, save Hell.

—*Archæologica Scotia III. Cure for the breaker of the peace*

I HAD just gotten myself at the age of 21 on to the local government electors' roll, as a lodger, when my chums and companions, none of whom had a vote, decided I should be put up as an I.L.P. candidate at a School Board Election. Another man, who later became the first Labour provost of our town, was to run in double harness with me. The election was fought upon the old cumulative vote system whereby if there were seven seats an elector could give all his seven votes to one candidate, or he could distribute them in any proportion he chose among the candidates. The system was P.R. gone crazy, or if you like, gone crazier, and it had some curious electoral results. At that particular election there were eight candidates for seven seats. I scraped in at the bottom of the poll and my partner in propaganda, Tom Gibson, was out.

Then the fun began. Possibly to keep me quiet and out of mischief I was installed as Convener of the Board's dud committee, the Evening Classes Committee, where I was expected to sign the registers of a winter's evening and witness the spectacle of sparse attendances of unwilling pupils, mostly possessed of a grievance against a parental authority which had decreed they should be barred twice or thrice weekly from fish and chip shops or horse-play in the streets, and ordered instead to improve their minds with mathematics or parsing (*i.e.* disembowelling) English. And yet, surprisingly enough, it was to be these evening classes which were to be the cause of much strife and schism in our community, and not the feeding of necessitous school children. Feeding these children had been a major election 'issue,' but somehow it became later a matter of almost general agreement. During the election we had been solemnly advised that to feed the drunkard's child would be an encouragement to the drunkard to drink more (and by parity of reasoning to allow the drunkard's child to starve would diminish the drunkard's thirst!); but in the end good sense and economics triumphed when the teachers protested the impossibility of imparting knowledge, or for that matter of it giving bible lessons, to a child who had had no breakfast. And we got an attendance officer who turned up trumps, and who later became a positive genius at buying large quantities of boots and clothing wholesale, despite some attempted frustrations by local merchants. Our necessitous child arrangements were first class, and attracted eager enquiries from other Boards; and some of our original opponents became enthusiastic supporters and displayed considerable pride in showing visitors round our public kitchen!

But it was on the evening classes that I blotted my copy book and roused the furies. An initial venture of a dancing class passed without great misgiving. I had conceived the idea of attracting increased Government Grants through increased attendances, and to get these increased attendances I had taken a public hall and started a dancing class to which young men and young women in regular attendance at another evening educational class under the School Board got admission free. Dancing pupils could choose their own education class—maths, sewing, English, mining, building construction, whatever they willed, and attendance at one of these classes procured a free ticket for the dancing class. We had a first class band, a first class dancing instructor, and the pupils themselves had to form their own governing committee to maintain discipline and order. Indeed the order maintained was draconian, any exhuberant being promptly and roughly conducted by a frog's march to the open air; the students' Committee took its duties very seriously. The experiment was a great success, and we had to limit the first dancing class to one hundred dancers. *Pari passu* the other education classes shot up in number.

Mothers sent letters of thanks in that they no longer feared for their daughters dancing at disreputable howffs; the ratepayers were saving money; further education was being promoted; we felt as if we were on top of the local world.

But alas, pride went to the predicted fall. I went farther and fared worse. I started a boxing class, calling it at first by the better sounding title of physical culture class. There were Swedish gymnastics, wrestling, and Indian club exercises, as well as sparring with gloves, but sparring and how to excel in it was the principal attraction, and so the class became known as the Boxing Class. The principle was the same as was being successfully operated in the dancing class; one attendance at an education class under the School Board secured a ticket for attendance at the boxing class.

Memories

We began with the bells ringing for us. The Drill Hall was taken; the first night the hall was filled to capacity and numbers were turned away; we had an accomplished instructor; and a local manufacturer—himself a skilled performer with the gloves—offered gold medals as prizes. Contestants on the first evening who disclosed holes in their socks or ragged or dirty undergarments only came so circumstanced once. Our education classes had to be duplicated: the rage for learning in circles which had hitherto resisted all the allures and appeals of educationists became almost phenomenal. We made a surplus on our continuation classes as a whole; the Education Department in Edinburgh played up splendidly, their inspectors becoming keenly interested in the boxing class project, and we actually got a Government Grant which amounted to half of our expenditure—upon everything from boxing gloves to Indian clubs!

But by this time, alas! the Kirks had been roused. Elders held meetings and we were denounced from pulpits with bell, book and candle; foremen in public works interviewed young apprentices and strongly 'advised' against attendance; letters showered upon the local press condemning our wickedness in teaching violence and bloodshed, and asking sarcastically when we were going to start breeding whippets, and teaching faro and roulette; clerical deputations waited upon members of the School Board, some of whom got windy; and the poor boxing (or physical culture) instructor, unable to stick it out, packed up and went off in disgust. It was in vain I had cried aloud that Glasgow University taught sparring; so did Ayr Academy: a Glasgow evening class had risked it too, and I went about with a quotation (upon which I am now unable to lay my hands!) from Dr. King Hewison, the great authority on the Covenanters, that they also had taught sparring. But I might have saved my breath to cool my porridge. The Holy Williams were too much for us; an experiment in higher—because more widespread—education had failed. Our embryo Eddie Beatties and Bennie Lynchs remained in embryo, and numerically our evening classes sagged again.

CHAPTER III

A TOWN'S AFFAIRS AND A
NEW TECHNIQUE

*... it is well that the traces of our old burghal history should be recorded,
ere we lose altogether our identity, and, swallowed up in some amorphous
agglomeration of city precincts—we a community that existed in pre-
Roman times when Glasgow was unknown, we who had a Christian
settlement before Columba was in Iona—are become a mere Post
Office district, a W.1. or a C.11.*

—*Prefatory dedication note to ' Old Kirkintilloch*

BEFORE 1929, at which date we were County Councilled, we had local
government; our town councils were held at night and we had a wide
range of choice in our councillors. Today so much of our business is conducted furth of the town and at daytime meetings, that we have lost a
large choice of vigorous personnel for our representatives, and have
in part substituted either a professional delegate group, who require the
allowances for time off from their daily avocations and whose employers
can afford to let them go, or in part a brigade of retired or ornamental
personages whose time is their own. Local newspapers do not report
County meetings as they used to report local meetings with their back-chat
and argument. Public interest has suffered in consequence.

Our local town council in the days of my youth was just of the right
size, twelve of us, and I have abiding memories of a Cleansing Committee
when we used to sit around a table and ruminatively chew horse beans,
thereby testing the quality of various tenderers for our custom, and protecting the town's horses from an inferior food supply. That at least was
the idea, but one observed that the councillors with false teeth did not
chew much, and any determinations they gave were therefore based upon
insufficient data. We had too as our Sewage Committee convener, an active
and genial coal merchant who invariably appeared at Council meetings
showing an elaborate expanse of stiff white shirt cuff, over hands from
which the grime of his daily employment had been imperfectly removed.

His impromptu speeches were a pure joy—"I did not ettle for to speak tonight for I have nothing proper thunk out," and so forth. But we had just missed the brave days of water works inspections before the town went dry by popular vote and shut all the public houses—the days when only fifty per cent of the inspectors would see the water works; the others took their whisky neat, or at least so it was no doubt sometimes libellously averred.

We did not feel unduly bound by use and wont; we pioneered. Thus before the war of 1914 there were disputations in our little realm over the non-democratic and wholly indefensible hour at which our police courts were held. Courts were held always of a morning, involving loss of time to a magistrate and to witnesses, both for prosecution and defence, and indeed interfering with justice itself, since potential witnesses to, say a street fracas, simply faded away whenever the police arrived, rather than give a testimony which necessitated loss of a day's work and wages.

To some extent public order was maintained extra-judicially and without witnesses by Sergeant Marr, "Big Geordie," who, a terror to evil doers and malefactors from the Ledgate to the Blackha', meted out justice of the high, the middle, and the low, with the aid of a little knobby cane stick. He too in his way was a pioneer, for he forestalled Mussolini. Once in Toddy John's public house, a character of ill repute had purloined a half sovereign. He was held and searched for the coin, but without avail. Big Geordie however shepherded him to the police station and despatched a messenger for a full bottle of castor oil; this was duly poured down the suspect's throat in the expectation that the coin had been swallowed. The expectation was justified and the coin recovered, Geordie claiming three-pence for his out of pocket expenses.

But these and other methods of trial by ordeal had to go, and finally—the sensible thing to do—we held our police courts in the evenings or the late afternoons, to the general public advantage.

About that period, early 1914, we broke out into Municipal Pictures. We had of course no statutory power to run pictures—the tablets of the law on the subject were frequently and solemnly laid before us—but there was nothing the Town Clerk could find in the law books to stop the Council fitting up its Town Hall with cinema projectors, screens, and all the appurtenances, and letting the hall so equipped to a small group of councillors who chose to call themselves an Entertainments Committee, and who hired a spare time manager. The success was immediate and beyond cavil. We reduced admission charges by from 25 per cent to 33⅓ per cent. Out of profits we provided to the children of the town, free Christmas treats, galas, and fêtes, with 600 prizes for the sporting events, and at one fête nearly provoking a riot among the contestants, there not being a prize for everybody. Again, out of profits from our cinema we brought first class lecturers and Beecham opera artists, and we imported the best army bands to play in our public park. Had we not so spent the bulk of our profits— we had in addition by the year 1920 handed over to the Town's Common Good Fund £1,043—I shudder to think of what the income tax authorities might have got away with. But these things were of the days before P.A.Y.E., and perhaps it was just as well that we were not an orthodox municipal committee, and were outside the *lex municipia*, for there were occasions when it was considered advisable that we should have some untrammelled capital to operate with, as for example when we bought surplus civilian suits of clothing and army kilts from Bradford at phenomenally cheap rates and retailed them, without profit, to our citizenry. The suits we bought at 50s. plus carriage from Bradford; we retailed them at 52s., and splendid suits and material they were. The Provost always wore one when he was giving official interviews, saying it gave him elegance and dignity.

One amusing memory of these Pictures during the war! It was a Saturday night; the hall was packed. There were music hall ' turns ' between the Pictures. Suddenly into the side room there blew the Provost and a tall dignified gentleman who was introduced to us as Lord Strathclyde, a great senator at the Courts of Justice, and a strong advocate of silver bullets (financial) for the war. We were informed that his Lordship would go on the stage and make a speech. The Committee protested that the audience had paid for their entertainment, and that silver bullets would be an unlikely result of breaking faith with them. But reason was of no avail, up went the lights in the middle of a Charlie Chaplin or a Fatty Arbuckle film, and the Provost and Lord Strathclyde stalked on the platform. The Provost's introduction passed in stony silence, but the storm, or rather the cyclone, broke whenever the silver bullet orator began. Yelling, cat calling, and " away to the Canal with him "; other disagreeable destinations indeed were loudly specified, and finally the poor gentleman could suffer it no longer, and with eyes staring in consternation he staggered to the wings, where a small Jew comedian from Glasgow, painted and attired like a tramp, stood waiting his call.

" What's wrong? " cried his Lordship. " What has happened? I've never been treated like this before."

" Awa', ye silly mutt," sneered the comedian, thinking his Lordship was only another ' turn,' " dae ye no see you've got the burd? "

CHAPTER IV

MUNICIPAL MEMORIES

Is this supremely successful experiment to remain unique? ... Have we indeed reached the limit of what municipal enterprise should be allowed to attempt, if we confine it to a single town? For my part I would as soon endeavour to imprison a volcano.

—*The Rt. Hon. Neville Chamberlain in his Preface to 'Britain's First Municipal Bank'*

WE PROCEEDED to apply our new technique of the non-statutory committee in municipal enterprise to Banking. Had we sought to go through the hoops that Lord Mayor Chamberlain and his Birmingham City Council had to jump ere they got their parliamentary powers to start a municipal bank we should have been jumping at these hoops still, and with a pretty bill in legal obfuscation for our citizens to meet. So we first decided as a Council, by a majority, in favour of the principle of municipal banking; no harm in that! Then we started a private Limited Company among such councillors as would join and pay 1s. for a share; again nobody could stop or interdict that! The private company was registered as The Kirkintilloch Municipal Bank Limited and the paid up capital was 7s. Every shareholder among the seven of us was pledged to hand over his share scrip to his successor when he demitted his councillorship. There was to be no profit earned, no directors' fees, no shareholders' dividend. The cost of floating the Company was £40 and a loan from the Common Good Fund of the town met it.

The *modus operandi* was simple. The new bank directors contracted for a nominal sum per annum with the Council (that was, themselves, in another capacity) for the use of the town's office, safes, and burgh treasurer's staff. A name-plate was put up on the office door: ledgers and passbooks completed our expenditure. Then we set out to explain to our citizens that when they in the past had deposited their savings in a Post Office or Trustee Savings Bank they got 2½ per cent interest. But when the Town Council (that is the representatives of the aforesaid citizenry) borrowed money for gas works or public parks or water works or any other statutory purpose they were compelled to pay anything from 3½ per cent upwards, and for temporary and short period borrowings as high as 5½ per cent. It was obvious therefore that if the citizens lent themselves money at 3 per cent they, the lenders, would gain ½ per cent, while the citizens as a whole, if they could borrow at 3 per cent plus a trifle for working expenses, would save large sums of money in interest every year. The bank was only a conduit pipe; the municipal treasurer was chief officer of the Bank, and he immediately transferred any monies deposited with him to some municipal department with the security of the rates behind it. Depositors therefore were absolutely guaranteed as to repayment. At the end of every year the Bank Treasurer and the Burgh Treasurer (the same individual, and whose integrity was covered by insurance anyhow) calculated what interest at 3 per cent was due to be paid by the Town Council to the Bank. When that was paid over the Town Council had borrowed cheaply and depositors had got ½ per cent more than formerly, and plus the trifle for working expenses.

The thing worked without a hitch; money poured in to us at 3 per cent; with this money we paid off the 5½ per cent lenders; we saved the town 3*d*. in the £1 on the rates, and ever since 1919 that Bank has functioned and no councillor of any party ever proposes to abolish it and add to the rates. A dear money cry would win no elections.[1]

The one question we had to face was, what would happen if there was a run on the Bank? It was not sufficient for us to argue that lenders would not be in the least likely to panic, since all their money was invested in their own waterworks, gas works, roads, etc., and if they withdrew their capital all that would result would be that the Town Council would require to borrow in a dearer market, and local rate burdens would be increased. That was sound logic and good psychology, but it was not enough; and so we got the S.C.W.S. directors to say that in such a crazy eventuality they would cheerfully lend us the necessary cash with good sound municipal securities behind it to meet a ' run.'

Other burghs followed suit—Irvine, Clydebank, Motherwell, Peebles, Selkirk, Cumnock, among them: Motherwell alone in eight years had deposits of £315,000—and I was introduced to public meetings as chairman of one of the Scottish Banks, and no doubt perhaps when eminent functionaries in Edinburgh heard of the description it but added to their displeasure and disgust at the entire Municipal Banking project.

At anyrate something had to be done about the matter and in 1926, by a Treasury Minute, a Committee of Enquiry into Municipal Banking, under the Chairmanship of Lord Bradbury, was appointed. The com-

[1] By the year 1950, this small burgh had £307,000 in its Municipal Bank.

position of the Committee, five 'City' men, enraged Birmingham, but we awaited, with some curiosity, their report, which we knew, as sure as two and two made four, would seek to hamstring the small Scots burghs' ventures in municipal banking. And it was even so. Lord Bradbury and his friends did not wait for their final report to the Treasury, but they

> "thought it desirable to inform the Treasury at once that in our opinion the first opportunity should be taken to prohibit the use in the title of any Banking Company of the term 'Municipal' or any other term which might suggest connection with a local authority."

And the Treasury obeyed. In the Companies Act of 1929 there was a clause (17) prohibiting any further use of the word "Municipal" by any new Banking inclined Council, but I am glad to record that Mr. Neville Chamberlain ostentatiously stayed away from the House of Commons during the division on the clause. The moneylending high priests had not only beaten off the Scots burghs, they had declared through the Bradbury Committee that they were "not in agreement with the general policy which brought it (the Birmingham Municipal Bank) into being." And the Birmingham Bank was Neville Chamberlain's child!

Henceforth then, the Municipal Banks in Scotland which were already in existence were allowed to continue without molestation, but no new banks using the word municipal in their titles would be permitted. And the only way to frustrate the frustraters was to call any new bank simply by the name of its town, as Kilsyth for example did—The Kilsyth Bank Limited.

Looking back upon these brave days of experimentation I recall, too, our municipal effort in pig feeding. We invited our citizens to segregate, so far as possible, their domestic food refuse, from their ashes and tin-cans; we collected the food refuse separately and fed young pigs with it, instead of, as hitherto, hiring a swamp or piece of waste land in the neighbourhood, dumping the waste food there, and feeding rats with it, and then hiring a rat catcher to kill the rats! For a year or two our pig feeding scheme worked well enough, but several of our young pigs died, it was said through improper feeding, and the project was abandoned.

Then we got a herd of goats for the land adjacent to our sewage farm: the goats' milk was to be reserved for tubercular children, and the scheme was started amid erudite witticisms such as "You are kidding us!" and "Do you take us for goats?"

A little before that the local Co-op had started a pasteurisation of milk scheme; in addition we got our Infant Welfare Centre to issue babies' food and clothing free to necessitous mothers, and to all other mothers at cost price (the mothers' saving on patent foods was considerable!); we ran a municipal cookery, or kitchen, and we had detailed balance sheets from 23 housewives showing that they had effected a saving, through buying the family meals at the kitchen, of from 2s. 9d. to 7s. per week according to the size of the family.

We even made municipal jam, and when we ran out of jam pots an appeal in the schools by the headmaster that any boy or girl offering a pot or pots to the municipal kitchen after 5 p.m., next day, would receive a halfpenny per pot, brought forth such a clamouring army of young offerers, who had raked their mothers' presses and larders, that the police had to clear a passage for horse traffic. The municipal kitchen ran for four years and made a net profit of £41 and the enterprise was only broken when it was overloaded by a more ambitious effort at a restaurant and tea-room in a less populous part of the town.

At any rate these dietetic and health experiments did have some effect upon our sickness and death figures, and our infant mortality fell from 162 per 1000 in 1915 to 128 per 1000 in 1916, to 93 per 1000 in 1917, and to 78 per 1000 in 1918, when it was the second lowest record in Scotland; in the last quarter of that year we had the lowest figure for all Scotland, and almost half of what it was in the rest of Dunbarton County.

We had three iron-foundries in the town; two of them made baths, but no moulder had a bath in his home, so we had to get municipal shower baths. These were mostly used, however, by school children; and in the six summer months of 1920 we had nearly 9500 bathers, and a net loss of only £123, or the cost of one tubercular patient for a year in a sanatorium. But the demand was for a bath in the home, and when the Addison Act in 1920 was available, the total liability to a Town Council being seven-eighths of a penny per annum no matter how many houses were built, the Government clearly carrying all liabilities over the seven-eighths of the penny, I did my utmost to persuade my colleagues to go in for a scheme of 500 houses.

Alas! the total capital expenditure frightened the majority of my colleagues, even though not our Council but the Government was responsible for everything over the seven-eighths of the penny rate. And no big city was tackling anything upon so vast a scale. We therefore had to be content with 200 houses and—almost incredible!—it was in the poorest quarters of the town that the ill-founded fears of 'reckless' municipal housing took firmest hold. At a municipal election two of my supporters were canvassing in a dingy, almost derelict property, called the Galleries, now happily demolished. Feeling their way in darkness along a rickety wooden lobby they came to a door and knocked. A householder arrived accompanied by a volume of chimney smoke which almost choked the canvassers.

Nevertheless they managed to begin: "We've come to see if you will support municipal housing." "Naw," shouted the irate householder, "I don't believe in your d——d municipal hoosing," and slammed the door, which thereupon, having long served its day, and being unequal to the exertion pressed upon it fell from its hinges in ruins, and left no barricade to the ancient cave dwelling.

At another *crannog* in the Townhead the only access was by an old wooden ladder, in parts held together by pieces of string and rope. The occupant was a strong opponent of municipal housing schemes, and he shouted down imprecations upon all canvassers who called upon him during an election day to record his vote for a new housing scheme. "Aye," he shouted, "I'll vote the nicht, but it'll be against ye." An exasperated canvasser, however, made certain that the vote would not be recorded, for he tore the rope ladder away, and left the voter sitting in his eyrie, and there he continued swearing and yelling murder until long after the polling booths had closed, and he was released from his imprisonment—and then arrested by the police for breach of the peace!

I think it was in these days of housing agitation that I must have begun to sense the foolish and indeed completely indefensible rating system which operates upon household property in Scotland—and only in Scotland. Many years later I was largely instrumental in getting the Sorn Committee set up to report upon the disastrous effect that system was producing upon our housing affairs: but even in the early twenties it had been obvious that rating arrangements which prevented and prejudiced repairs and improvements upon hundreds of thousands of existing structures, was insensate. Today in many areas deterioration in housing fabric proceeds at a greater rate than the new municipal houses can be built, and that simply because private houseowners (often family trusts) are unable, from the rents of their properties, to meet the rates and repairs obligation upon their properties. An owner's income is stabilised by the Rent Acts; but his outgo in owners' rates or repairs costs is not stabilised, with the result that in many cases repairs and renovations are withheld and properties slither irresistibly to decay: and when the last penny is extracted from them, are offered to unwilling Town Councils for bare feu duty relief.

Before the war too it was obvious that the private builder was boycotting the Scots housing market, so far as houses to let were concerned. During the year 1937, for example, over 72,000 new houses were produced by private builders for letting purposes in England and Wales; but in Scotland only 1,700 were so produced. One in Scotland to every 42 in England and Wales.[1] This disparity was not due to shortage of land or

[1] Committee on Rating & Valuation Cmd. 6595.

materials. We had considerable unemployment in the building industry; we required the houses—badly—and we had thousands of people willing to pay rent for added conveniences and amenities. I can suggest no reason for the figures 1 and 42 other than that the first indicates owners' rates with the sky as the limit, and the second that when the initial rent is fixed the owner is free of any anxieties that he may be swamped by subsequent increases in owners' rates.

Be that as it may, back in the twenties in our old burgh, side by side with our municipal housing campaigns, we did our utmost, in the tenants' as well as in the property owners' interests, indeed in the general public interest, to maintain existing fabrics. For example, we found that say during a period of severe frost tenement lavatories would be choked, or pipes burst, or after a storm, that slates had gone and roofs were leaking; but it was precisely to these tenement properties that local plumbers and tradesmen paid least attention; only after repairs on the bungalows and the villas—better paid and possibly less dirty jobs—did they go to the crowded tenements. This manifestly was bad for public health. And our Council then as a public health measure announced that it would mobilise its tradesmen from all its departments during emergencies, and at the request of property owners would undertake urgently necessary repairs at little over cost price. I suppose on an isolated sectional accounting we lost money, but I am sure the town's public health gained even in money; as certainly the tenants did in amenity. And *mirabile dictu* we had lived to see the day when property owners opted and voted for a works department!

Our burgh achieved some notoriety too in that it was one of the few in Scotland to go 'dry' by popular vote under the Scottish Temperance Act. And it is one of the still smaller number which at successive polls since 1920 has maintained its 'dry' decision. The Act is in some respects weighted in favour of the 'wets.' The 'drys' to win must poll more than a bare majority, but for the 'wets' to overturn that decision at a subsequent polling three years afterwards only a bare majority suffices. The most serious handicap, however, from which the temperance sentiment suffers is in the absurd and undemocratic limitation of the options upon which the electors are allowed to vote. By Statute they have only three choices:

a. continuation of the public houses in the area of polling.
b. cancellation of all licenses in the area.
c. limitation of licenses: the public houses to be scrapped being left to the decision of the licensing magistrates.

Now it is obvious that there are many concepts of what is temperance reform: many gradations of temperance reformers. There are those (a very large number) who want the profit motive eliminated from the sale of intoxicants, and who favour a Public House Trust or a Municipal Monopoly. There are those who would restrict public house sales to beers only, and would have spirits supplied by chemists upon a doctor's certificate. There are those who would have alcoholic liquors sold only with a meal. And there are those who would gladly vote for the closing of inn bars on a Sunday, and liquor supplied only with a meal.

But none of these groups can register a vote for their preferences, with the result that thousands of electors who never venture near a public house are—since they cannot go the length of complete no license being imposed upon a large minority—driven to support continuance of the existing system. Whatever else may be said for the Act of 1913 its options are too few and too restricted: a polling does not therefore register anything like the general temperance sentiment in a community; and the limitation of options, though that was never intended by the promoters, plays beautifully into the hands of the licensed trade as it now operates.

Yet despite all these handicaps our town, by a majority of 647, and amid great turmoils and excitements, voted itself dry. Two of my life-long friends, the late Bob Dickson (a leading industrialist) and Dr. Andy Cowan, played active parts in the No License campaign; the women's organisations in the town cast their strength at the ballot boxes, it was said to the last skirt; the temperance societies, with men at their head like William Fletcher, a generous minded Radical who later became chief Temperance leader in Scotland, conducted the struggle with religious fervour. But the high light of the contest came at a rather rowdy wet meeting in the town hall on the eve of the poll when the Provost jumped on a chair and openly accused the leader of the Publicans' Association of attempting to bribe him with £10 to come over to the publicans' side. If any single episode could have been said to settle the public house hash, that was it.

But lest this catalogue of what wicked innovations and disturbances hatched and operated in a small burgh during the first quarter of the century become over extended and wearisome, may I hasten in with but one last note. It is *in memoriam* of a Council which used its Gas Works buying powers to purchase and stack 500 tons of domestic coal as a public reserve, and supplied local coal merchants during periods of emergency. We found we could buy at 21s. per ton and sell at 27s. per ton.

And we supplied music and organised "promiscuous" dancing in our public parks, bringing in youths and maidens from villages and hamlets far afield in adjacent counties.

It was not only in Avignon that *sur le pont . . . tout le monde y danse.*

CHAPTER V

SCRIBENDI CACOETHES

My salad days
When I was green in judgement.

—*Antony and Cleopatra*

" *Do you know, Carter, that I can actually write my name in the dust on the table?* "
" *Faith mum, that's more than I can do. Sure there's nothing like education after all!* "

—*Punch*

IT WAS while I was at Lenzie Academy, having drilled into me Cæsar's Gallic Wars and such like memory exercises (so that today after the lapse of more than half a century I can recite the second book, beginning *Cum esset Cæsar*, right through to the end with barely half a dozen promptings!) that the revelation came to me about there being big money associated with the scribbling itch. In those days there were at least three weekly (or fortnightly) lurid publications, *Pluck, The Union Jack,* and *The Marvel,* which specialised in good hair-raising Buff Bill stuff for boys. And if you could write a " blood " about how honest Sheriff Wal Osborne, quick on the draw and capable of shooting a midge's wing at thirty yards, rooted out the brigands and budmashes and outlaws on the Sierra, and cleared the Grand Canyon of Pimply Pete and his nefarious gang, you didn't require to swot up the geography of the Mexican border; you just invented it, in the sure and certain knowledge that your reading public was as little primed on the matter as you were. But there had to be plenty of galloping along razor edged cliffs—one false step and you were plunged, you and your trusty mustang, into the abyss, high drama on every page, camp fires and pemmican and bison steak, and in the end victory for the righteous and the forces of law and order!

We had an English master called Lyall, who, when he discovered the source of my sudden bursts of affluence, volunteered to keep my wild western crudities within bounds. There was, of course, a higher class of

31

boy literature also on tap—*The Boy's Own Paper*—but I never sought to dabble there. And the only other early pen money episode I can recall is of a Burns Centenary competition promoted by a Scottish newspaper. Essays were to be original and confined to schoolboy entrants. The first prize, I think, was of £50; and I got second. But when the first winning essay was published, behold it was word for word the preface to Currie's "Life of Burns." Legal protests on my behalf were unavailing. The editor's decision was final; but he had slipped up badly.

At anyrate I had firmly determined I was not going in for law. Not for me, in Charles Lamb's words,

"A votary of the desk—a notched and cropt scrivener—one that sucks his substance as certain sick people are said to do, through a quill."

A brief day in an uncle's office where I was given foolscap sheets of elaborate legal blethers to copy, about first party of the second part and the like, sickened me; the more so as it was summer time, and I might have been away angling up a hill burn. So after some evasive and delaying action in junior clerical posts in iron-founding and insurance I got my heart's desire. An old gentleman—a cousin of my mother's—was persuaded to risk handing over to me one of his many subsidiary enterprises: a printing establishment and the editorship of two weekly papers. Of these publications one was a weekly largely concerned with grocers' grievances and specialised in *fama* derogatory to the Co-operative movement: the other a weekly newspaper where I could indulge at large in everything from editorials to profile drawings of local celebrities, the drawings being first cut on chalk plates and then the molten metal poured over the indentations to produce the blocks ready for printing.

Now that I had a printing press there was nothing for it but I must have a Scottish Socialist weekly as well. So the *Forward* was floated on a paid up capital of £60, and printing contracts arranged—after two years' operation our capital was still only £275. Mostly we were Fabians—Bob Pollock, a builder, Roland Muirhead, a tannery proprietor, who still, *clare et venerabile nomen*, remains the G.O.M. of Scottish Nationalism, William Martin Haddow, pioneer of school feeding, Dr. Stirling Robertson of Clydebank, Bob Maclaurin, the inventor and expert upon gases, Allan Wilson, an accountant, and myself, installed as *gratis* editor. William C. Ward, a retired naval engineer, acted as Secretary.

We would have no alcoholic advertisements: no gambling news, and my own stipulation after a month's experience, no amateur poetry; every second reader at that time appearing to be bursting into *vers libre*.

But we attracted many capable contributors. We got a full length novel from H. G. Wells. We had writers like J. Ramsay MacDonald, William Stewart, James Connolly, and as we backed the militant suffragettes, we got valuable aid from Mrs. Pankhurst and Mrs. Billington Greig. Willie Regan and John Wheatley drew us a considerable Catholic Socialist audience, and, although this was later, we got Upton Sinclair: and a great weekly comic strip known as the Adventures of Henry Dubb, from Mr. Ryan Walker in the United States. Dr. Stirling Robertson as 'Rob Roy,' with notable erudition, kept the anti-Marxian front well ablaze. He was a close personal friend of Keir Hardie, and he knew all about the European congresses and the platforms and the resolutions of the internationals.

Time and again it looked as if our ship was heading for the bankruptcy rocks, but somehow we always escaped. For our respites we had to thank mostly Dr. G. B. Clark, the crofters' champion, and Mr. Roland Muirhead, but I am thankful to record that we always managed to repay their loans. A witty but rather cynical friend used to say he always knew when the *Forward* was in exceptionally deep water; it would then come out with a specially strong Home Rule issue: that would be preparatory to ' touching' Mr. Muirhead for a loan!

There was a young contributor from Baillieston whose speciality (under the pseudonym of ' Myner Collier ') was the analysing of coal owners' balance sheets to show their fantastic profits, and when the *Forward* invested in a second-hand caravan (bought cheaply at Vinegar Hill) for propaganda purposes, we looked around for someone to organise the tours and gather in subscriptions to assist with the vanner's maintenance. So one night I got young ' Myner Collier ' into an Argyle Street tearoom and persuaded him to undertake the task. His name was Patrick Joseph Dollan, later to be Lord Provost of Glasgow.

And there was Tom Dickson, the cheeriest, wittiest man I ever knew. For years he was our chief sub-editor. He was a great Shakespearian scholar, and rather fancied himself in amateur drama, especially in declamatory parts. He had been a reporter on the staff of the *Scotsman*, and during the early stages of the first world war had been assigned for special reporting on naval occasions to a town in one of the northern islands. Time hung heavily, and the pressmen and naval personnel used to forgather at the village Post Office where the Postmaster would exhibit the official bulletins about the progress of the war. One day, after Tom had managed an adroit appropriation of a blank official announcement form, and after an equally deft sleight of hand at the window, the following important announcement appeared:

" *It is reported that the Turks have taken Cascara: and are evacuating to the south.*"

That interference with the solemnities of the war was overlooked—but only just. Tom was a born mimic and his burlesque of Mr. Ramsay MacDonald at his mistiest—Ah my friends, my dear friends, we must go on and on and up and up and up—was only equalled by his representation of Willie Adamson, Secretary of State for Scotland, in a wholly mythical performance of answering questions by always promising to give everything due consideration, especially when he would give due consideration to the promise of due consideration he had given already. When Tom was in the House of Commons as member for South Lanarkshire one of his greatest exploits arose during the period when Round Robins were being arranged to test the feeling of all parties in the House about the payment of M.P.s' railway transport to and from their constituencies. Just at that time the late Joe Sullivan, M.P., came to me in some distress, and asked me to intercede on his behalf with the Secretary of State to get remission of a police account against him for some £40. Apparently what had happened was this. One of Joe's friends, a Kilsyth miner, had been out walking with his Airedale terrier bitch, when she had leapt over a fence and worried a sheep in a nearby field. The miner had compensated the farmer who had owned the sheep, for his loss, but nevertheless he was cited to appear at Stirling Sheriff Court and show cause why the bitch should not be destroyed, under penalty of £1 per day to the Crown for every day that passed without the orders of the Court being carried out.

By the time the Sheriff had issued his decree of destruction of the bitch, Joe Sullivan had been hurriedly given the animal, and by the time the Kilsyth police traced it to Joe that gentleman was liable for forty days at £1 per day. And every day added another £1. So Joe sought clemency. The Secretary of State at my request consulted the Lord Advocate, then Lord Macmillan, and legal precedents, and due considerations rattled about Whitehall. Meanwhile Joe's indebtedness steadily increased.

At this stage Tom Dickson engaged himself in typing a flowery petition to the King to spare Joe's bitch; the offence had been purged; compensation had been paid; pups were expected and His Majesty surely would not knowingly permit the innocent to be punished for or with the guilty, and his petitioner's friends of the leal and trusty and well-beloved aforesaid Joe, member of the Order of the British Empire, would for ever pray, etc.

Now, while a debate on Members' travelling expenses was proceeding, this precious petition to the King about Joe's bitch was shoved before Mr. Lloyd George by an active Liberal member, Mr. Pringle. Mr. Lloyd George, his attention on the debate, without reading, signed, thinking it was a petition in favour of M.P.s' expenses. His signature was followed by signatures from all the Liberal front bench; the document was then passed to Mr. Baldwin and Mr. Austen Chamberlain, and in the end, signed by a majority of the House of Commons. In due course the front page, with the wording of the petition, was safely back in Tom Dickson's hands.

The joke might have ended there, but for the fact that somehow King George V got to hear of the ploy and sent Jimmy Thomas around for the document. The episode greatly tickled His Majesty and gave him cause for a sly comment upon how his country was being run—blindfolded. A fine lot of Privy Councillors!

And for all I know to the contrary the petition remains to this hour among the historical MSS. at Buckingham Palace. At any rate Joe Sullivan somehow got his penalties cancelled. (The Crown could never have gone into court with the possibility that the petition signed by most of the Party leaders and by many Privy Councillors could be dragged out to public merriment!) And finally when the pups arrived the one which was presented to James Maxton was by him christened: ' Comrade Macmillan,' in honour of the Lord Advocate of the day.

In the early *Forward* days I had compiled a rather pungent and scurrilous series of tracts purporting to be the undercover—or almost undercover—record of the great landowning families in Scotland. These tracts assuredly lacked little in vehemence, and they must have irritated many old aristocrats who, under the exactions of the tax gatherer, have now themselves disappeared. Although in their heyday many of these old families had ridden their powers with arrogance, selfishness and cruelty, still, looking back upon it, there were at least some descriptions in my collected tracts, *Our Noble Families*, which were historically one sided and unjust and quite unnecessarily wounding. The thing sold phenomenally—over 120,000 copies—it coincided with Mr. Lloyd George's Budget and Limehouse speeches; and it rankled in many an old family bosom long after it had left the market. And when a quarter of a century later, Colonel Walter Elliot and Commander Cochrane, then M.P. for Dunbartonshire, thought it might be appropriate if I were to be a member of the London Caledonian Club there were irate old aristocrats who arose from their corner seats and squelched the nominators and their nominee!

But it was in 1920 that my *History of the Working Classes in Scotland*, boosted by Tom Dickson with the glamour of American salesmanship, put the *Forward* well to the fore, and lifted our weekly paper out of the ' rag class.' Tom was appointed chief fugleman for the book, and he left nothing to chance. He whetted the public appetite by announcing that we were going to publish the book ourselves because we could not trust a capitalist publisher not to emasculate it, or indeed to keep it on the bookstalls once it was published. He told the public that Eugene Sue's *History of a Proletarian Family Across the Ages* had only been permitted publication in London in an abridged form and never repeated: and that an entire edition of Macleod's " Gloomy Memories of the Highlands " had been bought up and destroyed by agents for Highland lairds, zealous for the reputation of their overlords; and finally he issued collecting cards assuring everybody who would collect subscriptions from seven other purchasers that they would get a copy free for themselves. The result was that before we gave out the printing contract we had the money in hand for 6000 copies of a book selling at 10s. 6d. I should think that would be nearly a world's publishing record!

Tom Dickson's premature death was a great loss to his generation. He had become chairman of the National Union of Journalists, and everywhere in the Labour and Socialist movement he radiated gaiety and joyous abandon. Only one man—and he shall here be nameless—he could not think kindly of, and my last recollection of Tom is visiting him on his death-bed at Larkhall, when, between gasps for breath, he whispered: " Tom, the nearer I get to the golden gates the more charitable I become towards all men, but I draw the b——y line at ——! "

We had a " card " associated with our early efforts in securing advertisements for the *Forward*—an agent called Mandy McGettigan. He was a partner of John Wheatley's in business, and used to go about the streets of Glasgow in summer with a straw hat and an umbrella cushioned under his armpit. He had quarrelled with a Catholic priest and spent much time roasting him. He would make it his business to telephone an urgent call *in extremis* at midnight to the priest; the priest was wanted urgently at the bedside of a parishioner, and when the poor old gentleman would hurry along it would be to find his parishioner not dead, but dead drunk.

One of Mandy's neighbours some streets away had a beautifully tended lawn in front of his cottage. Mandy, knowing he was off on a holiday, strolled round one morning and awaited at his friend's front door on the appearance of a jobbing gardener who usually went the rounds looking for a day's work.

" Yes, my good man," said Mandy to the jobbing gardener, pretending he was the proprietor, " just dig up the whole lawn here, and I'll see you at night time." For some time thereafter the jobbing gardener, the real proprietor, and the police kept themselves busy, though to Mandy's relief without success, hunting for the man who gave the orders for the wreckage of the lawn.

When he went on a holiday to his native village in Donegal, Mandy would go around swaggering about his friend Lord de Rothschild, and how he was going to present new village halls and what not to the district, and he once had the nerve to change half a crown from the silver on the coffin at a funeral; possibly it was only his known friendship with Lord Rothschild that saved him from the astounded mourners. And it was Mandy who turned up at a Glasgow Catholic Socialist Society gathering, gaily attired in a tall hat and a white waistcoat and a gardenia, and roused the audience to fury by telling them that they would be better just to remain in poverty as they would not know anyhow what to do with finger bowls at dinner.

Undoubtedly the *Forward* made an impression on public opinion. Our circulation got up to 30,000. We specialised in socialist propaganda for key men and propagandists, and after some years of it I was flattered (and staggered) by a visit from an emissary of the late Lord Northcliffe, who offered me a four figure contract for a responsible post in London. I was not tempted, for well did I know that acceptance would mean parting for ever with any capacity I had for usefulness in the affairs of my world.

Then there was the famous suppression of the *Forward* on its New Year's Day issue, 1st January 1916, by Mr. Lloyd George, and high ranking police and military officers smelling through wastepaper baskets and old correspondence files in an endeavour somehow or other to find evidence *post facto* for an amazing and petulant and wholly illegal act of press suppression. What had happened was this. It was during the war; Trade Union rules and regulations were going by the board, but there was great apprehension about the high handed way in which the Ministry of Munitions appeared to be importing thousands of dilutees. Craftsmen saw their little safeguards disappearing, and this, added to the impact of thousands of strangers on an already over-crowded and inadequate housing system, created in every union branch a steadily growing resentment.

Mr. Lloyd George, then Minister of Munitions, was produced in Glasgow to talk the resentment away. His meeting in St. Andrew's Hall was carefully ticketed—in fact it was worse, every union member attending on the Saturday forenoon was promised reimbursement of lost time to the extent of six shillings—but a more unruly audience surely never gathered in Glasgow, and Mr. Lloyd George, charm how he would, failed to get a hearing; he even tried to praise his " friend " Mr. Ramsay MacDonald " and whether he is for the war or against the war, not one single word will fall from my lips against Mr. MacDonald " . . . " one of my greatest personal friends." There were many witty and uproarious passages, and the meeting broke up in disorder.

The *Forward* had a reporter, Mr. Tom Hutchison, at the meeting, and he had taken *verbatim* notes which were wildly at variance with the smoothly fabricated and all-was-well stuff that was handed out officially to the press, who were told that that was the sum total of what they were to publish. In the official hand-out the *Forward* was omitted, and I had friends in the press who cheerfully handed me their official orders that they were only to publish the cooked stuff. After carefully excising all references to military affairs from Mr. Tom Hutchison's report we published the lot: the columns interspersed with ribaldry, as for example: Mr. Lloyd George speaking:

" The responsibility of a Minister of the Crown in a great war is not an enviable one." (" The money's good " and laughter.) " I can assure you it is no laughing matter."

All this was too much for Mr. Lloyd George, who completely lost his sense of proportion and ordered a complete raid of all copies of the *Forward* in every newsagent's shop in Scotland; he even had the police search the homes of known purchasers. (There were some comic stories of what happened there—one police officer in an Ayrshire town misinterpreting his instructions and going round seizing copies of the *British Weekly*!) And he ordered a clamp down by police and military upon our printers.

The military and police sleuths got nothing from their searchings except embarrassment and ridicule. The *Forward* on the other hand got an advertisement worth thousands of pounds, and Mr. Lloyd George's chief Asquithian gadfly in the House of Commons, Mr. Pringle, eagerly seized upon the episode to make trouble for the Munitions Minister. The War Office disavowed any responsibility, and Lord Kitchener and Mr. Tennant, the representative of the War Office in the House of Commons, were running around privately looking for copies of the banned report as personal treasures. I of course kept publicly demanding action in the law courts and heavy compensation, and finally after five or six weeks of the hullabaloo Mr. Lloyd George bowed before the storm of ridicule and sent Mr. George N. Barnes (a member of the Cabinet) to " negotiate." A meeting was arranged with Mr. Lloyd George at his Ministry in London, and, accompanied by Mr. Rosslyn Mitchell, my solicitor, I had a most interesting time.

Operations began with the Minister effusively greeting me as if I were a long lost brother, and shaking my hand like a pump handle.

" My dear Johnston, you mustn't get me wrong. You really mustn't. I am the last man on God's earth to suppress a Socialist newspaper."

I laughed.

" My dear young man " (he was so ostensibly pained and distressed at my unseemly mirth). " My dear young man, don't you believe my word? Why do you laugh? "

" Well, Mr. Minister, you say you are the last man on God's earth to suppress a Socialist newspaper. You are. You did it six weeks ago, and no one has done it since! "

There thus being nothing of profit to be gleaned in the realm of political hocus pocus we proceeded to get down to business, with the result that I walked out free to start again, and " it had all been a mistake, and these things happen in the best regulated families, Ha! Ha! And we must see more of each other and be better friends in future."

But for all the gentleman's back slapping he was stone deaf to my hints about compensation.

And so a return to the writing of pamphlets and the editorial chair of the *Forward* where, until I was relieved by Mr. Emrys Hughes after a third of a century of it, I stuck without intermission. Millions of words I must have written in propaganda. But it was a good free life and I do not regret an hour of it.

CHAPTER VI

EDUCATION: ESCAPES AND ESCAPADES

*. . . Grant unto us purity of heart and strength of purpose, so that no
selfish passion may hinder us from knowing Thy will, no weakness from
doing it; but in Thy light may we see light clearly and in Thy service
find perfect freedom.*

—Sir Henry Jones's opening morning prayer,
Moral Philosophy classroom, Glasgow University

IN THE old School Board days the teaching profession—at least its more
vocal and clamorous elements—continually demanded wider administrative areas in education. They said they had all the experience of democratic control that they could suffer. The local clergyman, grocer, iron-
moulder, and roadman, were denounced in conference as incapable and
incompetent in making appointments and giving promotions; moreover
they the local public representatives aforesaid and the sheepish constituents
who elected them could only think in terms of small salaries for teachers.
Wider areas was the cure. Get away from local control, and vest the teachers'
fortunes among the more leisured classes in the country who could afford
to attend day time meetings, and who would be more likely to be men of
wider vision and culture, and who would appoint skilled full time officers
to run the business!

But when the teachers got their County Area Education Authorities
they were speedily disillusioned, the remote controllers showing no more
(if as much) concern for the status and remuneration of teaching than the
local and proximate controllers had done. But there was a substantial
increase in the administrative payroll.

In pre-County Authority days we had a small semi-rural single storey
school at Gartconner; the windows used to be cleaned on a Saturday
morning by an old cleaner who performed her task quite comfortably
standing on a chair. But under the new County dispensation things perforce
had to be better centralised and organised, and we had the spectacle of a

40

lorry with painters coming from (I think) Clydebank, say 20 miles to do the job. And in the old School Board days we had an aged lady who had a Saturday task of sweeping the room and the passages; under the new *régime* she was the heroine of a comic episode. A motor car with officials arrived from headquarters conveying an envelope with 52 insurance cards for her to sign. When they arrived the officials discovered that the old lady was 72 years of age and not eligible for insurance at all!

It is true that most of the more fantastic of these long distance administrations disappeared in due course, but along with a Tory ironfounder and a Catholic priest, I spent the first three years on the new 'Authority' struggling to get some real powers devolved upon the local School Management Committees; some functions likely to attract the services of men of energy and vision! But in vain. The School Management Committees were never intended to be anything other than stooges and dummies. So we left.

Feeling myself in need of the higher culture in moral philosophy and political economy, I found my way into the classes of Professor Sir Henry Jones and Professor William Smart at Glasgow University; and many years afterwards when the authorities of that ancient seat of learning were conferring upon me the degree of LL.D., the Professor of Spanish, who was reciting what he knew or thought he knew about me, declared positively that looking back he was not at all certain whether I had gone to Gilmorehill to be instructed or to instruct. Yet so far as I know the only possible justification for that jape would be some confused and wafted memories of certain (on my part) rather cheeky interpellations of the popular professor of Moral Philosophy.

Sir Henry Jones was a great character. He had begun life as a cobbler of shoes in Wales; he had become a disciple and friend of Edward Caird's and was winding up as a distinguished occupant of a Scottish University chair, and with a tremendous influence over his students. His classes began at 8 a.m., and he kept a wary and roving eye for those disciples who surreptitiously munched late sandwich breakfasts the while he would be discoursing upon the Hegelian Dialectic.

Being Welsh to the marrow of him, and a staunch Liberal in politics, he was greatly disturbed when at a Rectorial election, at which Mr. Lloyd George was nominated as the Liberal candidate, there was not only a Conservative candidate in the person of Lord Curzon, but a Labour candidate also, Mr. Keir Hardie. At that time I was chairman of the University Socialist Society, and as the election day drew nearer, Sir Henry could the less disguise his irritation, and would interlard his lectures with what he considered conclusive swipes at Socialist doctrine. Particularly did he pummel Sir Oliver Lodge, some of whose writing had inflamed him, and he orated with great eloquence upon how Socialism had failed in ancient Greece and Peru.

When he would make (as I thought) particularly controversial or questionable assertions I would go away back to the Students' Settlement, where I then lived, and indite long argumentative epistolary retorts, which I always knew he had read from the way his eye would smoulder as it rested upon me next morning. Then he would start out his lecture, and after a few moments, perhaps on Plato, would suddenly go on: " And if I may make an observation upon this subject, with Mr. Johnston's very kind permission. . . ."

This of course spread the news about the undercover controversy, and I would go forward with another retort by post, with, on one occasion, as an appendix, a compilation of books by the secretary of our Society which the Professor was recommended to study. The compiler was an ingenious and pugnacious medical student, Edward Glover, who later became a distinguished Harley Street psychiatrist. This rather impudent baiting of the learned Professor leaked out and caused such speculation that Glover had a wild idea of publishing the epistles as a pamphlet. But Sir Henry had the last word. When the votes for the Lord Rectorship were being counted, the chairmen of the three political parties were entitled to be present, and I, who had been well and truly plastered during the previous hour or two of polling with soot, rotten eggs, and tomatoes, and stank extensively, chose to stand behind Sir Henry during the enumeration.

When it was seen that Curzon had beaten Lloyd George and that Keir Hardie had polled sufficient votes (I think 122) which, had they gone to Lloyd George, would have secured his election, Sir Henry, who could contain himself no longer, turned and asked if I would mind removing my odoriferous and pestiferous presence a little farther to the rear!

One farther amusing recollection of that Rectorial! Some of our opponents had let loose the news of their intention to prevent by force the Keir Hardie supporters from recording their votes. Promptly our election committee despatched Glover to interview the leaders of the Glasgow Unemployed. At that time the unemployed were being processioned with banners in great numbers through the streets of the city, and the authorities were becoming increasingly anxious about the preservation of public order; Glover asked the unemployed leaders to make a public announcement that they intended organising a great march to Gilmorehill to see fair play for Keir Hardie's supporters at the polling booth; this announcement they of course gleefully made, and with some alarming elaborations.

Next day I was hurriedly summoned out of a Political Economy class room and whisked away by car to the Lord Provost's room at the Municipal Buildings. There I found the bewildered chairmen of the Curzon and Lloyd George committees, and when we three were ushered into the Lord Provost's room it was to meet an anxious and perturbed Lord Provost Bilsland, and an equally anxious and perturbed University Principal MacAlister, an officer from Maryhill Barracks, the Chief of the Police, and the Town Clerk. The Lord Provost began operations by addressing us three political party chairmen and saying he did not know which of us was which but that he and Principal MacAlister wanted assurances from each of us that the other two parties would be allowed to vote. This was an assurance I could cheerfully and easily give without waiting for the Principal's homily about the fear of the beautiful university buildings being destroyed by a mob, or the Police Chief's more specific and forthright declaration that he was darned well not going to have it. The gentleman from Maryhill barracks said nothing, rather to my disappointment, for I was hoping he would add a short piece about ball cartridge and riot acts. Anyhow the authorities got their pledge, the unemployed never marched; we voted; Sir Donald MacAlister slept the sleep of a Principal, relieved that the Bute Hall was not going up in blazes, and everybody was happy.

We had nominated Keir Hardie without his knowledge or consent, he being away in India at the time, and I was rather apprehensive lest when he heard of the escapade he would be annoyed and repudiate us. When he arrived at Southampton he was of course interviewed on many subjects by pressmen, one of whom shot at him out of the blue the query:

" What do you think of your chances for the Lord Rectorship of Glasgow University? "

That must have been a complete puzzler for the old gentleman, but the prompt reply surrounded by the traditional caution of his race, greatly relieved some youths in far away Glasgow when they read of it:

" Well you know, I have just arrived."

And a story still goes the rounds—I met it in America forty years after the polling—that Walter Elliot had voted for Keir Hardie and James Maxton for Lord Curzon. The legend ought to be, but is not quite true. Elliot at the University had been a Fabian Socialist, and Maxton, then all but indifferent to politics, had proclaimed himself a Tory. But they had both left for the outer world prior to the Rectorial of the year 1908, and while Elliot returned later as Conservative M.P. for the Scottish Universities, Maxton's next visit was as a Socialist leader to an uproarious meeting in the Students' Union. That meeting remains in my memory for an interruption which, for once, left Maxton speechless and retortless. Maxton by that time had grown his long tradition-like actors' hair, and during his speeches he would continually and with dramatic effect weave a lock away from his brow. At this Students' Union gathering he was set agoing at his most impressive oratory ... " *Three* millions unemployed (pause). Three millions *unemployed* (pause). Three *millions* unemployed (pause)." Amid the tense silence came a voice from the back:

"Aye, Jimmy, and every second yin a barber!"

CHAPTER VII

POLITICS: HIGH AND LOW

The Stoic Chrysippus found himself obliged to stand aloof from all participation in politics—" For if I counsel honourably I shall offend the citizens, and if basely, the Gods."

—*Rolleston's Epictetus*

Keir Hardie, the founder of the Independent Labour Party, once addressed a string of very wretched men who were waiting to scramble for a casual job at the London docks at dawn on a cold winter morning. They were the worst paid manual workers in London, and their poverty was being rubbed into them mercilessly by heavy rain. Accordingly Keir Hardie talked Socialist economics to them as their most urgent political interest. He then as a candidate for the local parliamentary seat, invited questions. Thereupon a man blotted against the dock wall for some half shelter from the downpour, stepped out and said he had listened to the speaker's able address, but had been surprised to find that it contained no politics. What they wanted to know he said were the speaker's views as to the disestablishment of the Church in Wales.

—*George Bernard Shaw: 'Everybody's Political What's What'*

I REMEMBER rather vividly my first step-up in the public oratory business. It was during a municipal election in Glasgow in the year of a Lloyd George budget, and a call for platform assistance had come to the University Socialist Society from the Labour Party organisers in the city. I was assigned to speak in support of the candidate for the Anderston ward. The candidate was a well-known lawyer called Walter Leechman who had a considerable police court practice, and who sported a black spade beard. The Anderston ward was mainly slum, and the meeting place a schoolroom in one of the dark and dismal side streets off Argyle Street. It was late October: the night was bitterly cold, and there was a depressing half-mist, half-rain. I had prepared my speech so thoroughly that I could almost recite it backwards—all about the benefits of municipal water, trams, gas, and, as I recollect, telephones—nevertheless I was as nervous as a kitten, and would have given much to be well out of it.

45

When we marched into the schoolroom, the whole platform party of us, three in number, the chairman, the candidate, and myself, I found that numerically the audience equalled us, for it consisted of two old women with shawls over their heads, who had evidently come in for a heat, and a man at the back who sat so immobile that it was not clear whether he was asleep or drunk. The proceedings started. The chairman was brief. Then the candidate for a solid half hour gave us a brilliant dissertation on the Budget and interlarded it with abundance of statistics and thousands of millions of pounds sterling, and wound up with an appeal to the audience to march unitedly to the poll at the forthcoming election and strike a blow for liberty and fraternity. Then, after I had recited my piece, and no questions being asked, the candidate and I walked back city-wards along Argyle Street. Greatly daring I said to him:

" I hope you won't mind, Mr. Leechman, and I hesitate, a much younger man, to make the comment, but you were about 1000 millions out in your Budget figures tonight! "

Walter Leechman stopped, and passed his beard through his hand.

" My dear boy," he said. " My dear boy, when you take a crowd like that tonight over thirty bob what the hell do a thousand millions matter? "

And maybe in that he was dead right!

Upon soul and conscience I never wanted the life Parliamentary, and most assuredly not in London. In 1917 and early 1918 I had resisted attempts to induce me to become a candidate, and it was not until James Maxton sent me a rather indignant letter saying he thought it most unfair that he should be landed for a contest in Bridgeton, while I should sit high and dry; in fact if fellows like myself were going to escape, he would jolly well get out too—not until then did I fall for the apparently ' hopeless ' seat of West Stirlingshire. But I lived on the borders of the constituency: a hired car could bring me home every night: the constituency covered the field of Bannockburn, the Wallace Monument on the Abbey Craig, and parts of the bonny banks of Loch Lomond, and touched Loch Katrine; and above all there was not the remotest chance of winning. And so became I entangled in note books, partisan controversies and strifes, and in back chat with interrupters, though I still managed for the most part to avoid open air oratory and the loud yelling exercises.

Then came the election of 1918. Sir Harry Hope, the Conservative, had secured the Lloyd George ' coupon ' of recommendation, and stood comfortably for sound finance and making the Germans pay the cost of the war: though how they were to pay, whether in ships, coal, or free labour, or what, was never condescended upon, for obvious reasons. His strong suit however was that he was for hanging the Kaiser; but so too was the

Liberal candidate, who had bobbed up in the person of Mr. R. B. Cunning-hame Graham; the electors, however, did not consider Mr. Graham would pull the rope tightly enough, and as I was obviously also lukewarm on the subject, Sir Harry romped home on polling day, beating both his opponents handsomely. During the election Mr. Graham enlivened affairs by denouncing the late William Ewart Gladstone and telling the electors that if they could not see their way to vote for Graham, to vote for Johnston and not for Hope.

Four years later, to my surprise and somewhat to my dismay, I beat Sir Harry by 815 votes and could henceforth irritate the country gentrice by asserting that I represented the Duke of Montrose and Lord Younger, the chief Tory whip, whose estates were in the constituency.

My firmest *silhouette* memory of the Parliament in the winter of 1922— it was before the days of free railway passes for M.P.s—is of the boredom and weariness of the week-ends we Scots M.P.s from the Clydeside had to spend in London. We had been well publicised as the turbulent wild red men from the Clyde, and some of our number on the strength of that publicity got speaking engagements, although, especially in Cockneyland, they had difficulty in making themselves understood; it was a singing of the Lord's song in a strange land; and David Kirkwood I remember became quite huffed because a lady clerk in a London hotel, failing to understand his polite English, was certain he was a foreigner of some kind—perhaps a Portuguese!

When there was no lecturing some of us would drift to the Scots kirk of St. Columba to hear the Rev. Archibald Fleming, and there was a Church of England parson in the east end whom McNeil Weir discovered, and who always put up a fervent word for strength and courage to the men from Scotland who had come down to Westminster to fight against needless poverty. We could, it is true, get an occasional break at Petticoat Lane on a Sunday forenoon, when thousands of people seemed to gather to listen to the cheap jacks' patter, perhaps to buy cheaply some remaindered articles, or, for that matter, stolen goods.

And once we got a laugh. Joe Sullivan, M.P., bought at a stall a cap for a shilling. He thought it was worth at least 2*s.* 6*d.*, and was proud of his purchasing skill as he saw it safely parcelled up, and was given it by the salesman with great courtesy—" Thank you, Squire! " But when Squire Sullivan got back to his lodgings and unwrapped the parcel, he found to his indignation, that the salesman by sleight of hand had substituted an old duster for the cap. Joe vowed that the next Sunday he would return to Petticoat Lane and beard the dodger (Joe called him worse than that!) at his stall.

When the next Sunday came, Joe accompanied by half a dozen fellow legislators, found the sleight of hand man now selling ties—" Three for a bob, pure silk, straight from the manufacturer, guaranteed the same as worn by the Prince of Wales! " and so on. Joe stepped forward for two shillings' worth, but refused to have the ties wrapped up; he had been done before. So, sticking them in his jacket pocket, he exultantly cried: " Ye're diddled this time, my lad! " But five minutes later in the press of the crowd Joe's pocket was picked, and by the time we all got back to the tie-salesman's stall, the dodger was offering the ties for sale again, straight as he said from the manufacturer and as worn by the Prince of Wales. Whoever wore them Joe never did; all he got was a threat of an action for slander and a charge that if there was any more protesting from him, a charge of breach of the peace and of disturbing public order!

About this time, and while most of my colleagues in the House of Commons were concentrating upon the grievances of the Unemployed, and urging a capital levy upon the war profiteers who were reported by the Board of Inland Revenue to a Select Committee of the House of Commons to be in possession of over £5000 millions of increased war profits, I had gravitated to Somerset House and interested myself there in researches into some of the higher level financial rake-off operations on the body politic.

One investigation blew me into notoriety. When the Government announced that it had guaranteed a loan of £3½ millions sterling to enable cotton estates in the Sudan to be irrigated, I discovered that the syndicate whose fields were to be irrigated had, if you please, paid 10 per cent dividend in 1916-17, in 1918-19 it had paid 25 per cent; in 1919-20 again 25 per cent and with in addition a bonus of 10 per cent; in the year 1920-21 the dividend was 15 per cent; and that the directors were entitled to 10 per cent of the net profits accruing after a dividend of 25 per cent was paid. One of the fortunate directors was a son of the then Liberal Party leader, Mr. Asquith. When I asked a question in which these facts and figures were incorporated, I was given the amazing answer that the loan to the syndicate had been guaranteed only after a deputation had been received by the Government on the subject, and that the deputation had been headed by Mr. Asquith and Mr. J. R. Clynes.

The question and answer raised a howl of indignation, and Mr. Asquith promptly made a personal statement that he had no financial interest in the syndicate, and that he had gone with the deputation, as Mr. Clynes had gone, in the interests of his constituents employed in the cotton industry. I was certainly at fault in that I did not notify Mr. Asquith of my intention to put a question indirectly referring to him, but it was the Government, and not I, who first introduced Mr. Asquith's name as leading the deputation which had urged the Treasury guarantee.

There were other curious benefactions disinterred during that Parliament: one, a British Italian Corporation, had received subsidies amounting to £283,000: it had actually been promised £500,000, but now it had intimated that the amount received was quite sufficient: it would refrain from asking for the balance. The Corporation had been promoted to edge the Germans out of Italian Banking control, and apparently it had succeeded. There was, however, to be no question of repaying any part of the £283,000 subsidy it had already received. That was for keeps and the sum figured solidly as the corporation's reserve fund in its balance sheet.

And so down the scale to the deposed Sultan of Turkey. He, poor fellow, was very much ex-Sultan, and very much on the dole, receiving from the British Treasury £100. Perhaps it was cruel on my part to enquire publicly whether he was being paid upon the then unemployed benefit scale, 15s. for the ex-Sultan and 5s. for each of his wives.

Upon the general attitude of the Labour Party to the British Empire (now the British Commonwealth of Nations!) I found I shared some serious misgivings with George Lansbury, and we teamed together to get a Labour Commonwealth group started. Most members of the Labour Party had inherited from the old Whigs and *via* the Radicals a curious if undefined prejudice in antagonism to the Empire; perhaps part of that prejudice was a hang-over from the Boer War; but the assumption that all colonial development was imperialist and anti-Socialist, and liable to embroil us in international strife, seemed to me to be as irrational and absurd as that we should endeavour to arrange nothing more in trade priorities, or in co-operation for security with our cousins, the five Labour governments in Australia (out of the six possibles there) than we arranged with the Tibetans or the Argentinos.

In Sir Charles Dilke's time antagonism to the Empire idea was the fashion in advanced circles. Cobden in his day judged the colonies to be very costly to the mother country, and he wanted them to be treated simply as foreign nations. In the nineteen-twenties the farther left you fellow-travelled in politics the more apparently you were persuaded that the best thing you could do with the Empire was to bust it up; the Communists in the sacred name of anti-imperialism actually ran around with the demand that the Sudanese should be handed over willy nilly to Egypt.[1]

Clearly there was something all wrong there. The self-governing parts of the Empire were in fact a league of British nations in being; the standard of trusteeship for other parts of the Empire was steadily improving, and

---

[1] Thus accurately forestalling the march of history.

there was no sense in decrying the fact that slavery was first abolished within the confines of the Empire. And obviously if we could not get common purpose and action among the peoples who had become accustomed to acknowledge one symbol of unity, the King, and who settled their international disputes by Privy Council arbitration, then there was but a poor chance of our succeeding with a League of Nations outside the Empire. On the lowest grounds of partisan politics too, there was simply no sense in leaving the Empire as a sort of stage property of the Carlton Club.

The Labour Commonwealth group, however, never became numerically strong—perhaps twenty or thirty of us at the most—but we had regular weekly meetings: we were addressed by overseas prime ministers, missionaries, colonial experts, and far travelled native leaders, black, brown and yellow. Gradually we acquired knowledge of the facts, and as gradually we effected a change in the outlook of the Party towards the confederation of British peoples. We could put up our members to speak with authority in debates in the House. Pethick-Lawrence (later to become Secretary for India) took an active part, as did Drummond Shiels: and Dr. Haden Guest created a stir, somewhat on the lines of Upton Sinclair's *Jungle*, with a report upon the conditions under which Levantine currants were packed, the packing comparing ill in labour payment and sanitation with the packing and drying of Australian dried fruits.

I for my part worked away at such schemes as the exchange of Scots salted herring for Jamaican citrus fruits. That one later on nearly succeeded. Since the war of 1914-18 the Scots herring markets in Russia, Latvia and other Baltic countries had all but disappeared, with the result that approximately 50 per cent of the herring fishermen in the north and north-east of Scotland had become unemployed, and millions of pounds sterling of public capital sunk in the herring towns on roads, housing, water-works, etc., were in danger of being lost to the nation. An alternative market for another 100,000 barrels of herring was desirable, indeed was vitally necessary; but where was that possible market? I suggested the West Indies with its population avid for salted fish, and possessed of a means of payment in their great surplus production of limes and other citrus fruits. Could not the surplus herring somehow be exchanged for the surplus fruits? We got the Empire Marketing Board, and later the Colonial Marketing Board interested. We had meetings with Mr. De Lesser, Chairman of the Jamaican Chamber of Commerce, and he and one of the directors of Messrs. Tate & Lyle, who had large sugar estates in the West Indies, thought there was something feasible in the proposal. So obviously did Mr. Oliver Stanley when he was President of the Board of Trade. Reports were called for from the Government of Jamaica and the Herring Industry Board; but the proposal I believe rather got shipwrecked over difficulties about merchanting. Neither this country nor the West Indies were yet ready for orderly disposal of surpluses in production, although Mr. Baldwin clearly nibbled at the idea (April 1924) when he suggested bulk exchange of surpluses with the Dominions.

" We must try and see," he said, " if it is not possible to enter into a scheme by which an enormous amount of the foodstuffs which we require from the Dominions could be obtained from them and distributed at cost price with the least possible margin; something of the kind should be thought out in order to obtain in exchange for it the free entry of our manufactured goods into those Dominions where they would not compete with their own."

And even as late as 1935 the courageous and sensible effort by the Potato Marketing Board to dispose of surplus potatoes in Durham county by selling cheaply to the unemployed, thereby benefiting both farmers and the unemployed, was killed after one successful year, by an organised press yell that this was a revolution which, if expanded, would destroy shopkeeping! But it did (and still does) seem to me that along the lines of administrative arrangement for ensuring that the peoples of the British Commonwealth of Nations swopped their marketable surpluses in production, lie possibilities of advance in human well-being almost beyond our imagining.

Some of the experiments in organised marketing into which I inveigled the Empire Marketing Board when I found myself installed as chairman of its Marketing Committee would, I imagine, bear detailed recording if the facts and figures have anywhere been preserved. There was, for example, the experiment dealing with the surplus prime Aberdeen-National Mark cattle. During a period of depression prices had crashed far below an economic level and threatened ruin to the farmers in the north-east of Scotland. To avert this the Empire Marketing Board got together a team of about 50 women canvassers and endeavoured to sell the surplus cattle. Suburban districts in South West London were chosen and the canvassers were let loose upon the householders to explain the superiority of Scots National Mark beef, and how important it was that the housewife should, if she wanted that beef and paid for it, be assured she was getting it and not some lower quality substitute. Whenever the housewife showed interest the canvasser supplied a leaflet with the names of firms in the vicinity who stocked the prime Scots quality, these firms having been previously canvassed and having agreed to stock it and to exhibit posters. It was really wonderful how speedily the experiment increased the demand for the best beef, and

how the surplus was taken off the market by the teeth of the London consumers. Two of the large Co-operative Society organisations, the Royal
Arsenal and the South Suburban, with 90 shops between them, undertook
to stock Scots National Mark beef, and so successful became the venture that
we actually had to circumvent an attempt to send Buckinghamshire cattle
to Aberdeen for the purpose of qualifying for the extra $2\frac{1}{2}d.$ per lb.
quality price on the London market.[1] Similar methods were used to boost
Irish butter in Lancashire.

But our most spectacularly successful experiment I imagine was the one
relating to milk in the Lanarkshire schools. Here I had persuaded the
Empire Marketing Board to venture a sum of £5000. Then I got £2000
out of the Distress in Mining Areas Fund, and by this time, having been
appointed Under Secretary at the Scottish Office, I had the key to other
doors. I cadged—cadged is the operative word—a sum of £477 out of
the Dairy industry. I then collected two able medical enthusiasts, Drs.
Leighton and McKinlay, and we set about seeing what would happen
were we to supply a milk ration per school day to half the school population
in the County of Lanark over a period of four months.

First, all the children were weighed and measured; then, by ballot,
10,000 children were chosen as 'feeders' and another 10,000 were given
no milk ration, but were kept under observation as 'controls.' After a
four months' test all the 20,000 were again weighed and measured; a most
remarkable fact emerged: at age eleven the boys who had been on milk
ration had increased in weight by $6\frac{1}{2}$ oz. over the boys who had got no
milk ration, and at the same age the girls on milk were $12\frac{1}{8}$ oz. heavier in
increase over the girls who were not on milk ration. And both boy and
girl 'feeders' had gained in height over the boy and girl 'controls.' Lesser
increases took place at younger ages; figures so emphatic and so indisputable
could not be ignored and they formed an irresistible argument for the milk
in schools scheme which was later launched with the approval of all parties
in the State.[2]

One other experiment of mine at that time, however, failed miserably.
I had persuaded the Empire Marketing Board to give me money for an
attempt at organising co-operative marketing of eggs in Skye. In some
parts of the island the crofters had only been receiving 4d. per dozen for
their eggs from the merchants who came round with their vans peddling

[1] This method, assisted by a circular appeal to Local Authorities to stipulate wherever possible
home produce in their hospital purchases, caused the sales of Scottish sides of graded beef to
increase on the London market from 237 to 2,547 per week; and the price improved.

[2] I ought to place upon record thanks for the services of Dr. John Macintyre, the Chief
Medical Officer of the Education Authority in Lanarkshire. E.M.B. members such as Dr. Addison
(later Viscount Addison), Mr. Amery, and Mr. Walter Elliot also strongly supported the
experiment.

clothing, black puddings, bootlaces, and other commodities. To inaugurate a better egg marketing system we opened a store at Portree, and offered to purchase for cash at (I think) 1s. per dozen, all the good quality eggs we could get in the island. We candled and graded the eggs and wholesaled them in the best markets on the mainland, and whatever sums over the 1s. per dozen rate we got, were to be returned as bonus later to the people from whom we got the eggs, in proportion as were their sales to us. We printed literature, sent Department of Agriculture exhorters round the townships, and we promised that immediately the organisation was in full swing we would hand it over *gratis* to the crofters to run themselves.

We even tried to bring the merchants into the scheme, but when some of these merchants began offering 1s. 1d. cash down and the crofters, forgetful of our later promised dividends, foolishly took the merchants' bait of the immediate extra penny, our effort dried up, and when it was out of the road the price per dozen eggs slithered down again.

There was one other matter of public policy in the Labour Party's programme in the Parliament of the early twenties which occasioned, to some of us, a perturbation of spirit. It was the free and unrestricted importation of goods, even when they could be classed as ' sweated.' There we were as a party struggling to raise standards of living among the producing classes, urging factory acts and all manner of restrictions and penalties upon employers who underpaid labour and worked child labour for long hours, yet as a party committed to an extreme free trade in the importation of sweated goods, always provided of course that these goods were produced abroad.

Not only had the jute bags of Dundee to compete against the child labour produce of Bengal, but also, it appeared, against the prison labour produce of Belgium. The coir mats of England had been swamped by the coir mats of the prisons of Travancore; the sun-dried raisins of Australia possessed of decent labour standards had to compete in our markets against the dried fruits produced under the miserable standards of the Levant; from Shanghai came liquid eggs packed by labourers working 13 hours daily for seven days a week, and I kept a cutting from the financial columns of the *Manchester Guardian* which seemed to carry the free imports case to its logical conclusion.

" COTTON TRADE LOST TO THE JAPANESE."

" If we are to make any headway there will have to be an increase in the hours of labour and lower wages because Japanese sweated conditions are capturing our markets in the Near East."

Discriminatory tariffs to some of us were no satisfactory remedy: they would have left the competition of 'sweated' goods in foreign markets quite untouched, and in any case the very mention of the word tariffs was a blasphemy and a defilement in the temple of labour during the nineteen-twenties. But with the powerful aid of John Wheatley and Arthur Greenwood I got the Labour Party to appoint a committee to consider and report upon Sweated Imports and International Labour Standards. John Wheatley and myself were appointed as members of the committee. Philip Snowden was to be chairman—an insurance that the Ark of the Free Trade Covenant would be respected—and Arthur Greenwood was appointed secretary.

I must say the Committee turned up trumps. Among its members were Arthur Henderson, Sidney Webb, and Tom Shaw. When the facts were fully laid before them we got an unanimous report, which I think did more to shift the Labour Party away from traditional Whigism than did anything else of which I can remember. We declared for an international boycott of goods produced by countries which failed to implement the Washington Hours Convention regulating the length of the working day. The length of the working day was precise and measurable. There were only 24 hours in a day everywhere in the world. The number of hours worked could not be confused as could money values and exchange rates and purchasing values.

We showed that there existed precedents (always a certain buttress even to a good case!) for complete prohibition of certain classes of imports; not for tariffs or imposts upon price to make them dearer, but for complete and absolute prohibition by law; books which infringed the Copyright Acts: goods proved to have been produced in foreign prisons: indecent books and prints: infected animals: clocks and watches infringing the Trade Marks Act, and so on. And we knocked out the free traffickers by citing the fact that Messrs. Cadbury, the cocoa manufacturers, had to their credit induced the other British and German cocoa buyers to boycott absolutely the slave grown cocoa of San Thome and Principe in Portuguese Africa.

Moreover our proposals, as we were careful to note, were only to be applied to commodities where there were alternative sources of supply. We might have to exclude from our attention oranges, Brazil nuts, mahogany and bear skins; one step, provided it were big enough, was enough for us; but a new conception was here; an improvement in the status and conditions of labour in other lands with an accompanying rise in the standard of life and purchasing power would open up for us new and expanded markets!

And one amusing recollection! It is of a debate in the House of Commons in March, 1925. I had, with some difficulty, procured a tin of liquid eggs from China with which to illustrate my argument. The tin I had deposited in an umbrella stand at the Palace Yard entrance during the morning. But Bob Murray—I'm sure it was he—punctured the canister, and during the day the liquid had oozed out and had corroded the enamel of the stand (incidentally it was from these concoctions that many of the meringues which ladies consume with their afternoon tea are, or were, derived!) When the hour of the debate came I carried the canister into the House of Commons under my jacket, guessing of course whence came the smell, and wondering how long it would cling to my clothes. The canister lay at my feet in the chamber until I was called upon to speak, but the effluvia increased with the period of waiting, and resulted in my colleagues ostentatiously shifting their seats away from my neighbourhood. After the debate, during which I had illustrated my argument by holding up the ' sweated ' goods, I was naturally faced with the difficulty of knowing how to dispose of my unwelcome canister.

Fortune led me to a House of Commons attendant as I was making with it to the River Thames.

" Would you mind disposing of this for me? " I asked.

" Certainly sir," he said most obligingly.

But some days later, when I was going through the lobby with Sidney Webb, I ran into my attendant friend again.

" And did you throw my tin into the river? "

" Well, no sir. I took it 'ome, an' the wife fried the heggs with the 'am, and it was all right, sir, for two or three days, but then the heggs got a bit 'igh, sir, and the wife gave 'em to the Jewish mission for the poor! "

And there was another egg story of the people's food worth remembering—it was fathered upon Dr. Wellington Koo, the Chinese Ambassador in London, but I understand that that gentleman later, although somewhat diplomatically, repudiated parentage. During the First World War our troops, and the troops of our allies in Europe, received enormous quantities of tinned pork from China, the Chinese villagers being encouraged by high prices to send their pigs to the canning factories; in time, it is alleged, there was a shortage of pigs: the supply ran dry. But a trade like that was too good to lose, and village dogs here and there were collected, killed, skinned, and the carcases sent to the factories as pigs. Then in time even the supply of dogs gave out, and the Chinese authorities protested to the managers of the canning factories that village dogs were the scavengers in China, and if the scavengers were to be taken as pork then there was imminent danger of plague! And would the factory managers please therefore discontinue canning the sewage system of China into food for allied soldiers!

As Mr. Samuel Smiles puts it, in his essay on *Thrift*, there is a place for everything, but I question if the fighting men would have relished such an anecdote, whether fabulous in whole or in part, about the origin of their pork and beans, and we had to respect the wishes of our ally China.

In any case there was henceforth for me and mine a rigid prejudice against a foodstuff which, however succulent and edible, might have been village dog.

CHAPTER VIII

THE ZINOVIEFF ELECTION IN 1924

In one of the Loyalty islands, Uvea, so great is the eloquence of the people that they employ oratory to catch fish, whom indeed, they regard in their legends as half human, and it is believed that a shoal of fish thus politely plied with compliments from a canoe will eventually and quite spontaneously beach themselves spellbound.

—Havelock Ellis, ' The Dance of Life,' p. 14

LOOKING BACK upon the election of 1924, I think we probably exaggerated the effect of the Zinovieff letter on the result. The letter was let loose on the Saturday before the election day, when most men and women had their minds or their prejudices already fixed as to how they should vote. Moreover the method of disclosure carried with it all the smell of an election stunt designed to bear upon the central issue of the election: the proposed treaty with and loan to Russia. The propaganda experts opposed to the treaty had already done their best, and with great artistry and power. Sir Robert Horne had talked about Russian lice. Sir Thomas Moore had authoritatively exposed how women had been nationalised by the Soviets, Mr. Churchill dramatically had conjured up:

" Russia, self outcast, sharpens her bayonets in her Arctic night and mechanically proclaims, through half starved lips, her philosophy of hatred and death."

And *Punch* with a cartoon entitled " On the Loan Trail " featured an unkempt ruffian in Whitehall carrying sandwich boards: one hand in his trouser pocket, and the other holding a red flag. The board had the words " *Vote for MacDonald and Me.*" Beyond doubt the populace that was liable to be scared had already had attention from the best practitioners.

Moreover these skilled artists possessed first class material upon which to work in what is known as the Campbell Case. The Attorney General in the Labour Government, Sir Patrick Hastings, had initiated a prosecution against the editor of a Communist weekly paper, because of an article written by a Mr. J. R. Campbell in which soldiers had been incited to refuse to obey orders if these orders involved interference in a trade dispute. When Sir Patrick Hastings learned that the editor had been decorated for gallantry during the recent war he abandoned the prosecution. I surmise, however, that his decision was aided by a discovery that the Communists were going to put Mr. Ramsay MacDonald, the Prime Minister, in the witness box, and be examined about a speech he had delivered in the House of Commons in 1912 in defence of Mr. Tom Mann, when that gentleman had also incited the armed forces to refuse duty in a trade dispute.

Of course the Communists loudly proclaimed their disgust that the Campbell case had been withdrawn; a great propaganda had been denied them. On the other hand the episode provided the opponents of the Labour Party everywhere with first class debating material about political interference with the course of justice!

What however gave the Zinovieff letter a high place at the political election feast in 1924 was its apparent acceptance as authentic by Mr. Ramsay MacDonald, who had gone to the trouble of drafting a reply to it. Labour candidates who had been backing the Russian treaty were embarrassed by the almost crazy irresponsibility and anti-treaty spirit evinced by the letter. If the letter were authentic a government capable of sending an incitement to conspiracy, to armed insurrection, and to civil war in a country with which it was ostensibly engaged in pacific and trade treaty negotiations, was a government which only an abuse of words would class as a friendly, or indeed as a sane government.

Zinovieff, the alleged sender of the letter, was at that time President of the Executive Committee of the Third International; and the letter itself was supposed to have been sent to the Central Committee of the British Communist Party. To this day it is doubtful whether or not the document was an election forgery. Zinovieff himself, liquidated in a later purge of the faithless, is not available as a testator, and of the two Committees of Enquiry set up by the Labour Party, one composed of J. H. Thomas, James Maxton and William Graham, could get nowhere and had to admit defeat, while the other, which included Philip Snowden and R. C. Wallhead, got the length of the Foreign Office and some secret service chief, about whom they were apparently pledged to secrecy; years afterwards, however, 'Dick' Wallhead confided to me that this secret service chief did most definitely believe that the Communist Party Committee in London had received the Zinovieff letter, and under cross-examination by Philip Snowden had—although after much hesitancy—given as the reason for his belief a statement that he had two under-cover agents or correspondents in the Communist Party executive, the one not knowing of the other's Government contacts; but when the reports of both these agents agreed he accepted their reports as true. In this case they had both reported receipt of the Zinovieff letter in London.[1]

And further, according to 'Dick' Wallhead, Snowden had asked whether any of the services—Army, Navy, Air Force—ran special counter-espionage departments, and whether it was possible that some of these other departments had also representatives among the Communist hierarchy. That was possible: just possible, though not likely, was the reply. But it all provided Wallhead with a variety of interesting and humoursome speculations about the under-cover personnel operating in the Communist Party, and its cost to the nation.

Some collateral support for the Dick Wallhead narrative is to be found in Sir Austen Chamberlain's speech in the House of Commons (15.12.24) where he asserted that the Government had got four copies of the letter, all from sources independent of each other, and which did not know that the Government had any other sources of supply.

My opponent in the 1924 election was an energetic, breezy naval commander, who, one gathered, had a difficulty in understanding why Socialists should be called Reds: Black for them was more appropriate—Black as sin! He specialised in orations about how the Socialists betrayed the British Empire at Shanghai, and he buttoned his reefer jacket and let us have it straight from the quarter deck. He certainly had the courage of his beliefs, was good fighting material, and I often wondered why, after one brief spell in Parliament, his party dropped him, or whether he had just dropped his party.

Some of my supporters in my friendlier villages used to concoct strange queries for him at question time: queries such as:

> "Does the candidate think it right that a man should get up to work at five o'clock in the morning if he has the strength to lie in his bed?"

And at one place, Banknock, a colliery audience arranged in advance that they would follow a leader who (whenever he thought the gallant commander had committed a whopper or an excessive foolery) was to place his cap upside down on his, the leader's, head. All the rest of the audience had then to do likewise with their caps upon their heads, but not

---

[1] On the other hand, for the contention that the letter was a forgery, see Mr. Emrys Hughes, M.P.'s " Bolshevik Bogey in Britain," recording the critical examination of the document by M. Rakovsky, then Russian Ambassador in London. M. Rakovsky for example shows that while the letter was headed " Third Communist International," there was never a *first* or a *second* Communist International. There was a third international, but never a third Communist one. And Mr. Marlowe, the Editor of the *Daily Mail*, himself confessed to the *Observer* four years later (4.3.28) that he had two copies of the Zinovieff letter, one in which the recipient was Mr. Arthur McManus, the other in which McManus was purported to have signed the letter.

a word was to be spoken. This dumb insolence was too much for the commander, who wanted to challenge the leader to fight. But the leader happened to be Eddie Beattie, the boxer, and it took my Committee all they knew to escort Eddie home before any damage was done.

Some of the Commander's supporting orators were evidently hot stuff, and once to a rural Blane Valley audience, where practically everyone was his backer, a speaker began by announcing that the first interrupter was going to be immediately thrown out upon the roadway by two hefty looking importees who stood beneath the platform flexing their muscles in expectation.

Scarcely had the orator begun ere a swing door at the rear of the hall was pushed open and an inebriated ploughman entered with the shout, " Goo' ole Fanshawe " (my opponent!). Prompt came the demand to the importee stewards to do their duty, gentlemen! It was expeditiously done, and the ploughman frogmarched and thudded to the road.

Meanwhile another gentleman had risen to a point of order. He had wanted to explain that the extruded ploughman was a good Tory supporter, and that he himself was a committee man. But he got little time to explain matters: the importees got after him too, and had his wife not hurriedly dragged him down to obscurity in time he also would have been for the outer world. I should have liked to have been able to record that the evictions and clearances of supporters continued, but, alas for that, peace and decorum thenceforth reigned, even as if the audience had been Kulaks before Commissars, or as sheep before shearers, so they opened not their mouths any more during the rest of the evening's exhortation.

And one night during that same election my election agent arrived with a doleful countenance at my house. I would require, he said, to go back and hold another meeting at Cambusbarron, and Mrs. Johnston would require to come with me on the platform.

" But why? "

" Well, they have started a story about you there, that every Saturday night when you come home drunk you give your wife a hammering."

How my agent managed to persuade my wife to appear I to this day know not, but the upshot of it all was that we three, my agent, my wife and myself, and a local chairman (almost my only known supporter in the village) bravely stumped on to the platform at Cambusbarron for a repeat election oration, this time before a crowded audience.

When the chairman had finished his brief introduction I rose to my feet and, as I rose, I caught sight of two old men with ear trumpets in the front seat. And one of the old men, with the penetrating voice of the deaf, who always imagine they must shout to be heard, cried to the other old man:

" A kent yon was a dampt lie! "

" Whit wis a dampt lie? "

" That b——y man couldna bash that b——y woman."

My reputation as a drunken wife beater may or may not have contributed to the election result. Anyhow my opponent won, and, alas, I did not have sufficient sense to take a rest and indulge in some form of public service which would not necessitate my living in London. But next thing I knew I was adopted as candidate for Dundee to fill a vacancy caused by the untimely death of Mr. E. D. Morel, the man who killed a Belgian King's private exploitation of the Congo with its forced labour cruelties and terrors. Morel's shoes were impossible for me to fill: his knowledge of foreign and colonial affairs was unique, and, had he lived, he would indubitably have been one day Secretary of State at the Foreign Office. But within a few weeks of the general election I found myself entering Westminster by another door to take Morel's place, and this time a-straddle of nearly 13,000 of a majority.

Dundee was a two member constituency and my sparring partner was a Prohibitionist and Evangelist, Mr. 'Ned' Scrymgeour. How non-teetotal Dundee tolerated us both at the same time is, I confess, to me an abiding mystery. Ned would have shut the pubs by Act of Parliament: I for my part would have left the closing to be done by local option. But perhaps the citizenry only suffered us both lest worse befell them, somewhat after the manner of the Aberdonian who, subsequent to a wicked and riotous life, decided to join the Church. The minister was putting the new communicant through his paces, " And do you love God? " he asked.

" Weel, Minister," he replied, " aboot that, I dinna richt ken, but I'm awfu' fleggit for the ither fellow! "

CHAPTER IX

A NATION ONCE AGAIN

A man called John Lundie, a blacksmith, had practised as a horse doctor in Scotland. Later in Northumberland he had blossomed out as a successful medical practitioner. He told Sir Walter Scott that he used two simples upon his patients—laudamy and calamy.

"But John," said Sir Walter, "do you never happen to kill any of your patients?"

"Kill? Oh ay, maybe sae. Whiles they die and whiles no: but it's the will o' Providence. Ony how, your honour, it wad be lang before it makes up for Flodden."

—Lockhart's 'Life of Scott.'

IN THE year 1925 there was a great entertainment staged at Westminster Hall—the hall where William Wallace was tried and ordered to be decapitated and dismembered. Glasgow Corporation had promoted an Extension of Boundaries Bill, and since London at that time insisted upon keeping an even tighter grip upon Scottish affairs than she does now, the examination of Glasgow's case and the pleas for the opposition by contiguous local authorities had perforce to be held in London. So to London there went flocks of witnesses, skilled and only moderately so: doctors, lawyers, town clerks and their assistants, engineers with their deputies, education officers and gentlemen from the Faculty of Advocates with their wigs and gowns. The fun lasted for several weeks and Members of Parliament were permitted, indeed entitled, to escort small parties of visitors without charge to witness the proceedings.

The tribunal itself was selected from Members of Parliament: none of the Members were Scots; and it was reported that only one had ever been in Scotland, and that was upon an occasion of a grouse shoot; he would therefore, I suppose, be the nearest to breaking the rule about impartiality and freedom from bias. One other of the Members was so far away from knowledge of what he was supposed to be deciding that he thought the town of Yoker in Dunbartonshire was a drink!

The costs of the enquiry by the time the Commons side of it was over were alleged to be in the neighbourhood of £200,000, but whether or not that included the disbursements from the Town Clerk's Fee funds, I cannot say. One skilled witness for an hour and a half in the witness box netted £250. There were over twenty advocates, some of them at £1000 down —cash on the nail: it was called a retainer!—plus £40 a day as a refresher. I do not recollect whether a Committee of the House of Lords insisted upon a rehearing of the evidence and the cross-examinations, but the farce is worth remembering as an illustration of how, in the twenties of this century, government of the people in Scotland, by the people, and for the people, was preserved.

These private bill extravagances and dripping roasts for the lawyer men had gone on for so long that they were almost sacrosanct. I have a pamphlet reprint of a series of articles in the old *Glasgow Mail* dealing with the period 1883-1885 wherein is quoted an official return in the House of Commons secured by an M.P., Mr. Craig Sellar, showing that the cost to the Great Northern Railway Company of its parliamentary promotions amounted to £590,355 plus another £172,722 in securing leave to make alterations in its orders, a total of £763,077 for obtaining leave to construct 245 miles of railway, or £3115 per mile.

Always in Scotland there has been a strong current of nationalism. George Buchanan—the George who flourished in the sixteenth century— the greatest master of the Latin language since it died as a vernacular, reminded the learned world in his Epithalamium, that it was only in Scotland that the onrush of the Roman legions was stopped, and that here they had to build defensive walls for themselves against the Caledonians. The armies of Bruce and James IV defied, it will be remembered, not only the English enemy, but the dread curse of papal excommunication in their struggles. And in the days before the Union we are told that when an English lawyer called Attwood published a book wherein he maintained that England had direct superiority over Scotland, our Parliament in Edinburgh ordered copies of his book to be burned by the common hangman.

Nor did the treaty of Union between Scotland and England in 1707 do anything to stem that current in Scotland. Sir Walter Scott fed it with his Malachi Malagrowther when London made an attempt to obliterate the note issues of the Scottish banks. Burns fed it with his immortal ode of ' Scots Wha Hae,' and he has told us in prose how

    " The story of Wallace poured a tide of Scottish prejudice into my veins which will boil along there till the flood gates of life shut in eternal rest."

And to this day our concerts carry a haunting nostalgia of Jacobite songs, and beerified workmen of a Saturday night when the public houses scale, sing loudly at street corners to Prince Charlie:

> " *Will ye no' come back again*
> *Better lo'ed ye canna be,*
> *Will ye no' come back again?* "

But Jacobitism is only a song: an air on the pipes. Bonnie Prince Charlie (who was half a Pole) is but a melody. And once at a Labour gathering during a by-election, I remember being tormented by an angry republican who was inflamed about the oaths of allegiance being taken by Labour M.P.s, until I asked him who would be the first president of a Scottish republic if chosen by popular vote. While he was pondering over a reply to that one, I said there was only one possible who would poll ten to one against all comers—and she was the present Queen![1] The roar of applause from the audience finished the interrupter, who indeed took it as a notice to quit!

Probably there are fewer English haters today in Scotland than at any time in our history; if one man avows himself an English hater he will get the press headlines (thereby of course indicating his unusualness!), competing with the symbolists who demand that the Queen should have another crowning in Scotland, and with those who complain of the absence of a Scottish representation upon our coinage. This latter grievance, by the way, was once replied to with rather more than a suspicion of contemptuous levity by the Master of the Mint, that gentleman affirming that the bronze currency with the symbolic figure of Britannia had as " the original model for this figure a Scottish lady." No doubt too but here and there diligent search might discover people so hotted up in their nationalism that, as Mr. C. M. Grieve in his Lucky Poet notes: " They'll be wanting a national geometry next."

The real bellows which blow the fires of Scots nationalism are not the symbols upon the coinage, but the absence of adequate supplies of it. The real flame-throwers are the frustrations and irritations of government and administration by a long distance bureaucracy. Sometimes the Scots people —who by the way have treaty rights with England—feel that they are regulated as if they were a branch post office; sometimes as if they were an animal disease; and at the outbreak of the last war I had, as Regional Commissioner for Civil Defence, the utmost difficulty in explaining to the London Food ukase issuers for example that their British schedule of prices for tomatoes had taken no account of climatic differences, and would,

[1] Now, of course, the Queen Mother.

64

unless amended, just about ruin all the tomato growers in Scotland, thereby occasioning civil discontent and imperilling the national unity then so necessary. London administrators had fixed the prices, evidently according to the periods at which tomatoes ripened in Kent and Surrey, not knowing that Scots fruit ripened a month or so later, and that the Scots fruit would come on to the market only at the cheap glutted price rates which would then be ruling. The English tomatoes would have had higher prices a month earlier; but never was there to be any higher compensatory prices for the Scots.

Right down too until the middle of the war the Crown lands in Scotland were administered by the English Minister of Agriculture and Fisheries, and we actually had to get a Bill through Parliament to enable him to be divested of his control. And there must literally be thousands of business executives, local authority representatives and civil servants, continually trekking to and from London on the trains, and by air, attending Committee meetings in the great Metropolis where they are always in a hopeless minority; and that quite apart from the time and expense incurred in attending the meetings.

Another effective blower of the bellows for many years was the almost perpetual preponderance of our unemployment figures *vis-à-vis* England and Wales; we were always from 5 per cent to 7 per cent worse. In the period 1932-1937 there were 3217 new factories started in Great Britain, but Scotland got only 127 of them, or one in every twenty-five; and during the same period we closed 133 factories, so we actually lost on balance. We had serious emigrations of our healthiest stocks of citizenry; we had 300,000 houses without water closet; our maternal mortality was 50 per cent higher than in England and Wales, our infant mortality was 25 per cent worse; our army rejects were 6 per cent higher; control of some of our banks was moving south to Lombard Street.

Yet with all these facts and figures and distresses continually inciting public opinion in Scotland against the long distance government from Whitehall, held to be largely blameworthy for our miseries, and despite the steady growth of a nationalist spirit, the protagonists of self government for Scotland have still to overcome two major difficulties: one, the apprehensions of employers and business men generally that a Scots Parliament would speedily mean the erection of tariff walls upon our borders, with baggage examination and delays *à la* Ulster and Eire, and considerable trade handicaps to some of our Scottish industries: and second, so far as the Trade Unions are concerned the fact that they have been of necessity driven, most of them, to organise upon an all-British basis.

Yet though neither our Chambers of Commerce, nor our Trades Union

Congresses show any disposition so far to sever the bonds that tie them up with their class fellows south of the Cheviots, clearly Scots sentiment is preponderantly behind the new Covenanters. For myself, I had always put Scottish Home Rule on my election programmes—as Keir Hardie did upon his—believing that Imperial Parliament was so increasingly being choked with world affairs that it had little time for attention to Scots domestic problems.

Indeed I should not have been at all surprised if imperial necessity at Westminster had ere this compelled great devolutions of power to a Scots Parliament. But for many years past I have become, and increasingly become, uneasy lest we should get political power without our first having, or at least simultaneously having, an adequate economy to administer. What purport would there be in our getting a Scots Parliament in Edinburgh if it has to administer an emigration system, a glorified Poor Law, and a graveyard! Surely at least it is expedient that we spare *some* part of our propagandist energy towards securing an aircraft production industry: if possible—even at this late date—a motor car industry: recover our trans-atlantic shipping services: be less dependent upon other countries for our cement production, and make the maximum use of our natural resources, by research, and by co-operation among ourselves. Hence the reason why, although I seconded my friend the Rev. James Barr's Home Rule Bill (albeit with some misgivings about the proposal to take all the Scots Members away from Westminster, thereby leaving us with an even more diminished home rule over such important reserved subjects as Foreign Affairs), I also was resolved upon the establishment of the Council of Industry (and Development).

This Council of Industry, under the energetic guidance of Lord Bilsland is, thank Heaven, so far, independent of partisan politics, and acts energetically as a promotion agent for Scots industrial interests. We got the Council appointed with the concurrence of all the living ex-Secretaries of State for Scotland during the war, and any critical comment I could make of it today would be as to the superfluity in its title. The " and Development " might well be nipped off.

Yet while, as I see it, there is vital need for emphasis upon the prior attention that should be paid to our industrial economy, and while there is no instance in the world's history of a people who had achieved economic power being denied political power, there is no denying that the political covenanters, with their over two million signatures, have crystallised national sentiment for native political control in Scotland. All parties must henceforth take stock of these signatories.

CHAPTER X

PEEP SHOWS ON INDUSTRIAL INDIA

If a man in a village has a daughter he is pestered by recruiters. Some people post notices on their doors—" No daughter for factory work in this house."

—Labour recruiting—Japan International Labour
Review. Oct. 1925

THE JUTE operatives in Dundee, balancing themselves precariously from year to year on the border line of hunger, and being repeatedly advised that their poverty conditions were due to a competitive pressure from low waged jute goods produced in Bengal, asked John Sime, the secretary of the Dundee Jute Workers' Union, and me, to go out to India in the year 1925 and to report.

We joined the *Caledonia* at Marseilles, where the quay was filled with sword swallowers, weight lifters, fortune tellers, musicians who played God Save the King, and furtive retailers of filthy postcards, the latter being darted after vigorously by the police. The day was warm, and we had been recommended to a temperance drink—a mineral water of some kind which had the taste of Rochelle salts, and of which having partaken, we at once retired. After a quarter of a century the memory of that nauseous alleviator lingers, and at any rate, due to its potency, we did not witness the arrival of our fellow traveller, the Maharajah of Patiala, with a suite of some 30 persons, mostly in turbans and whiskers, and a major domo in green-grey uniform, and swaggering a huge gold stick. The serene highness had 15 tons of luggage, pianos and what not, and in his person he provided a lasting topic of speculation among his fellow passengers, about the number of his wives, one Anglo-Indian asserting emphatically that the figure was over a hundred. When later during the voyage I met Patiala, I found his chief interest apparently was on deer stalking in the Scottish Highlands, and why did not the Clydeside M.P.s wear the kilt in Parliament? But I did not care to ask him to settle the current bets aboard about his connubial affairs.

Memories

We had other interesting fellow passengers; one, an Arabic scholar who assured me that during the fast of Ramadan, which lasts for a whole month of days from sunrise to sunset, there were wee frees so orthodox and so strict that they would not even swallow their saliva, which, for working to rule, beats anything recorded so far among our narrower brethren in Scotland; and there was an Egyptologist who told me much about Thothmes III and Cheops, but what I particularly noted at the time was that when the Suez Canal was opened in 1875 the then Khedive spent £4,200,000 in festivities. There was also among the passengers an Anglo (or rather a Scots) Indian mine manager called Mason, who operated in the Manbhun region; he hailed originally from Fife, was a keen Socialist, and a doughty champion in the political debates in which I got involved with the saloon passengers.

Perhaps three hours' sailing down the Suez Canal lies El Kantara, the base of operations for our Palestinian army during the war of 1914-18. And here were still the ruins and wreckage of that base—railway lines, the sleepers blown over with sand, sheds in decay and decrepitude, acres of tin-cannery, cement blocks, and telegraph poles. There were half a dozen awry date palm trees with their wrinkled elephant leg stems, and two churches still standing, one said to be a Christian church for soldiery who held by the doctrines of Nazareth, and one a Mahometan Mosque where the muezzin would summon Allah's faithful to prayers, ere they sallied forth in the chartless sands to kill and mutilate other worshippers of Allah. And there was a railway station notice board "Sinai Military Railway," indicating the thoroughfare to Mount Sinai, where Moses got his ten commandments, including that one about Thou shalt not Kill (to say nothing about the one about not stealing!) which the faithful have not hitherto adopted.

A man at my side, who had been an officer under General Maude in the pursuit of the Turks away up to Jerusalem and beyond, stared reminiscently at the ruins of El Kantara. "Faith," he said, "I remember this accursed place . . . over there an English boy who was only fifteen or sixteen had given an older age to be accepted into the army; he had marched two days on end . . . in that heat, that infernal heat, and then he was put on sentry duty. . . . He wasn't asleep really, but he must have been drowsy and he did not answer the challenge promptly. . . . That under Maude was a serious offence, and they tried him by Court Martial and shot him at dawn. Not by the men of his own regiment, no, but by the men of another regiment.

[1] Some doubt has been expressed as to the locus of this incident, if it were at El Kantara, then General Maude was not responsible. He was in command over at Mesopotamia, not Palestine.

68

And General Maude's widow got £50,000 cash down from Parliament, while that poor boy's mother, away in some English village, or in some crowded English city street got nothing but a polite official intimation that the Secretary of State for War regrets. . . . The boy had died not by a German bullet, but by an English one fired by an official order, and now he lies out there, his mother knowing not his resting place, and mercifully not dreaming of the true manner of his dying away in a far sandy drift in the Holy Land, where, let us hope, protected from the kites and crows, he sleeps at peace!

And so across the Red Sea, which, by the way, is turquoise blue, to the great crucible where the 2000 main castes and tribes, with their 3000 sub-divisions with 222 separate languages, and the 319 million people, two-thirds of them living in appalling poverty, and with only 82 per 1000 over five years of age literate, are being pounded together into what is hoped will emerge one day as a political unity. Bande, Materam! Hail, Mother-land!

> " *We have no mother,*
> *We have no father,*
> *No brother, no wife, no child,*
> *No hearth, no home.*
> *We acknowledge nothing, save the motherland.*
> *My motherland, I sing;*
> *Thou art my head, Thou art my heart,*
> *My life and soul art Thou;*
> *My soul, my worship and my art*
> *Before Thy feet I bow."*

Anyone curious about the conditions of labour in India in the first quarter of this century can be safely referred to Miss Kelman's *Labour in India* or to the Indian Year Books. When we arrived in Bombay in 1925 the city was in the throes of a great cotton strike, over 150,000 workers struggling against a reduction on their average wage of £2 3s. 0d. *per month of 240 hours.* I sent cables home, and sufficient funds from British Trade Union sources were forthcoming, so that in the end the 20 per cent cut sought from the miserable wages was obviated.

But the wage rates were not the worst of it—not by a long long chalk mark. There was no Truck Act; there was an infant mortality of 572 per 1000, and an official investigation by the Health Department of the Government of Bombay in 1922 showed that out of every 1000 children born in *one room tenements,* 828·5 died in their first year; the chawls (tenements) I was taken over by the Strike Committee turned my stomach, foul smelling, pitch black holes they were 8 feet by 6 feet, in rows, ashpits and water taps adjacent: the lavatories, little boxes containing a drain for urine and a hole for excrement—the boxes I was told were removed once a day in a basket; it was not the death rate in conditions like that that amazed me, but the living rate!

Foremen and clerks in the mills had a levy system of their own, whereby they took 8 annas per month from the wages of all women workers, and when I asked the proprietor of the Swadeshi mill (an Indian) about the practice, he admitted, but said he could not stop it. At another mill, the Hindostan (and possibly it was the general condition in all mills!), the monthly wages system bred the Bannia or moneylender in great profusion, and the millowner there had started a competitive "tick" system of his own: that was, after a man had worked 14 days he was entitled to apply for an advance of 14 days upon his month's wages, but he had to pay an interest rate of from $\frac{1}{2}$ to 1 anna per rupee, i.e., $37\frac{1}{2}$ per cent to 75 per cent upon the advance, or rather in fact upon the money which he had already earned. And when I asked the chairman of the Millowners' Association (a Parsee!) how upon earth he justified that unconscionable usury the answer coolly was that "It is less anyhow than the rate charged by the moneylenders outside!"

It was in 1925 too that Miss Katherine Mayo arrived from New York to get material for her book *Mother India*—a book which later shocked the civilised world and certainly enraged the Hindus—about the child marriage system; she may have fallen down here and there, particularly when she had taken some story upon trust, as for example when she repeated the quotation often fathered upon Sir Partarb Singh—that if the English departed, "three months afterwards not a rupee or a virgin will be left in Bengal." The story in fact had been vehemently denied years before by Sir Partarb.[1] When Miss Mayo was in India I did not meet her, but I often wondered why no one apparently had taken her to see in Bombay the amazing Grant Road-Falkland Road system of wooden compartments for prostitute women. In front there were iron bars; behind sat, or lolled, the women; for all the world as if they were animals caged in a zoo. Tram cars clanged down the middle of the street, a busy thoroughfare; a thousand women of almost every race, except British, beckoning and bargaining, and now and again an iron gate would be opened and a customer would enter. I took photographs of this amazing scene, nobody objecting in the slightest, and published them on my return to Scotland, in the hope, which proved vain, that they would carry conviction of the incredible.

[1] Miss Mayo's *Mother India*: a Rejoinder by K. Natarajan, Editor, The Indian Social Reformer, Madras.

Peep Shows on Industrial India

Mr. S. M. Edwardes in his *Crime in India* (1924) quotes a flybill for the Ripon Theatre in the Grant Road of Bombay:

RATES OF TICKETS

						Rupees.	Annas.	Pice.
Gallery	..	..	..	..	..	0	8	0
Pit	..	..	..	..	..	0	4	0
Ladies	..	..	..	..	..	0	4	0
Prostitutes	..	..	..	..	..	1	0	0
Stalls	..	..	..	..	..	1	0	0

Persons shall not be allowed according to our will.

Men behaving ungentlemanly shall be driven out without returning the money.

I am not sure if it was to this particular theatre that John Syme and I, accompanied by a British police inspector, paid a surprise visit. But at an Indian theatre in the area one night our presence among the audience was clearly a great embarrassment to the actors, and detracted the interest of the audience from the stage: obviously there was expectation of imminent arrest of somebody: an actor disguised as a Rajput warrior made a poor shape at fighting half a dozen demons simultaneously, but the conditions were against an engrossed attention and he must have been greatly relieved when we filed out.

We saw little evidence in Bombay of untouchability. There are said to be between 50 and 60 million outcasts in India, who are taught that their sad state is due to wickedness in some former existence. But Mr. N. M. Joshi, the secretary of the Indian Trade Union Congress, and Mr. R. R. Bakkale, the secretary of the Textile Union,[1] declared that in the large industrial areas the mill factory system was wiping untouchability out. Just as Sabbatarianism cannot be sustained during clashes on a battlefield so too must complicated industrial processes be incompatible with the untouchability of sections of handlers or producers. And up at Ahmedabad, when I got there, I found the Textile Labour Union in high feather because it now had got a piecer in the Laxmi Cotton Mills, an untouchable called Bhagat, elected unopposed to the local municipality. But Ahmedabad was within four miles of Gandhi's home, and Gandhi, to his everlasting

[1] Neither Mr. Joshi nor Mr. Bakkale were of the lawyer-politician-careerist type so common, we found, among Union builders in India. They were the ablest men we met in Trade Union circles in India, and they were members of the Servants of India Society, who voluntarily restricted their incomes to £2 per week.

credit, had bravely warred all his life against untouchability, declaring that "Nobody is untouchable to God!"

Over to Nagpur where a stocky Glasgow keelie soldier in a Highland regiment walked about the railway station maintaining order. He had a half cigarette over his ear, and he good-humouredly moved the crowds about with such adjurations as "Come on, Granpaw!" and "Move along, Whiskers!" Everybody obliged him as he shepherded the various theological groups to their respective drinking water stations. One water station was placarded "Drinking water for Christians": another "Drinking water for Hindus," and a third "Drinking water for Mahometans." I never saw any watering provision for Jews or Untouchables, but when I enquired of the soldier boy on the subject, he dismissed the problem airily by saying: "Ach, it's a' the same watter onywey. It's a' the yin wan!"

It might in truth be the same water, but the various denominations, before they drank, bought clay bowls for the purpose from the potters, who did a roaring business, and the bowls were all smashed on the station platform after being used, I expect lest anyone should service them again, mayhap at a polluted water.

Across India to Calcutta. Peasants in the wheat fields: cheap, almost pathetically cheap, gimcrack shoddy village temples, shrines with stucco bulls: black buffaloes wallowing in the clay puddles: towards evening the peasants following their cattle home: and everywhere the acrid, but not unpleasant, smell of burning dung, the common fuel of rural India.

In Calcutta where was a Durga Pouga (I hope I am spelling it correctly!) a great religious procession, perhaps a mile long, with emblems and bannerettes: and there was a band in the procession playing—and I could scarcely credit my hearing—the tune of

> " *Wha saw the tattie howkers,*
> *Wha saw them gauin awa.*
> *Wha saw the tattie howkers*
> *Marchin' tae the Broomielaw* "

—picked up almost for a certainty from some Scots army band!

Of course we visited the temple of the goddess Kali and a priest showed us around for two rupees (3s.). In the Ganges, flowing past, there was a dead dog with a kite perched on top, and people were washing themselves for holiness. Here too was a burning Ghat, where a dead boy was being incinerated, his legs doubled up below him, and the body laid upon a row of logs: another row of logs was placed on top of the body, a fire was lit below and the relatives squatted around two yards off. The priest said they burned all except the navel, but he could not tell me how they stopped at that. Then we passed through rows of beggars and holy men to the temple of the goddess herself—a huge brass (or gold) tongue, leering eyes, a grotesque fearsome face, a squat figure. Before her the pilgrims bow, the bell booms, and the priest takes the cash. Nearby is a tree laden with small stones tied with thread, and other similar offerings to the goddess by child-less women, with a promise or vow that if they have a baby they will return after six months and deposit a lock of the baby's hair at the foot of the tree. Beside the tree lay large quantities of black hair!

But our main preoccupation in Calcutta and in Bengal was the economics and practice of the Jute industry, and especially in its competitive pressure upon wage standards in Dundee. I must say that most of the men in a position to assist us in our enquiries gave us that assistance without hesitation, and it was obvious that men like Mr. R. N. Band, then the president of the Jute Employers' Association, and Sir Alexander Murray, a prominent industrialist, were as anxious as Mrs. Santosh Kumari Gupta, the wealthy little lady who founded and largely financed the Bengal Jute Workers' Association, to lift the stigma from the industry and to stop the scandalous levy commission upon wages called the Sardar system.[1] The sardar is a foreman, and he levies, for his own pocket, a commission or bribe before a worker is employed. There was no fixed tariff, every sardar screwing what he could out of his underlings. Some weavers paid as high as 75 rupees, two or three months' wages, for permission to work, but the average or normal levy was about 10 rupees. Nobody escaped. We were told of an assistant sardar who had a demand made upon him for 1500 rupees.

But that initial capital levy upon future wages was only the first toll. There was a regular backsheesh demanded after that, upon pay day every month, of a penny or twopence per employee. When the employee was unable to meet the sardar's demand he went to a Kabuli, a moneylender, and he, getting no security for his loan, exacted a rate of interest up to 300 per cent; and we saw these Kabulis at the jute factory gates, large hefty fellows with turbans and beards and big sticks, engaged in collecting their dues. The millowners and managers to whom I spoke professed their inability to stop this sardar robbery system, but Mr. Addyman, the manager of the Bombay Woollen Mills and chairman of the European Association in Bombay, had ruthlessly stamped it out by sacking the bribe takers, and he told me that the workers had enthusiastically backed him in his struggle.

In the jute industry in Bengal there was in full swing one ingenious

[1] So far as we could learn no white foreman engaged himself in the nefarious business. Indian foremen only.

trick of factory act evasion. No registration of births was in force and factory doctors were in the habit of examining teeth and armpits of children to see that none but children over twelve was permitted to work in the mills: but once passed, there was a double shift system whereby a child could work six hours in one mill and then go to another mill for six hours.

I interviewed everybody I could in Calcutta, from Lord Reading, the Viceroy, down through proprietors, agents, missionaries, political leaders of all schools of thought, Government officials, and newspaper men, and I went about the jute villages addressing meetings of workmen, until we got at last a pretty complete picture of the facts about the jute industry in Bengal, which was later published in pamphlet form in Dundee.[1]

But not quite everybody helped us in our quest. There were about 800 to 900 Dundee white assistants in the Bengal jute factories, and we tried a publicly advertised meeting for them, but with poor results. The hour of our meeting was actually altered in the press advertisement without our knowledge or consent, to the impossible one of 9 p.m. And as we discovered later the press was instructed to make the alteration in our advertisement (for which we had paid) after the hall authorities had privately discussed the matter with a prominent jute millowner.

And there was another comic interlude. Mr. Goswami, one of the Swaraj left wing leaders, handed in disgust to John Sime, a letter signed by twenty Dundee communists, asking him (Goswami) to report week by week to the aforesaid twenty as to whether we were indulging in " corrupt banquets and hospitality." What had made these worthy Communists suspicious was that while the Trade Unionists of Dundee had been prepared to pay the expenses of our Indian visit, I had mysteriously and inexplicably declined, and had insisted upon paying my own travelling charges, and, continued the epistle, " this makes us somewhat uneasy regarding his intentions." Some phoney work must be afoot! John Sime refused to treat this " I spy " business as comedy and vowed he would have it lantern slided and published broadcast from Lochee to Broughty Ferry, when he returned home, and fulfil his vow I believe he did.

Some of the village meetings were of interest. One at Kankanarrah, I remember, was addressed under an awning which bore the inscription in huge letters:

WELCOME
GOD SAVE YOU. LOOK UPON OUR POORNESS

And one spoke with pigeons or parakeets fluttering about, and dogs, goats and buffaloes ambling in and out. And at another poverty stricken place,

[1] *Exploitation in India*—Johnston & Sime.

Jagaddal, there had been inappropriately placed opposite a mill an advertisement:

HAIG'S WHISKY

INSIST ON HAVING IT

He was a hopeful gentleman, the advertising agent who selected that site!

Many of the *bustees* (houses) in the Jute area were indescribably filthy, and I collected a dengue fever inspecting a group of them, so that, on recovery, I was not in the slightest sorry to leave Bengal. To Dundee I could send, however, a message that the relative efficiency of the Dundee millworker to the Indian millworker was at least as 3 is to 1, and that a Government nominee on the Bengal Legislative Council, Mr. Chowdhry, had supplied us with figures showing that in the ten years 1915-1924 profits distributed to shareholders in the Bengal industry, plus profits placed to reserve, totalled £300 millions sterling, or 90 per cent per annum on the capital invested. There were from 300,000 to 327,000 workers employed at an average wage of £12 10s. od. per annum. A profit of 300 millions sterling arising out of the labour of 300,000 workers in ten years is £1000 per head.

That means £100 per annum per worker, and as the average wage was £12 10s. od. it follows that the average annual profit was eight times the wage bill.

Moreover the land and buildings were worth, in most cases, from 10 to 15 times the sums at which they stood in the companies' balance sheets.

About sixty per cent of the jute company shares were held by Indians. And that, by and large, was the economy of the industry which threatened the life of Dundee.

Then off on the grand tour. First, to Darjeeling, twenty-four hours by rail, but to a temperature drop from 86° in Calcutta to 39° at Darjeeling. Awe-inspiring mountain scenery, Kinchinjunga almost as far in the clouds as Everest; the nomenclature translated means The Abode of the Gods. It is always wreathed in snow, and wild gales sweep its fastnesses. In the vicinity of Darjeeling British army bugles sound for meals; women, thousands of them, many with babies aft and bags before, were plucking tea leaves, but I was not sure about the dietetic effect of the not uncommon practice whereby a handful of plucked leaves would be used for sanitary purposes with the babies, and the leaves then thrown back to the bag. On the spot I almost became a coffee addict.

We inspected one tea estate, Major Little's, and there the Nepalese population appeared cheerful and well-fed and comfortable; their housing was good. But I could not understand complaints made about the Church

75

of Scotland school teachers, who were said to have a wages rate of only 20 rupees per month; that was 30s. The school children, Ghurkas, looked fine, free, happy youngsters; they sang action songs to us, and wound up with God Save the King; they looked indeed happier than their teachers.

We could hardly get away from Darjeeling for the station-master holding up the train by salaaming us and saying " Your Honours "; finally I made him happy by assuring him that I would let both the King and the Viceroy know what a treasure of a station-master they had!

I had intended, if I could, to see some of the hereditary caste of thieves, whose children were being compulsorily educated by the State (the only compulsory education in India!). I failed in that; but I did manage to make contact with some Bhoyans and low caste Santals in the Jheria-Asansol coalfields; both ate rats and snakes; they dug the rats out of the paddy (rice fields) after harvest, and ate both the rats and the rice which the rats had stored in their holes against the winter. To one Bhoyan who had a smattering of English I put the question as to whether he did not consider mice to be a morsel sweeter than the rats, but he said ' no, sahib, there was not so much eating on a mouse ! '

In the coalmines there were still some 60,000 women workers, all (I think) carrying tubs on their heads with the coal excavated by their hewer husbands. In the Asansol area working five days (3 tubs per day at 7 to 8 annas per tub) hewers could earn about 10s. for the week, but at Raniganj coalfields I was assured the shifts were of 24 hours at a stretch, although of course the workers were not actively employed all that time. The houses, called dowrahs, were much superior to the houses in either the jute or the cotton factory areas.

Benares is a very holy Hindu city filled with temples—the Monkey temple, the Gold temple, and so on, and as Macaulay said in his essay on Warren Hastings " rich with shrines and minarets and balconies and carved oriels." Holy mendicants abound, sitting in dirt and hair, and with alms dishes extended; there is a stench of burning flesh from the ghats, and floating down holy mother Ganges are many half-decomposed corpses, kites sitting on the bodies picking steadily. Nearby, four miles off, is Saranath, where the Buddha first taught, and the Dhamek Stupa, built by King Asoka about two centuries B.C., and covered over by Mahometan conquerors and forgotten until (one at least up for that viceroy!) Lord Curzon's time, and under his direction restored.

Nearby to our hotel I was intrigued by a doctor's shop announcement:

COMPLICATED DISEASES

TREATED EXPLICITLY

and I am to this day sorry I did not think out an imaginary disease, go in, and speculate a rupee or two for the fun of the thing.

At night in our hotel we had Mohammed Buksh, said to be the greatest conjurer in India. His skill was hereditary: a brother was conjuring at the Wembley Exhibition; and he himself was a marvel. We sat two yards away from him, and he produced eight small living birds from below an empty basket; he made a rupee run up the back of my hand without his touching it. He allowed us to pick a card from a pack, tear it in pieces, and hold one piece; he then put a lid over the remaining pieces, and lo, there was the card complete except for the part we had kept. He told us that his grandfather had performed the rope trick at Barrackpore, but that no one had done it since. This is a trick whereby a rope is made to grow upwards from a flower pot, a boy climbs up the rope, and disappears. I was prepared, after the rupee running up the back of my hand trick, to believe much, but the authenticity of the rope story has been repeatedly challenged.

Then to Agra and one of the wonders of the world, the Taj Mahal, a poem in white Jaipur marble, precious stones, and beautiful gardens, where realisation far transcends expectation. Built in the seventeenth century— " time of Shah Jehan " as the guides date it, a tomb for the Shah's beloved princess Mumtaz-i-Mahal, it still today commands the awe and the admiration of the world. But the Shah by modern standards was in himself a most disagreeable person. Manucci, the Venetian traveller, records that he kept at his court several baskets of poisonous snakes for the purpose of biting offenders. This method of capital punishment was sometimes varied by guilty persons being thrown to mad elephants who tore their victims to pieces. And Manucci tells us of a curious punishment Jehan reserved for military commanders who fled from battle. Not only were they made to suffer in their own bodies, but rats were placed in the trousers of their wives and daughters, and to a westerner, the fact that the Taj was built by forced labour does somehow detract intangibly—it may be irrationally—from its beauty. Perhaps a worthier monument is that one at Ghazipur to the Lord Cornwallis who died there, after having fixed a system of land rent restriction,[1] and where to this day the ryots worship or salaam his tomb as they pass.

At Delhi we ran into an able secretariat of the government of India— Sir Clement Hindley, of the Railway Board, Sir Charles Innes of the Commerce Department, Sir Bhuphendra Nath Mitra, Advocate-General Das, and others, and were piloted about the capital, Himayams tomb and Kutb's tomb, by a son of Principal Clow of Glasgow, who is now Sir

[1] *Cambridge Modern History* IX, 713.

Andrew Clow of the Gas Board in Scotland. Delhi Fort, with its peacock throne of gold and jewels, had been pillaged by Rajput invaders, but had also been savaged by British troops after the mutiny; exquisite marble work had been stolen or damaged: a beauty room had been converted into a cookhouse, and priceless decorations four centuries old, blackened with smoke. On one lintel of a room which had been converted into a military prison, two of the prisoners had carved their names, " J. McCabe Belfast " and " D. O'Brien."

South then to the native Indian state of Jaipur, its capital thoroughfares between 30 and 40 yards wide: its garishly dressed populace: its flocks of camels in the main streets heaving their way through the crowds; elephants too and thousands of peacocks, pigeons, kites, goats, bullocks, buffaloes; and marriage processions with weird tom-tom music, and bridegrooms arrayed in red and gold with their brides tied to their mantles. The buildings mostly of pink stone; abundance of mice and lizards in the hotel bedrooms, but it is an offence to kill, since all life is one. No income tax or municipal tax—all revenue being raised by a levy of about one-fourth of the standing crops. Wages low—lower than in British India—coolies earning only 8 to 12 annas per day.[1] Right in the midst of the city is the huge decorated maharaja's palace, the zenana, or women's quarters, at the back being protected by a lake filled with alligators. The protectors or feeders of these alligators are royal servants who, at certain stated times, go down to the lakeside and shout *Holo* and throw huge pieces of mutton tied to the end of ropes into the water. The alligators crawl landward after the mutton when the ropes are hauled in, and one old fellow allowed a keeper to clap its forehead. But the others were ugly brutes, and one I saw snapped at a man's leg.

Some of the artificers in the bazaars were splendid workmen: the enamel workers in brass and ebony carvers I watched for hours, especially the enamel workers, whose secret processes had been handed down from father to son for generations. In the School of Art magnificent designing and craftsmanship were displayed and taught, but the teachers were rewarded shamefully—assistants 12 rupees per month (18s.) and head teachers anything from 20 rupees (30s.) to 40 rupees (60s.) per month. One man I saw, a creative architect engaged in designing a monument for Calcutta, had only 20 rupees (30s.) per month. Outside the city, at Sanganer, I saw white paper being manufactured from jute and lime and water on hay reed frames by a process which had been a secret for 1000 years; the price was 1s. 6d. per quire of double sheets, 26 in. x 18 in.

The British resident, Colonel Cator, got us a royal elephant, a huge

---

[1] Eightpence to a shilling.

beast called Mohan Mala, 'beloved Garland,' to carry us up the steep hill at Amber, the old deserted capital, where monkeys with curled tails run along the walls and green parrots build their nests in the windows; and tigers prowl at night by the lake at the hill foot.

And Colonel Cator told us that in Jaipur, girls were married from age six upwards, the poorest fathers paying 200 rupees in dowry, which most frequently had to be borrowed, the money lenders charging 60 per cent interest. Almost the entire population was living under crushing burdens of usury.

On to Ahmedabad, Gandhi's town, a congeries of small factory cotton hells with a Sathi (" Companion " is how the word is translated) system in full blast, and which I had not encountered elsewhere in India. Jobbers or touts scoured the villages, taking charge of boys for a term of five years. The parents were paid 30 to 40 rupees and the boys went off with the Companions. Often the boys would be resold at a profit and forced to work for ten hours daily, mornings in one mill and afternoons in another, the boys' wages going into the pockets of the Companions. The victims lived in a semi-starved condition.

There was a Textile Workers' Union which ran a co-operative grain shop at 10 per cent lower than normal market prices, but I could not understand why it did not compete the other traders to a standstill. Wages were 14 per cent lower than in Bombay. In some mills there were no women's urinals: the employees in the mills were said by a Government Official to be living below the standards prescribed in the Bombay Jail Manual for Prisoners, but he begged of me not to quote him, lest the Indian millowners would declare this to be a British attack upon the Swaraj or Indian independence movement. Gandhi's temperance crusade in 1921, he asserted, had been converted into an anti-British crusade—" Don't drink in Government shops," and the bibulous ones were assured that immediately the British were driven out they would be able to " brew their own drink without hindrance ": for all the world like Shakespeare's Jack Cade who promised that seven halfpenny loaves should be sold for a penny, and the three hoop'd pot have ten hoops: it would be a felony to drink small beer, and all the realm would be in common—when he was King!

I made my stay short in Ahmedabad, and stepping over some stark naked animal-like men lying on the pavements, made off for Gandhi's ashram, four miles out through cotton growing land, and droves of monkeys by the wayside. Unfortunately Gandhi could not cancel engagements he had contracted at Wardha, but his son deputised for him, gave me food, and showed me around. The place was plain and simple, a single storey veranda, with some 200 people mostly being instructed in weaving. There was a fine herd of cows, and there was a framework of red pomegranate blossom.

Gandhi, the Mahatma (great soul), I had met once in London. He came of Government official stock in Kathieawar, was married at age 13, and had a son before he left for his law studies in London. After he became a barrister he was sent professionally to South Africa, where he was outraged at the way his compatriots were treated, and when he himself was bundled roughly out of a railway carriage at Maritzburg as a species of coolie, and told although he had a first class ticket that the place for him was the van, and was left to freeze on a station platform, he became Indian nationalist. Twenty years of his life he spent in South Africa fighting Indian trader grievances in the law courts. Returning to India he gradually developed his belief that the only way to secure his country's independence was through non-violent, non co-operation with the British. But when his theories were tried out on a large scale the non-violence disappeared and there emerged murders and martial law. Promptly Gandhi displayed the great moral courage which was his by calling off the civil disobedience campaign, and at Nadiad declaring publicly that he had made a " Himalayan miscalculation " in starting it. India was not ready for the stern disciplinary conditions and sacrifices of non-violence.

Parts of Gandhi's living creed were beyond my understanding. I could not for the life of me grasp, for example, how he could find religious objection to cows' milk but not to goats' milk, nor what he found wrong with the eating of hen's eggs, even when they were sterilized. I suppose there is bacteriological life in a lettuce, and that the only way one can refrain from destroying living organisms is simply not to eat at all. But Gandhi was a great old gentleman and exercised a profound and beneficent influence upon millions of his fellow countrymen; hundreds of thousands literally venerated him, and when he was a prisoner at Poona, and suffered from appendicitis, it must have taken an exceptional act of courage on the part of the prison doctor (an Englishman, Colonel Maddocks) to decide upon an operation. Had that operation failed and Gahndi died, all India would have declared the British Raj had foully murdered him!

In appearance the Mahatma was like the pictures we used to see of Indian famine victims; he had wretchedly bad teeth, peered at one through nickle plated spectacles, and arrayed himself in rough homespun, to a westerner so insufficiently, that he always gave the impression of being a skinny man about to take a pneumonia.

Back to Bombay, where I made speeches about the factory hovels and the death rates which excited and irritated the Swarajist press; I was editorially advised to get off back to Dundee where housing was bad enough and leave the chawl owners in Bombay to manage their own affairs. And the British police authorities, wondering what kind of wild fowl of a Briton I must be to be in the bad books of both Indian and British millowners, put their C.I.D. agents on to me, disguised as taxi drivers and the like. One police agent taxi driver was embarrassed every time I winked to him. I hope he reported the winks!

CHAPTER XI

THE SAVIDGE CASE

*The Court of Star Chamber hath abounded in extravagant censures . . .
for divers causes where there hath been no offence.*

—*The Grand Remonstrance,* 1641

LATE ON the night of 15th May 1926, before we had become familiar
with epithets like " the police state " or " the iron curtain," a House
of Commons attendant searched me out in the library; there was a gentleman called Savidge in the lobby looking for me. The visitor had an extraordinary story to tell. The first part of it was common knowledge, having
been widely splashed in the press.

Sir Leo Money, a well-known economist and ex-member of the 1914-
1918 Government, had, along with a young woman called Irene Savidge
(my visitor's daughter), been arrested and charged with improper behaviour
in Hyde Park. The case had been heard at Marylebone Court, but the
magistrate (the equivalent, I believe, in legal grade of our Scots stipendiaries)
had been so dissatisfied with the police evidence for the prosecution that,
without calling upon the young woman for her testimony, dismissed the
case and awarded a penalty of £10 against the police. A few days later the
Home Secretary, Sir William Johynson Hicks—" Jix " for short—authorised
an investigation into whether or not the police had committed perjury.

Still some days later, the 15th May, at 2 p.m., a police car had called
at the works where Miss Savidge was employed, and, while a woman
police officer remained seated in the car, two sergeants got out and asked
for the Welfare Officer. To that gentleman one of the sergeants made the
request that he send for Miss Savidge. When she came the sergeant explained
that there were a few matters to be cleared up at Scotland Yard about the
case recently disposed of: that there was a policewoman in the car outside,
and would Miss Savidge mind coming along? The Welfare Officer evidently
demurred, saying the request was unusual, and asked the girl if she was
willing. The sergeant declared the matter was urgent. The girl agreed
to go.

Not a word was said that she was going to be examined, and a statement taken from her. Not a word that she could be accompanied, if she wished, by a friend. Not a word about advising her mother where she was going, although the car passed the end of the road where the Savidge family lived; but off the party went in the car to Scotland Yard. When it reached there the policewoman was dismissed, and Miss Savidge became the subject of a severe (and according to her story) at times an indelicate cross-examination, lasting for over four hours, by two skilled police interrogators, one of whom was Chief Inspector Collins. Statements alleged by the young woman to have been made by her interrogators, though later emphatically denied by the police at the Tribunal set up to determine the truth, as: " Now you are a really good girl, and you never had a man, have you? ": " but there are several things you can do without really sinning; do not be afraid to tell us as, we are looking after you "; and " Don't tell lies to us: we know everything and if you tell lies, both you and Sir Leo Money will suffer," and others of a like kind continued a long time.

Then after something like four hours of it, allowing for a brief tea interval, the young woman was escorted back to her home in a police car about 8 p.m., and there she collapsed. Her mother, by the way, had been telephoned by the police about 6 p.m. that she was not to be anxious about her daughter's absence.

The details of the young woman's statement were supplied to Sir Leo Money's solicitors, and, although Mr. Savidge and his family shrank from the publicity that further action would entail, he thought in the public interest something should be done about it.

I agreed I would raise the matter in the House of Commons conditionally upon Sir Leo's solicitors—a most reputable firm—coming to see me next morning with confirmatory evidence, and giving me a copy of Miss Savidge's signed statement of what she alleged had occurred at Scotland Yard. Next morning a lawyer duly arrived and we went over Miss Savidge's statement in detail. Thereafter I put down a special notice question asking whether all this was done with the Home Secretary's approval, and later, on the adjournment, retailed to an astonished and angry House of Commons what, as I had been advised, had happened.

The Home Secretary, and the Prime Minister, Mr. Baldwin, were manifestly disturbed about the whole business, and especially about the possible reactions of the general public towards the Metropolitan Police. The Home Secretary admitted that an interview had taken place at Scotland Yard: that Miss Savidge had no legal adviser or friend present: that the woman police officer had been told her presence was not required at the interview: that Miss Savidge had never been warned that anything extracted from her under the examination might have implicated her in another action. On the other hand some of the third degree and indelicate suggestions were denied by the interrogators. But he, the Home Secretary, was gravely anxious about the proceedings—even that part of them that was not denied—and would set up a Tribunal of Enquiry at once. Sir John Simon, a former Home Secretary, cried " If this had happened to my daughter . . ." but the end of his sentence was drowned in a burst of cheering from all parts of the House of Commons.

An enquiry was promptly held ; Mr. Norman Birkett was counsel for the police, and Sir Patrick Hastings for Miss Savidge, and after some hard swearing and perjury somewhere, the Tribunal by a majority of 2 to 1 accepted the police version of what had transpired at Scotland Yard. Mr. Lees Smith, M.P., signed a minority report, accepted Miss Savidge as a truthful witness, and gave his reasons for discarding some of the police evidence. But all members of the Tribunal were agreed that it was most reprehensible that the police should have called for the young woman at her place of business and not at her own home, have failed to warn her of the " possible consequences " of making a statement and in not having a policewoman present at the interview. The legal journals, the *Law Journal* and the *Law Times* sided with the minority report, and they were especially emphatic in condemnation of the action of the public prosecutor, Sir Archibald Bodkin, who had actually sent a letter to Sir Leo Money's solicitors on 17th May—that was two days after the Scotland Yard gruelling of Miss Savidge—to say that he wanted a fresh statement from Sir Leo Money and that " there is no necessity for me to obtain your consent, or indeed to consult you in any matter whatsoever." And the last paragraph of this minatory letter ran: " If you decline I must take other steps to procure what is essential for me to have before me."

But this, while it might have worked with a young woman in a factory, miscarried when applied to a firm of solicitors.

All that eventuated from the Enquiry was a series of new directions to the police for the future in accordance with the views of the Tribunal, forbidding the authorities from repeating some of their " usual practices " as they claimed them to be.

No law abiding citizen wants to hinder the police in the proper discharge of their duty, but every law-abiding citizen insists upon fair and open public trial, and, when a verdict is given, no surreptitious retrial by police agents under the pretext of enquiry into something else. To public prosecutors and others whom it might concern that was the chief and, let us hope, abiding lesson of the Savidge Case.

CHAPTER XII

O CANADA

Nova Scotia—the name speaks for itself—and as for Canada, why it is as Scotch as Lochaber—whatever of it is not French.

—Noctes Ambrosianae. No. 46, Septbr. 1829

THE DELEGATES from the Empire Parliamentary Association to Canada in the autumn of 1928 must have given their Chairman, Lord Peel, many an exciting headache. For we were a mixed and often discordant grouping, as indeed was perhaps proper and desirable, since among our members we had always someone who could appeal to any kind of audience in the great amalgam of races and coherencies which constitute modern Canada. We had Indian Swarajists, Australians, New Zealanders, a man from Zululand, a Maltese, a speaker from a Boer Parliament, members of Mr. De Valera's Government, high Tories like Sir John Marriott, and Clyde Socialists like David Kirkwood. We had aristocrats, colliers, lawyers, engineers. and ex-policemen: and nobody pulled his punches.

Sir John Marriott would tell audiences which included Boers, Indians, and Celts, about the superiority of and domination by the Anglo-Saxon race over lesser breeds. David Kirkwood, at a ship's concert, chose to sing "Stirling Brig" and prefaced his song with an explanation of how "we leathered the English!" An Irish delegate told an astonished Canadian gathering that it was an Irish saint, Brendan by name, a navigator in his spare time, who had discovered Canada in the sixth century—this was proved, he said, by old writings and by mythology. He also boosted Irish whisky and declared that Scotch whisky was not a drink for a man, but only for women and aged gentlemen taking toddy before going to bed. The Scots delegation did not rise to that fly; but the Irish were not always in agreement among themselves, and one of them, Senator Barrington, provided a caustic commentary upon the compulsory teaching of the Irish language, declaring it to be the exact equivalent in fatuity of what would be a compulsory tuition of the language of the Objibway Indians in the schools of the United States, or teaching Scots children "Scots Wha Hae" in Pictish!

The delegate from Zululand too was at some pains to explain in the presence of the Boers that there were in South Africa 15,000 natives who were on the electoral rolls, and that in every constituency they voted for an Englishman in preference to a Boer. And there was one glorious occasion in the Annapolis valley when a local judge, who had strongly fortified himself for the occasion with fermented liquors, gave us a great speech of welcome. Lord Peel was to reply. I enjoyed every minute of the judge's oration, which concluded with the peroration: " The freedom of the city is yours. I will suspend all the sentences! "

Perhaps the only occasion on which I can have caused serious offence was over the miner-harvesters from Britain. The idea of the harvesting scheme in itself was splendid—unemployed miners in Britain encouraged to accept assisted passages to Canada to help ingather the harvest. Wages guaranteed to a minimum of £3 per week plus board and bonuses. Many of the men, it was hoped, would settle down permanently in the Dominion; if not, their return passages were to be provided for. The Shipping Companies played up well in transit with first class food. Unfortunately the screening by the Ministry of Labour in this country was not always too good; perhaps in some cases local labour exchange officers would be only too glad to get doubtful or difficult characters off their books. And an ingenious bureaucrat in London had devised a declaration which all the married men volunteers had to sign: it was tantamount to abnegation of poor law relief rights by the dependents they left behind. Here was the declaration:

" I............declare that during my absence in Canada, I have made provision for the care of my wife and children . . . that her parents are willing to care for them and provide for them "

(man)

"............I agree that above statement is correct."

(wife)

Nevertheless there were all told about 8000 volunteers, and inevitably a percentage of them misfits, workshys, chronic grumblers, and sore-bellies; and there were some genuine physical weaklings who could not stand the rigours of the new life, and who should never have been passed as fit. On the other hand there was also a proportion—a small one perhaps—of the farmer employers who were not too accommodating, or ready to make allowances, and some few who were openly accused of breaking the terms of the contract with the men, and of underpaying them. Yet with all these handicaps almost 70 per cent of the harvesters set their teeth, surmounted their difficulties, and made a success of the scheme.

But one night at a Winnipeg railway station, Tom Shaw (later Minister of Labour) and I had seen a group of the returning 'misfits' penned behind locked railings, and with an armed guard; and next day, at a public luncheon where I was an official speaker for the delegation, I had let loose some commentary upon the episode. This caused great offence, Lord Peel and others declaring my remarks to be an abuse of Canadian hospitality, and that if there was to be any more of it they were going home. Bluff Tom Shaw however insisted that my statement of facts was correct, and the lid was clapped upon the incident when Dr. Anderson, the leader of the Conservative Party in the Saskatchewan provincial legislature went far farther in public denunciation of how some of these miner-harvesters had been treated, than I had gone.

On therefore swept the mixed delegation from coast to coast, travelling outwards on Canadian National, and returning on Canadian Pacific Railways, putting up our orators in rotation wherever our train stopped, and leaving behind us, we hoped, fresh enthusiasms for Empire Marketing and co-operation for security, and for common purpose in the world. And we could all unite in singing led by a French Canadian with a high pitched tenor voice:

> " *Alouette, gentille alouette,*
> *Alouette, je te plumerai.*
> *Je te plumerai le dos*
> *Et le dos*
> *Et le cou*
> *Et le pattes*
> *Et le bec*
> *Et la tête*
> *Oh!* "

Almost one-fourth of Canada is of French descent and of its French-Canadian population 870,000 at the last census reported that they could not speak English. They multiply in families of from 12 to 16. Birth control is at a heavy discount in the province of Quebec. In the Maritime Province, on the other hand, one-fourth of the population still speak Scots Gaelic; the wealthier among them make pilgrimage to Scotland and search gravestones and kirk records for trace of their ancestry; the poorer go to ceilidhs, and when I was in Canada they still had a monthly Gaelic newspaper. One night at a dinner I was placed next to a French-Canadian, who was Minister of Public Instruction. His name he pronounced as Frasie-eh. But his grandfather had been a Fraser Highlander in Wolff's army, and when his regiment was disbanded at Quebec he just stayed on with his Gaelic Bible and a

87

photograph of old Simon Fraser, Lord Lovat. At Cape Breton you can journey all day past Scots names on the railway stations, and there even the negroes speak the Gaelic. Scotland gave names to the Fraser and Mac-Kenzie rivers; and all over Canada, Scotland raises its head and, loudly and stridently, its voice. At the census of 1941 there were 1,403,974 declarants (including their families) who certified they were of Scottish origin.

In the Prairie provinces there are considerable colonies of Ukrainians, Galicians, Ruthenians, and the like, classified slangily as Bohunks, and frequently you could get no reply from them but " Nichts Verstehen " (Nothing Understood!).

Nevertheless King's English has many inflections, and I have a memory of strolling one night in Toronto with David Kirkwood and some others of the Empire delegation. We had rather lost our direction, so Kirkwood stopped a girl and began politely:

" Ma lassock, we're but strangers, and hae nae kennin' o' the roads hereaboots——"

" Good gracious," cried the girl, rather shrinking back, " another Bohunk! "

And a memory of Toronto comes to me. We were out on a conducted drive round the city: the driver obligingly pointed out to us the house at 211 University Avenue where Mary Pickford was born.

Sir John Marriott (University Don), always anxious for information: " Who was Mary Pickford? "

This staggered the driver, but he later registered a facetious come-back by showing Sir John a street where a Scotsman had lost a dime!

In our travels we were permitted to see many marvels: the *Caleche* of Old France, high wheeled and gimcracked, from Louis XIV's time, swaying through the narrow streets of Quebec with an American millionairess and her tortoiseshell glasses aboard: the families of Huron chiefs selling Indian shoes to visitors; at Truro, marigolds—the size of plates; at Prince Edward Island under prohibition 14 out of 17 prisoners inside for bootlegging alcohol; at Nova Scotia it was the Tories who, after an appeal to the Privy Council, abolished the second chamber by appointing sufficient senators to vote their office out of existence; and the ingenious Gideons, the Christian Commercial Travellers' Association of Canada, who make presentations of Bibles to hotels and ensure that they are read by pasting on the fly-leaves such injunctions as " Study Psalm 37, if trade is poor "; the " commercial " who turns up Psalm 37 is rewarded with such key messages as:

O Canada

" A little that a righteous man hath is
better than the riches of many wicked,"

and

" The wicked borroweth and payeth not again."

We marvelled too at some cockeyed 'revolutionaries' who objected to organised British immigration, but protested not at all at organised Bohunk immigration from the Balkans; and especially did we marvel at one queer labour spokesman at Sault Saint Marie on Lake Superior, who thought there was every chance of a good revolution seeing that one had succeeded in England in 1914; that was why he was not bothering about a Co-operative Society or a Trade Union, of which there was neither at Sault Saint Marie; what precisely he did 'bother' about we could not fathom, since the steel workers were enjoying eleven hour shifts, and there was no Union; and who elected him a labour spokesman was anybody's guess!

We also saw a memorial stone erected in Dundas County, Ontario on the site where the first chance seedling of the fine Macintosh Red apple settled and fruited: and another memorial cairn, which I must say annoyed me greatly; it was at Jaspar Station in the Rockies, where a huge Indian totem pole, perhaps forty feet high, had been brought from the Queen Charlotte Islands, and re-erected; a precious, priceless relic of the Massit Haida Indians, and there now it stood, and vulgar barbarian hoodoos had amused themselves by carving their initials upon it; one crazy fellow had cut his folly high upon an eyeball " E.W." The desecration restored my belief in the necessity of capital punishment.

And there was the covering overpowering romance of it all, back to our boyhood days with Fenimore Cooper and R. M. Ballantyne: the very names " Sioux Look Out ": " The Caribou Pass," " Moose Jaw ": the sign posts " This way for the Yukon Valley and the Emerald Lake." The glories of the Indian summer when the maple leaves turn fiery red; the majesty and great silences, and the snowy mutches of the Rockies, and in the morning the unforgettable red glow of the sun upon the peaks.

But I thought the show-places like Banff and Emerald Lake were rather cheapened a bit by the staged side-shows, the cowboys, the bison, the tame black bears, and the still tamer Indian warriors in wigwams, who would smoke a pipe of peace for two bits, or less, and if the visitor had no currency with him, it could be marked up on the slate and the hotel would pay later. One Indian chief, a Stoney, who was put on show to us, we irreverently nicknamed Spitting Eagle, for he could spit all right and he certainly wore the feathers.

The amazing fruit crops of British Columbia—tomatoes eight to fifteen tons to the acre; in the Okanagan Valley the apple yields so great that the trees have to be propped up with poles.

And the amazing live wire Conservative and Orangeman Prime Minister of Ontario, Ferguson, whose programme apparently was public ownership of all monopolies, and who went about boasting that the public ownership of electricity on the northern side of Niagara was selling power and light to 1,000,000 Canadians at less than one-third of the rate charged by the private corporations operating the electricity drawn from Niagara on the United States side. I did not need any converting, but after spending half a day with Premier Ferguson I solemnly registered a vow that if ever the opportunity came my way I would assist in doing for the economy of the North of Scotland, through the public harnessing of its water power, what Sir Adam Beck and his colleagues had so successfully accomplished on the St. Lawrence. Fifteen years later my opportunity came.

But I never tired of asking questions about Canada's great achievement in co-operative marketing of her wheat—surely the greatest attempt ever seen in the world at orderly and profitable marketing by the producers of food! In the prairie provinces there were 144,000 farmers in a huge and capably handled organisation possessing 1400 elevators, and effecting saving in transport and marketing to its members estimated at 8 cents per bushel, and in saving from ironing out the speculators probably twice that figure. Canada exported more wheat than the U.S.A., and the Argentine together. How imperative then that her great primary product should be efficiently and economically marketed!

PART TWO

CHAPTER XIII

COMPULSORY UNEMPLOYMENT
BETWEEN THE WARS

It is going to be a great problem in the world, and a great problem in the next generation too. What is to be done with the surplus output of the mass production which will take place in many countries?

We shall have to leave that problem for its solution to those who are responsible when it becomes more acute than it is.

—Mr. Stanley Baldwin, Prime Minister, at Sheffield 8.5.30

IMMINENT DISASTER. UNITED STATES PRODUCING TOO MUCH WHEAT. . . . *Only a severe failure of the coming wheat crop can save America from a financial disaster of the first magnitude.*

—*Central News. Press Service* 14.3.30

IN THE years between the two world wars, in Britain unemployment was the major problem. Over its cause(s) and cure(s) there were innumerable debates and disputations. Mr. Ernest Bevin produced a pamphlet plan for dealing with two million unemployed, mostly through pensioning off ageing workers and raising the age of compulsory attendance at school—devices which in substance were taken up later by Sir Oswald Mosley. Mr. Lloyd George told the electors how we could " conquer unemployment." There were Douglas schemes: J. M. Keynes schemes: Neo-Malthusian schemes: Sidney Webb schemes and Page Croft, Beaverbrook, Sir Alfred Mond—" Free Trade " Within The Empire—Garvin £100 Million Loan For Empire Development, schemes. And Lord Inchcape had a simple solvent of his own: emigrate the unemployed overseas![1]

Yet despite all the diagnoses, alleviations, and remedies, the army of our unemployed grew steadily until in 1933 it reached the appalling figure of 2,400,000, plus 300,000 on poor relief; moreover, between the armistice in 1918 and the year 1933, we had spent £380,000,000 on relief, and unem-

---

[1] There was of course a school of thought which held that the problem had no solution: it was insoluble: an act of God: Sir Arthur Steel Maitland, who was Minister of Labour in 1927, openly espoused that thesis in a debate I had with him at Gray's Inn.

ployment insurance benefit, and got in return for that expenditure not one brick laid upon another, not an extra blade of grass: nothing! The older workmen had taken to dyeing their hair in striving to keep their jobs: the physical condition of the people in many areas had manifestly deteriorated. There were English and Welsh counties with 42 per cent and 45 per cent, and over all Scotland, 35 per cent of the male workers unemployed.

No longer was unemployment blamed upon sun spots as Professor Stanley Jevons had blamed it in 1868: no longer did anyone declare that involuntary idleness was due to the victim's double dose of original sin, his drunkenness, his slothfulness, shiftlessness, or improvidence. Men in all classes now saw that productive capacity, inventiveness, labour saving devices, were steadily outrunning permitted consumption of goods. Improved techniques were increasing year by year the actual and potential wealth of the world. The problem now was the problem of the glutted market, the electric navvy, the combined harvester; it was one of how to distribute the greatly increased wealth that was pouring from the machines.

In the United States it was reported by a study group of scientists that in agriculture one man could now do in one hour what it required 3000 hours for him to accomplish in 1840; in the steel industry productive capacity had increased ninefold between 1887 and 1929.

Some crazy expedients were being devised for getting rid of the surpluses. Walter Nash, who became Finance Minister in New Zealand, told me in the middle thirties of what he described as the prize insanity in the world's history; it was the scheme of the American Government for subsidising American farmers who would kindly oblige by refraining from swelling the glut in the pig market; *the American farmers were given a bonus not for raising pigs: but for not raising pigs*, and an American farm journal published the following delightful satire which Nash recited to appreciative audiences:

" Dear Sir—a friend of mine in New England has a neighbour who has received a Government cheque for a thousand dollars this year for not raising hogs. So my friend wants to go into the business himself, he not being very prosperous just now; he says in fact that the idea of not raising hogs appeals to him very strongly.

Of course he will need a hired man, and that is where I come in. I write to you as to your opinion of the best kind of farm not to raise hogs on, the best strain of hogs not to raise, and how best to keep an inventory of hogs you are not raising.

The friend who got the thousand dollars got it for not raising 500 hogs. Now we figure we might easily not raise 1500 to 2000 hogs, so you can see the possible profits are only limited by the number of hogs we do not raise.

The other fellow had been raising hogs for forty years and never earned more than 400 dollars in any one year. Kind of pathetic, isn't it, to think how he wasted his life raising hogs when he could have made so much more not raising them."

And Dr. Nansen, who had been Famine Relief Commissioner for the League of Nations, turned up at St. Andrews to deliver a Lord Rector's address to the students at the University, and painted a gruesome picture of the Russian famine in 1921-2 when thirty million people in the Volga region were " starving and dying " because of drought, while at the same time there was such an abundance of maize in America that the farmers were having it burned as fuel in the railway engines!

The solution, as Dr. Nansen clearly pointed out, was for the unemployed and the needy to be permitted to take food surpluses off the market with their teeth. But that was too complex and revolutionary for even the Socialist parties in Britain—certainly for the Scottish Socialist Party! We did manage, it is true, to persuade Parliament to allow the surplus milk to be consumed in the schools (incidentally saving the milk producers from ruin, the children from ill health, and the public purse from much expenditure upon hospitals!). But Lord De La Warr and the Potato Marketing Board were only allowed one year for an experiment at Bishop Auckland in Durham County to dispose of a local glut of 200 tons of potatoes by selling them to the local unemployed at 4d. instead of the normal price of 9d. per stone. These interferences with the natural laws of supply and demand aroused great and foolish opposition. Better that the potatoes rot in the pits, the hungry go with empty stomachs, and the farmers with empty pockets; the situation would right itself next year anyhow, for the farmers would grow fewer potatoes. Lord Boyd Orr and the others of us who had conceived of something on the lines of a national dividend from increased production and from the bounties of nature, had to bow before a united opposition of those on the one hand who thought we would wreck the commercial system of profit taking, and those on the other hand who thought we would shore it up and perpetuate it.

A similar fate met the well-intentioned effort by Dr. Ryan, the Minister of Agriculture in Eire under Mr. De Valera. Here the trouble was a surplus of fat cattle, 60,000 of them eating their heads off; so the minister arranged to buy the animals at the rate of 1000 per week, the price he paid being only 25s. per cwt., live weight; the cattle were sold through the usual channels at maximum prices of 5d. per lb., to every family on Public Assistance or Unemployment Relief in Dublin. But the Irish pundits and the Irish press, no more than their British counterparts, could understand such an economy, and Dr. Ryan had to bow himself and his scheme off the stage.

When you fail to make any impression with what you take to be fundamentals you fall back upon half measures and alleviations, hence the reason why many of us backed the Lord St. Davids' committee upon unemployment grants. There was no Socialist upon the committee; its respectability was guaranteed by its prominent members, Lord St. Davids and Sir William Plender, the accountant; it had examined, and approved of, relief scheme expenditure by local authorities down to the year 1929 to the value of £104 millions; it had given grants in aid to these schemes to the extent of £40 millions, and it reported that

" the results obtained are of undisputed and permanent benefit to the localities concerned."

The schemes had employed *in cumulo* 610,000 men for a year; they had been the means of improving roads, eliminating blind corners, draining marshes, and the like; other 11,900 schemes had been approved—and then the axe fell! Henceforth the Treasury and the Government would only give grants in aid to local authority schemes from the very depressed areas.[1] And inasmuch as the very distressed areas were suffering from enormous local rates for poor law purposes, they would be the least likely to indulge in road widening or any other schemes. And so the usefulness of the St. Davids' Committee was beautifully hamstrung.

In the late twenties I had come firmly to the conclusion that there were many important issues in our public life which ought to be lifted entirely out of the arena of partisan political strife; unemployed relief works was one of these issues. So I diligently set out to persuade first the Labour Party and then the House of Commons that, for example, a blind corner on a public highway was a blind corner and a manifest danger to road users, whether travelling on Rolls Royce or on proletarian bus: that water supplies were equally necessary to Socialist, Tory, and Liberal consumers: that land drainage, afforestation, Empire Marketing Boards, and dozens of other projects for adding to the national wealth and providing rational employment for our people could surely be discussed on their merits without our being first lined up into groups whose settled policy was to frustrate any other political group from doing anything. There were always ingenious groups of M.P.s who could start long filibuster discussions about the habits of grey seals, or whether Moses led an Egyptian campaign,

[1] Circular 15.12.26.

not because they had the slightest interest in grey seals or Moses or Egypt, but simply because they wanted to delay some other business coming forward.

In March 1927 the Labour Opposition was officially committed to a resolution in the following terms:

> " That a select Committee be appointed to consider schemes of work of national benefit designed to provide employment . . . that the Committee do report to this House at intervals not exceeding one month during the sittings of this House."

And although we got the powerful support of Mr. Lloyd George we lost —on a partisan vote—by 252 to 142.

And when in May 1930 I had been transported from a back bench to the post of Under-Secretary at the Scottish Office I repeated the plea that relief work

> " is too big for any one Party, harassed by strong opposition, to undertake, when it is open to all the obstruction and delays inherent in a partisan political struggle. . . . Until we can get Unemployment and its emergencies regarded as an all-Party question in this House: treated as questions were treated in the emergency of the war: obstruction swept away, the pettifogging delays which take place in this House over legislative proposals abolished: an all-Party committee responsible to Parliament, making recommendations to Parliament—unless the House can rise to such a conception of its duties, I do not believe it is possible, quickly, to expand the area and the scope of relief works in this country. . . . Everything is impossible unless we are prepared to regard Unemployment as we regard the work of the Empire Marketing Board, or the Public Accounts Committee, or the Local Legislation Committee, or other matters which are regarded as being on a non-Party basis."

And it is worth recording that Mr. J. R. MacDonald as Prime Minister in November 1929 said that if the Opposition were willing to co-operate he would be willing to receive representations. Nothing then came of the all-Party select committee in continuous session idea, but some day, who knows? Parliament may return to it, to the all round advantage of the citizenry of these islands.

There was one other alleviation of Unemployment that I thought could have been more vigorously applied. Who first devised the export credits guarantee I know not, but he was well on the right rails, and deserved a Dukedom. The general idea of the scheme was that if a British trader could secure a foreign order, but was hesitant about taking the risk of non-payment, or long delayed payment, by his foreign customer, he could insure up to 75 per cent of his risk with a Government financed insurance committee, called Export Credits Guarantee. Inaugurated in the autumn of 1919 it was—down to 1930 at anyrate—rather tightly operated and at unduly excessive premium rates. Nevertheless it was facilitating an export trade of £4 millions sterling per annum; the losses by defalcation on the part of foreign customers were negligible, and in fact the Fund was making a profit to the Treasury. But the usefulness of the scheme could have been greatly extended.

In vain I pled that the deliberate exclusion of the Russian market from Export Credits Insurance was suicidal for our own workmen and our own national economy. The Norwegian Government were reported as giving credit facilities of £830,000 for fish products to the Russian market, but no such alleviation came the way of our only half employed fishing fleets. And when for a few brief months in the finance crisis of 1930-1931 I was (on my part reluctantly) lugged from the under-secretaryship at the Scottish Office and installed as Lord Privy Seal in charge of unemployment—so the press announcements of the joke were phrased!—I made one hurried dive for the Unemployed Grants Committee, and induced them to bring Russian orders within the scope of their insurance policies.

The Committee was not easily persuaded; I had to show them that private finance houses in London were charging as high as 13 per cent interest upon trade credits to Russia, an almost prohibitive obstacle to any trade at all; that the German government was charging its nationals only 2 per cent for the same trade, and that the Italian Government was levying only from 1 per cent to 4 per cent according to the length of credit demanded.

Finally the Committee agreed to a premium rate of 9 per cent for an insurance of up to 60 per cent of the value of the order, on Russian orders, and they agreed to a two years' credit. The terms were still stiff enough; it had to be remembered that 40 per cent of the value of the order had still to carry an interest rate up to 13 per cent levied by the private finance houses; yet despite that I was able to get Mr. Sokolinkoff, the Russian ambassador, and Mr. Bron, his trade adviser, to place at once orders to the value of £6,000,000 for engineering tools in Britain,[1] while Moscow announced its intention of placing a minimum of £20,000,000 of orders for ships, fertilisers, dyes and metals. Moreover we were discussing with the Russians projects involving £100,000,000 of iron and steel orders to be spread over three years, when our Government collapsed and new dealers

---

[1] In getting these orders speedily placed I was greatly indebted to Sir Walter Citrine (now Lord Citrine) of the British Trades Union Congress.

were brought in to hold the cards. All I know further about the £6,000,000 orders for engineering tools is that the accounts were met in full on the due dates, although the Russians used to allege that payments were made unnecessarily difficult by such trickeries as newspaper scares about ticks being in a cargo of Russian butter, held ready for sale to get the funds to meet their bills.

CHAPTER XIV

AT DOVER HOUSE AND AS KEEPER
OF THE PRIVY SEAL

Don't shoot the pianist; he's doing his best.
—Placard in Mining Camp Saloon

TOWARDS THE approach of the general election in 1929 I had intimated to my election committee that I would not again contest Dundee. There had been some rather disagreeable local squabbling between the Independent Labour Party and the Trades and Labour Council. Ostensibly the cause of the trouble was that the wife of the I.L.P. Secretary, who kept a newsagent's shop, sold copies of a blacklisted daily newspaper. This had given offence to the Trades and Labour Council, who insisted that the lady should discontinue selling the offending newspaper ; either that or the I.L.P. should " discipline " its secretary. The lady continued to sell the paper and the I.L.P. refused to discipline its secretary. And thus the squabble began!

By the good sense of both sides I, as Member of Parliament, had been kept outwith the ring, but when the Trades and Labour Council disaffiliated the I.L.P., and because I was an I.L.P. nominee, I judged it right to announce my withdrawal from the constituency at the forthcoming general election. Other Unions, the Jute and Flax workers, for example, offered to stand sponsor for my candidature, but in view of my long association with the I.L.P. I persisted in my withdrawal.

When the election came I was adopted for my old constituency of West Stirlingshire and winning the seat this time, and a minority Labour government emerging—Mr. Lloyd George politely telling it to behave itself or else![1]—I was ' sent for ' by Mr. Ramsay MacDonald. When I reached his room there was Mr. Willie Adamson awaiting. He had been Scottish Secretary in the first Labour administration, and everyone con-

[1] " The mandate of the Government ends when it fails to pursue a Liberal policy. The very hour the Ministry decides to become a Socialist administration its career ends."—Mr. Lloyd George, 13.6.29.

fidently expected he would occupy that post again. Mr. MacDonald began by distributing some saponaceous lather and then told Mr. Adamson he would like him to go to the House of Lords; he could be titular Secretary for Scotland, and sit in the Cabinet, and "do the ceremonial stuff" but that I, if I would take the under-secretaryship, could take charge of Scottish business in the House of Commons. He hoped we would both agree quickly, for he was very busy, and time was precious, and he had other appointments.

I said I was quite willing to work under Mr. Adamson and Willie then shook hands with me, and said he would go to the Lords!

"Thank you both," said the P.M. "But not a word about this until you see it announced in the newspapers."

"Can I no' tell my wife about the Lords?" asked Willie.

"Oh you can tell your wife," replied the P.M.

"And my son?"

"Your what!" shouted the P.M. "I didn't know you had a son. That arrangement is off. I am against appointing peers who have heirs to inherit their titles."

And so suddenly was blotted out a noble lord, and the Scottish Office had to run with the usual administrative set up, although Mr. Adamson was enjoined to see that I got plenty of rope. "But don't hang yourself with it," was the P.M.'s parting benediction.

I find it somewhat difficult to write unless in terms of what might appear exaggerated affection for "Old Willie" Adamson, as we commonly called him. Not only did he allow me to do as I liked, with never a remonstrance, but I know too that he went out of his way to share some displeasures which I was to incur in high quarters. I tried to reciprocate and to assist him as best I could. He had his peculiarities, as we all have, but he was the soul of loyalty and good comradeship.

He was an old collier from Fife, was caution personified with a capital P; he carried on for years a relentless warfare with the communists in his county, and his motto in that warfare as I once told him was the motto on the Covenanters' banner at Tippermuir: "Jesus and No Quarter." To most supplementary questions in the House of Commons he had a stock answer: it was that he would give the matter "due consideration." And once when some of his interrogators became annoyed, and one of them, Mr. Pringle, asked whether after he had given the due consideration to the due consideration he had previously promised, he would give due consideration to the advisability of giving an answer to the question, Willie imperturbably replied amid roars of laughter that he would give the point raised by the honourable member due consideration!

We were in opposition when the English Prayer Book debate took place, and the Scots members of the Opposition front bench decided that as it was almost entirely an English issue, it would be unjust and improper for us to vote. But we sat—Willie Adamson, Willie Graham, Tom Kennedy and I—and listened to the debate. There came a powerful oration from Mr. Rosslyn Mitchell against the new Prayer Book and as it proceeded there fell something like a sob from Willie Adamson: "Tom," he whispered, "I couldna' look ma forefolks in the face if I didna' vote the nicht." And vote we all did!

He and James Brown, the first workman Lord High Commissioner to the Church of Scotland, were great friends, and Willie and I went to the Commissioner's garden party at Holyrood to support him. That was a never-to-be-forgotten spectacle: the bus loads of colliers who arrived in honour of Jimmy Brown: some of them in tall hats that had never been out in use since the Disruption, and placidly smoking their clay pipes; and Willie Adamson and Jimmy Brown, two old colliers, representing the King's Majesty at the ancient castle. I would not have missed that sight for much.

Willie for some reason or another was rather terrified of Philip Snowden, and I got the task of going as commercial traveller for Scotland to the Treasury whenever money was wanted.[1] But he was awed by few other men. Once I recollect his ringing me down to my room and beseeching me to come up and help him with a most difficult deputation which was just arriving. It was from the country *gentrice* of Ayr, who wanted to take over an old county jail building for, I think, territorial army purposes. They had wanted the building *gratis*, and Willie could not give it *gratis*, and now the forces had arrived to state their case with vigour and vehemence to the Scottish Secretary. It was a formidable deputation headed by a gentleman with a beard and a monocle, and as the speakers warmed up they became more contemptuous and, I thought, more than a shade insulting; indeed they became so much so that I whispered to Willie that I could not stick this kind of thing any longer and was going out of the room before I burst.

"Bide a wee," whispered back the Secretary for Scotland. "Juist bide a wee, and I'll let ye see hoo tae haunel thae birds."

Then he would smile and invite the deputation to proceed with its case. And when they were exhausted, Willie said: "Well, my Lords, and gentlemen, we hae heard whit ye have tae say. It's been verra interestin'. Yes, I'll say that—verra verra interestin', and ye may rest assured that your

---

[1] There used to be a joke at the Treasury that so persistent were demands from the Scottish Office for money that they ran to take in the cat's milk when they heard us coming.

words'll be given due consideration and you'll be communicated wi' in due course, and we're much obleeged tae ye, and d'ye see that door: It's aye open for you."

And the deputation was out on the street before Willie's *double entendre* about the door had dawned upon them. The door only opened outwards so far as they were concerned.

After the deputation had disappeared Willie turned to me: " Tom, wull ye tak' a word o' advice frae an aulder man than yersel'? I saw ye were losin' yer temper wi' that gang. Never lose yer temper. If ye canna gie a man whit he wants, ye can aye gie him a kind word. It costs damn a'!" And Willie was an old Baptist!

There was one other amusing story of my old chief which went the rounds at Dover House. Willie had been visited by two civil servants, one an eloquent and loquacious gentleman, who had harangued Willie for ten minutes. Then Willie began to stem the spate with an occasional " Imphum" and " I see " and head nodding. But that, not stopping the flow, Willie said he would give the matter his consideration.

" You won't decide now, sir?" asked the importunate civil servant.

" No, I'll consider it," said Willie.

Whereupon the two interviewers left. As the door almost closed upon them, Willie called the quiet one. " A meenit, Mr.—— Tell me, what on earth wis that mannie talkin' aboot?"

It was in those days that the Prime Minister, Mr. Ramsay Macdonald, devised an ingenious scheme to keep some of his potential trouble makers quiet. He would appoint a Committee to produce schemes for dealing with unemployment; the chairman, Mr. J. H. Thomas, then Lord Privy Seal; Mr. George Lansbury, the Commissioner for Works, Sir Oswald Mosley, the Chancellor of the Duchy of Lancaster, and myself, the Under-Secretary at the Scottish Office. A more ill-assorted team could hardly be imagined and looking back upon it I can well understand the sardonic glee with which its appointment was received. It was openly asserted that the Committee was set up so that the critics would confound each other: dogs were to be kept busy eating dogs.

At our second meeting Mr. Thomas made a speech to the other three of us. He was filled with a notion that somebody had given him, of how unemployment could be tackled; he was going to Canada and taking samples of Welsh coal with him. He was going to enter into large trading barter arrangements with Canada; the Dominion was to take Welsh coal, and we were to receive in return wheat, but—and here was the point, said Mr. Thomas, slapping the desk!—we were to get raw wheat and not milled wheat; this would mean the erection all along our Western British shores of milling plants and stores; it would mean cheap offals for British farmers; it would mean employment for hundreds of thousands of our fellow citizens. And there you were! As easy as that!

Foolishly I put a few questions about what would be the reaction of the existing milling interests in Canada, and what would happen to the British firms now supplying Canadian markets if their customers in Canada went into bankruptcy and the like. But I was told that the answers to these questions had been thought about and would be revealed in time.

So off went our missioner to swop coal for unmilled wheat, and the other three of us went our several ways, Mr. Lansbury to run a Lido, Sir Oswald to devise schemes for increasing pensions as a means of taking aged workers out of industry and leaving jobs for younger men, and raising the school age as a means of preventing so many new recruits to industry; while I started to get national (as opposed to local) relief works started.

First I wanted to get a road right round the shores of Loch Lomond as a great tourist attraction: but the Duke of Montrose, the major proprietor, had given some sporting and other leases which he could not break. He offered me, however, the toll-bar coaching road from Aberfoyle to the Trossachs. Here, I thought, was a great chance of constructing a splendid motor road with a circular tour round the Lady of the Lake country; and giving each local authority in the west its quota of young unemployed men a job on construction; the country would receive a solid asset for its money, and thousands of young men would get a self-respecting and physically rehabilitating employment in the construction of the road.

Moreover it was the year of the Walter Scott centenary, and I had a tentative promise of participation of the Prince of Wales and the American Ambassador in the opening ceremony. I visualised that ceremony—pipers with beards swaggering about among the heather and artistes playing Rob Roy and Helen Macgregor on Loch Vennachar; and I would have cargoes of American and foreign visitors spending money and——

But we at once ran up against opposition from the local sporting lairds; we had to face actions and threats of action for interdict, both from the lairds and the L.N.E. Railway Company (Craigie Aitchison, then Lord Advocate, was a great hand at contriving methods of dealing with and circumventing the interdicters! and in the end the compensation some of them got through compulsory arbitration was less than they had been offered voluntarily for speedy acquiescence!). But the greatest delay and disappointment we had was over the frustrative non-co-operation of the Perthshire County Council.

I had to persuade the local authorities in the depressed areas to make a small financial contribution, according to the quota of men they would get on the scheme, always remembering that the new national works were to be constructed outside their areas. That settled, I next had to tackle the Perthshire Council, but, alas, instead of seeing a great tourist attraction in their midst, and some national return for the moneys being poured out from the Unemployment funds, they were persuaded by some of the sporting *gentrice* to refuse to have anything to do with the road; and had it not been for the good sense and vision of two men on the Council, the late Lord Mansfield and the factor for the Duke of Atholl, the road would never have been built at all, and a great asset to the nation would have been lost. As it is, to this hour, the road, although perhaps a million or two visitors have passed over it and delighted in the glorious scenery, has not yet been formally declared open. Payment of the opening ceremony expenses was offered by the late Mr. Henderson of Lawton, the Convener of the Roads Committee, but even that bait was not enough, and the Prince of Wales and the pipers playing in the heather, and Rob Roy had to stay away.

Of course, all the dashed hopes and frustrated expectations in these national relief schemes were not on one side. I recollect being taken up to Ness on the Butt of Lewis to inspect a proposal that the State should spend many thousands of pounds in rebuilding a harbour which had been washed down in a storm. There were only two or three fishermen in the vicinity, and why ever a harbour should have been built there originally was a problem I could not answer. There was not a hope of rebuilding at that time anyway. As we marched back we passed two men who, in hoarse whispers, were overheard asking one of the locals who had accompanied me: "Is there ony hope?" And the answer, also whispered: "It's a' on the lap o' the gods noo."

But to return to the Unemployment Committee in Whitehall. Mr. J. H. Thomas had arrived back from Canada and he in due course summoned us to consultation. We met in the Treasury Chambers, and, to our surprise there had also been invited most of the heads of departments. Lansbury, Mosley, and I flanked Thomas and behind stood a well-known Treasury official, Mr. Eddie Marsh, with a monocle. On the mantelpiece beside Marsh was a brown paper parcel.

Then the fun began. Thomas, in a few well-chosen declamatory sentences, told the meeting of the magnitude of the unemployed problem; said he had been surprised at one or two things brought to his notice since his return from Canada (not a word about the coal for wheat project: it had just died!) and in particular he had asked a chief officer from the Post Office to be present that day. Was he here?

"Yes, sir!" said a gentleman with a white pointed beard.

"Well," said Thomas. "You see the wooden boxes with the two little bells on them that's in every telephone kiosk?"

"Yes, sir."

"Where do you get the wood from?"

"From Sweden, sir!"

"Just so," said Thomas. "From Sweden, and how much does each box cost you . . . on a haverage?" (Jimmy was lapsing into the vernacular!)

"About 10s. 6d., sir."

"Well," said Thomas triumphantly. "Eddie, let me see that box"; down came the brown paper parcel from the mantelpiece. Then—to the Post Office representative—"That box is not made of foreign wood, but of British steel, made by British labour, and it don't cost 10s. 6d., or 8s. 6d., or 6s. 6d. but only 4s. 6d. Now what 'ave you to say for yourself?"

"Well, sir," replied the Post Officer. "My box has two bells on it, and machinery inside it, and yours has none!"

Lansbury in glee kicked my ankle beneath the table, but Thomas never batted an eyelid: simply wrapping up his steel box in its brown paper he declared we would go farther into this matter on another occasion. And the audience filed away with stoic faces, but I am sure with large laughs bubbling up for subsequent explosion.

That was the end of the Unemployment Committee as such. We never met again. In fact we had only met twice in six months, but of this the Opposition remained in blissful ignorance. Then in January 1930 Mosley asked Lansbury and me to associate ourselves with a memorandum of over 25 pages typed foolscap he had drafted for submission to the Cabinet, through Mr. J. H. Thomas. In general we agreed with most of it, but he had contrived to widen his front of attack and bring in monetary policy and long term planning of permanent economic reconstruction, and there were already indications that he was preparing his ammunition for a break-away movement, and *that*, as we both told him, would get the unemployed nowhere. So he signed his memorandum himself, and when Thomas rejected it, he resigned from the Government. Later he formed a new party, which later still became the precursor of the British Union of Fascists.

I suppose it is now futile to speculate upon when and under what impulses Mosley began his political *decensus Averno*, shouting anti-semitic slogans, wearing black shirts, and parading about as a miniature Musso-Hitler, indeed parading himself into detention as a menace to his country during the war; but there was a time in his life when—despite some *post facto* commentators—there was no sign of these aberrations. He might have been of great service to his generation; no doubt he was ambitious, but he was not too wisely handled, and he grew up and shot out the wrong way.

After unemployment had got the better of Mr. J. H. Thomas's efforts, and after Mr. Vernon Hartshorn had died, the Prime Minister sent a message for me to come to his room. There I was told he had ' decided ' to appoint me as Lord Privy Seal. I demurred: said I was quite happy where I was: had a lot of irons in the fire, and was waiting on my ships coming home. But J.R.M. turned on the heavy appeal. He was in difficulties: needed help: needed somebody to put up real unemployment relief schemes. I was the man, and so on. Reluctantly I yielded.

It was, he told me, urgent. Two days hence I would have to go to the Palace to be sworn in, but in the meantime not a word to a soul, as the King was very wroth when he read of appointments in the press before he had sworn in the appointees. I wanted to know what kind of clothing and headgear I was expected to wear when I went to the Palace; was told to see Sir Maurice Hankey about that. I replied rather argumentatively that at anyrate I would have to disclose matters to Sir Maurice. Oh, of course, but he was different. And I was ushered out.

Rather disobediently I phoned home to Scotland for my funeral hat (being Scots, I was not going to buy a new one!) From home over the phone came an enquiry as to who was dead, to which I replied that I couldn't hear very well. Then off to a ready made warehouse, Messrs. Barkers in Kensington, to get a white shirt and a black waistcoat and trousers. I had a promise of a loan of a frock coat from Sir John Lamb, the Permanent Secretary at the Scottish Office (which borrowing involved another leakage of State secrets!).

The morning of the swearing-in day arrived. When I started to dress at the Scottish Office it was discovered that through some mischance I had got a pair of trousers so wide that I could have stuffed a pillow down the front, and the pillow might have been lost. Hurriedly a messenger was sent up to a shop in the Strand for safety pins, and Sir John Lamb and Adam McKinlay, M.P., my private secretary, got me pleated, and the pleats pinned together at the back, Sir John averring that nobody would know, for the frock coat hid all.

Everything at first went with circumspection and according to Cocker. I had bowed myself past the Privy Councillors present and was kneeling as per instructions on the little footstool in front of the King, when—zipp! —the pleats broke from the safety pins; and I missed the rest of the ceremony in wondering how I was going to juggle myself out of the room with my trousers all in concertina such as the clowns wear in circuses. The King asked me if I was free for a talk upon affairs, and I hitched myself into a little side room, where the King and I sat down at a fire, and he toasted his feet at the embers. The old gentleman had a happy knack of being able to put people at their ease, but I'll swear he never had a more difficult case to operate upon than he had that day.

Yet somehow without mishap and without undue attention being drawn to my habiliments I got outside to a taxi, and back to the Scottish Office, where I recounted my experience to Willie Adamson. It was too good a joke for Willie to keep to himself, and later I learned he had passed it on to J. H. Thomas. He in turn—a great *raconteur*—had passed the story, probably with some expansions, to the King. Some time later, when the Government had resigned and the Cabinet was back at the Palace handing over our seals of office, we filed in separately. When my turn came, after shaking hands, and just as I was leaving the room the King, in a hoarse chuckling whisper, asked: " How are your trousers to-day! "

Elsewhere[1] I have recorded my estimate and recollections of the world finance crisis of 1931, which broke the first Labour Government and brought into being a coalition to save the pound sterling and the gold standard.

The dismemberment of Austria at the end of the First World War: the raising of the Austrian banks' overdraft rate to 12 per cent: the bankruptcy, first of the Boden Bank, and then of the Credit Anstalt: the vain attempt of the British Treasury through the Bank of England and in association with Messrs. Rothschild to shore up the Austrian finance system: then the crashing of the German banks, beginning with the Darmstaedter, and the ' run ' upon London, where the Banks held over £400 millions of foreign short term currency: the rapid fall in our gold reserves: the intimation to the British Government that it would require to back a heavy borrowing abroad to save the Bank of England, and that this borrowing could only be secured from New York and Paris provided that the British Government would balance its accounts by, among other economies, slashing the unemployed benefit rate—these are now history.

There was no bankers' plot—the bankers were the most scared of all the citizenry at the time. Mr. Montague Norman, the Governor of the Bank of England, had to go off in the midst of the crisis to Canada to avoid a breakdown, but there was some mighty unscrupulous political propaganda ; for example, Mr. Runciman at Newcastle-on-Tyne brazenly declaring that the unemployed had eaten up " a substantial part of the assets of the Post Office Savings Bank," and there was a steady and persistent press story that Paris was draining London of its gold day by day.

This Paris story was to the majority of the Cabinet inexplicable. If the pound sterling went, the chances were that the franc would immediately follow, and Mr. Arthur Henderson, who was the Foreign Secretary and who was leading the majority in the Cabinet against the cuts in the social

[1] *The Financiers and the Nation* (Methuen), 1934.

services then being pushed by Messrs. MacDonald and Snowden, was particularly worried. After discussion with him I went off to Paris to see M. Flandin, the Minister of Finance, and M. Pierre Laval, then Prime Minister, and I had with me as a witness and, if necessary, interpreter, Mr. Ralph Wigram from the British Embassy in Paris. Both Messieurs Flandin and Laval, when I saw them at the Quai D'Orsay, swore emphatically that France was not draining gold from London and that the Governor of the Bank of France, M. Moret, had indeed offered to lend money to London to save the pound sterling, and that upon at least two occasions when the Bank of France had bought gold, it had done so at the direct request of the Bank of England, and this request was made "for purely regulatory and administrative reasons."

But back in London the French draining of gold scaremongering propaganda had served its purpose in adding to the finance panic and confusion. The Government as constituted, had lost its cohesion and confidence in itself, and amid bitter recriminations the minority, led by the Prime Minister and the Chancellor, went over to a Coalition with the Liberals and Conservatives—a coalition which later swept the country. Many months afterwards, on 4th May 1932, when the mischief had been done, Mr. Winston Churchill told the House of Commons that there was "a good deal of exaggeration about the crisis . . . and a certain amount of manipulation"—the which saying for *naïveté* and understatement of the obvious reminds me of the *Daily Telegraph's* report of the British bomber during the war, when over Berlin, and being subjected to a terrific barrage of "flak," flaming onions, and the like, wirelessed back a message: "The natives appear to be hostile."

CHAPTER XV

INSIDE (UN)HOLY RUSSIA

The high rate of interest (7 per cent) which is paid by this loan stands out in bold relief against the background of the situation in capitalist countries, where interest on loans is being constantly lowered, and loans yielding high rates of interest are being converted into loans paying 2, 3, and 4 per cent interest.

—*Page 121, chapter on ' The Second Five Year Plan Loan ' in ' Scientific Construction in the U.S.S.R.,' published by V.O.K.S. (Soviet Union Society of Cultural Relations with Foreign Countries). Printed at the Trust Mospoligraf, Moscow, Filippovski per 13.*

He spoke of cases of cannibalism, which were reported by the Society's evangelists, including authentic reports of women who had cooked and eaten their babies which had died as a result of malnutrition.

—*Report of lecture on " The Truth about Russia," by Rev. F. J. Miles, Editor of the " Friend of Missions," Belfast Newsletter, 1.11.34*

IF I WAS not a fellow traveller to Russia in the autumn of 1934 I was at least a traveller there. Perhaps owing to my activities as Lord Privy Seal in 1931 in procuring improvements in Russian trade terms, I was regarded as one of the Soviet's white-haired boys, and when I sought information from Intourist Ltd. about probable costs and conditions governing a holiday in Leningrad and Moscow I was offered every assurance that my journeying would be facilitated. I could go anywhere and see (almost) everything I wanted to see, and Mr. Maisky, the Russian Ambassador, busied himself procuring introductions. It was the year after the trial of the six British engineer employees of Metropolitan Vickers for espionage and sabotage—the trial in which Mr. Vishinsky, the public prosecutor, first emerged to prominence; it was the year when things were beginning to cook up for the big purge of Communist members in 1938, the purge during which, according to Mr. Walter Duranty, hundreds of thousands, anything up to half a million Communists in Russia were " liquidated, executed, disappeared, exiled or expelled from the party."[1]

[1] *U.S.S.R.* by Walter Duranty, p. 228. Duranty, English born correspondent for the

Inside (Un)holy Russia

I made it clear that I had no desire to go on any conducted tour in the Soviet Union such as one was given to understand was frequently arranged for easily acquiescent and readily assimilative tourists. I was a journalist by profession, accustomed to weighing evidence; I did not want to go in blinkers; I wanted to see the rough as well as the smooth. Could I, for example, get into a criminal trial, and into the Kremlin, and speak, unaccompanied, with priests and Kulaks, and see an arboritarium, and marriage and divorce proceedings? That, I was assured, was all right. There were my visa and my letters of access to all the authorities.

So armed with my *laissez passer*, I set off in the *Cooperatzia* from Hay's Wharf, London, with a mixed passenger list of returning Russians, Argentinos, Oxford youths, and long hairees, making for the land of their dreams. I kept up my national status with a defiant Kilmarnock bonnet.

Discipline on the ship was quite good—no attempt visible at interference with the captain, unless it was the insistence with which somebody kept turning on a shrill tenor gramophone record about a song of partisans in the Far East, and which seemed to annoy the captain. He would order the record to be turned off, but five minutes later it would erupt again, and this went on for days. I hoped against hope that some O.G.P.U. would emerge from the struggle.

The food was good, borsch soup, sliced tomatoes and onions, chicken, fish, tea, and good brown bread, a much superior bread to the terrible smelly stuff we got later in the hotels in Moscow. The ship berths were clean and comfortable.

We arrived at Hamburg: took on more passengers, mostly French, vivacious and critical of the Soviets. Hitler's dock detectives kept staring as if mesmerised at the ship, but made no attempt to interfere with those of us who paraded up to the city. There we found about one in every six adult males had gotten himself up in a uniform, black, brown, blue, green; fresh combinations evidently were only prevented by the colours running out: great salutings too of each other were taking place on the pavements, and there was much swaggering about in black polished military boots.

One of our French engineer passengers (obstreperously anti-German!) went into an hotel.

" Heil Hitler! " said the porter.

" Heil pommes de terre," said the Frenchman. " I do not speak politics. I speak potatoes! "

He could only, he said, get 1½ potatoes to each meal in Germany and in

---

New York Times, lived in Moscow through the period 1921-1941. According to him it was the purge in Russia which misguided Hitler about Russia's strength, and induced him to his fatal war upon the Soviets.

consequence was emphatic that Germany was no good. Hitler, he thought, would last but a year—if that!

Then up the Baltic with much polyglot oratory in the crew's rest room —the Chinese and the Portuguese orators excelling; concerts on deck with sailors as *impresarios*; singing in various languages: Russian dancing, particularly good, by Russian lady passengers. I resisted appeals to dance the Highland Fling.

I arrived at Leningrad and was supplied with a lady interpreter (whether the supply source was Intourist or the Foreign Commissariat I could not be sure). She had, she declared, been educated at Oxford and her father had been a great friend of Tolstoi's. She began by testing me about the Materialistic Conception of History, and was obviously disturbed when I told her that the slaves had been freed in the British dominions and that Britain had actually paid compensation for the freeing of them. This clearly was not in the Russian textbooks, and I was left in peace from propaganda after that.

The Astoria, where I was accommodated, was a most swagger hotel; it had been built pre-war by a German company, and had been acquired by the new dispensation: compensation nil. In the basement was a Torsgin shop filled with ikons from old churches and valuables looted from bourgeois or aristocrat houses. While I was inspecting some ikons a man sidled up to me and whispered in English:

" Want to buy roubles, sir? "

" No."

" Cheap, sir. One hundred to the pound."

" No."

Then five minutes later another importunist wanted to sell me roubles at 150 to the pound. But I was not falling for that; and I strongly suspected that these black marketeers in the rouble were deliberately planted upon me to see if I would be tempted to buy roubles at $1\frac{1}{2}d$. each which I could then use in a Torsgin or foreigner shop where goods were priced low, but where the rouble was valued at 3s. 6d.[1]

I must say I liked Leningrad: its smart traffic policemen: its Red Army groups marching through the streets singing the Budenny March or the Gipsy song " Tabor," or the Song of the Red Air Fleet: its Tsarist show palaces; its Marinsky Theatre with its ballet; its Hermitage with its pictures and its Scythian gold ornaments of over 2000 years ago; its monument to the Emperor Alexander III with its new and revised inscription:

---

[1] The foreign and home rouble valuation business is not easily explained. But the simplest examination of it I know is given in Lord Citrine's *I Search for Truth in Russia*, one of the most objective accounts of a Briton's view of life in the Soviet Union.

" Scarecrow. My son and my father were executed and I reap the harvest of immortal shame. I am standing here as a cast-iron scarecrow for the country which has forever thrown off the yoke of despotism."

And round every corner is a history: Father Gapon, Rasputin, the long trees on the long road to Tsarskoe Selo where the Whites in the civil war were said to have hanged a Red prisoner from each branch: and the Tsarina's apartment still there with 600 ikons over her bed. I did not care so much for the Leningrad Park of Culture and Rest, thinking it much inferior to the Moscow one; and the St. Isaac's cathedral, widely publicised as an anti-religious museum, did not impress me; the chief propaganda I saw in the cathedral was a swinging pendulum hanging from the roof designed to prove that the earth moved and that the Church was wrong in asserting otherwise; and there was a lot of statistical evidence showing that the Church had always sided with the Tsar and of how Patriarch Tihon (was it?) in a year of famine, when he was asked to use the Church funds to buy wheat, refused, saying it was wrong to divert money left for sacred to profane purposes, and cursing all those who had proposed or backed the idea.

There were said to be about 40 Greek churches still functioning in Leningrad. One was in the main thoroughfare, the old Nevsky Prospekt, now renamed as the street of the 25th October; in that building when I visited it the worshippers were almost all aged people, kneeling and kissing the stone floor. The priest, tall, dignified, with black curly hair, was obviously struggling against grave difficulties. He was not regarded as a citizen: had no food card: and how he lived on the meagre contributions which were all the poor folk could give him I could not guess.

At another church, the Sennaja, in the street of 3rd July there was a crowd of about 600, most of them going in turn to kiss a huge ikon. Beside the ikon some sanitarian had hung a towel and many of the worshippers before kissing used the towel to clean the ikon. The priest's sermon as translated to me was on the necessity of sacrifice for the faith. His mitre was of imitation gold and jewels which glittered and sparkled in the candle-light. The music was splendid, but there were no seats, and a priest came round for a collection and distributed blessings as he steered himself, and some following appellants with trays, through the crowd. I gave him what must have been to him a munificent donation, for they are brave men, these priests, whatever we may think of some of their dogmas. When he saw what was now on the tray he gave me a startled look and his eyes shone with sudden tears.

Outside the church there was a string of ragged beggars, sufficient in number to start a new Charity Organisation Society. At the approach of a foreign tourist a waif would fall down most artistically upon the church steps, and when he was brought round he would be ready with a good story of how he lost his parents in the civil war. There was current a malicious accusation that the Church authorities reaped a commission from the takings of these artistes during the holiday season. I hope the allegation was unfounded, but curiously enough I never saw any more than one performer at a time at the door of any church. The stances seemed somehow to be carefully allocated.

Despite obvious embarrassment to my interpreter, on my motor journeys I would suddenly decide to direct the car driver down some side road, and visit sad slum villages, and once or twice a poor ragged priest; I came across gipsy encampments but no Kulaks, and there was a Lombard or pawnshop near the Astoria hotel which I visited once or twice. Here a cash loan was given upon goods, and the rate of interest charged was three-quarters of one per cent upon values up to 15 roubles and one per cent upon values over 15 roubles. In addition there was a small charge per month for depreciation of security, but all told the people who deposited goods with the Lombards—and there were thousands of depositors in Leningrad—were only charged an annual rate of about 12 per cent.

In the new tenements the flats were generally of three rooms. Often there were two or three families to each flat, an allowance of nine square metres to each person. Occasionally, but not often, I found two families to one room. On the walls outside the tenement there were placarded particulars of the winning room for cleanliness and tidiness, and by contrast particulars of the worst kept room. On one tenement of which I took particulars, out of 486 apartments 57 in one week were classed as dirty, and the occupants had been fined by the Comradely Court or the Hygiene Commission. The Comradely Courts for the tenements were selected from the tenants, usually two or three women and two or three men; they adjudicated upon and settled petty quarrels. When there were two or three families sharing the same apartments quarrels were frequent and not always petty. For hygienic delinquency the Comradely Court could fine up to 50 roubles.

I have my doubts, however, about whether the publicity on the black boards downstairs had any shaming effect upon some of the worst sinners whom I saw before the Courts. It had to be remembered of course that many thousands of these new tenement dwellers had been suddenly and without any preparation dragged from the villages where sanitary arrangements were primitive; moreover they were only a year or two away from complete illiteracy and were possessed of the craziest kind of belief in devils and witches and wizards; in any case they and their families in the tenements had to share the use of a water closet with other families. Maybe given the same origins and conditions few of us would have behaved any better than these new industrial Soviet citizens.

The rents were low, about 55 roubles per family per month: they had a theatre, they had crèches, restaurants and shops attached to groups of tenements, and there was one set of tenements with hundreds of houses near the fortress of Peter and Paul reserved for old revolutionists who had been sent to Siberia in the Tsarist days. That was the best building scheme I saw, and somebody had given orders for it to be continually decorated with flowers.

Tremendous efforts were being made in public health improvement. (By the way all medical aid, false teeth and optical glasses were free, though specialist treatment was charged for, on a sort of means test basis.) But the infant mortality statistics, despite some 30 splendid Maternity and Child Welfare institutions, for example the one in Skorachordhva Street, were terrible. Dr. Bogen, the chief M.O.H. for Leningrad, gave me his child mortality figures.

1911–1913	.. ..	23·8%
1919–1922	.. ..	22·4%
1932 ..	.. ..	16·2%
1933 ..	.. ..	16%

Note the per cent, not per thousand. And while the official explanation of these appalling statistics was that they were the result of other governments' interventions and blockades, there was no doubt but that the main causes were the unduly high proportion of production that went to capital goods and armaments; the habits of the people; the conditions under which they were housed; and the war on the Kulaks, who had retaliated by killing much of the live stock, and so created the milk and meat scarcities.

I had not been long in Russia before I abandoned any attempt at equating prices to British prices. There was, to begin with, the vast difference between the pegged value of the rouble for foreigners and its value in the home market; perhaps the ratio was about 10 or 12 to 1; and then there were different price rates for rationed goods and free market goods. Into the so-called free market at Leningrad there went ragged peasants with skinny hens or decayed cucumbers in the hope of disposal for old shoes or clothing. There was meat too, third class looking stuff, and ancient apples, and still more ancient salted herrings, which I would not have eaten at £1 per bite. ' Free ' sugar was sold at 4 roubles to the pound, while the rationed sugar in the co-operatives and official shops was retailed at 2½ lb. for one rouble. ' Free ' tea sold at 8 roubles to the quarter pound, ' regulated ' tea at three roubles.

The black bread and the ' white ' bread alike repelled me, although both grades were just about of the same degree of odour and unpalatibility as those served up to me later in one of the best hotels in Moscow. The purchasers at the ' Free ' market would include the stateless people who had no ration cards—the clergy, " the ex-servants of religion," the old Tsarist police, people who had fought in the White Army, and other despised groups, but there were also child beggars about, who whenever they spotted an Angleeskee suit of clothes, would crowd around crying " Moaney! "

At the registrar's office—ZAGS (Bureau of Registration of Civil Acts) —I saw two marriage ceremonies performed. They were most casual and offhand affairs. A young woman, the registrar, sits at a desk with a red bandana on her head, and sells marriages with the same disinterest and *insouciance* as if she were a railway clerk selling tickets. The registration room itself looks like a rural railway station waiting room in urgent need of repairs. A man and a woman enter: declare they want to get married: no previous notice: no witnesses. They are simply asked their names, addresses, employment, age, and whether married before; and please sign on the dotted line, and the charge is 7 roubles (about 2s. 4d. in our money), of which 4 roubles go to the Committee in charge of homeless children and 3 roubles to the Government. Out the couple walk, man and wife!

Divorce was even easier. I timed one—four minutes; only one of the parties requires to appear, saying he or she desires a divorce. The first intimation a woman may hear of her divorce is when she gets the formal notice served upon her that she is no longer a married woman; no previous notice to the other party is required by the applicant for a divorce. You discard the partner of your joys and sorrows, your bed and board, with the same *sang froid* as you discard your old coat or your holey socks. No questions are asked as to the reason for divorce, but, unless otherwise agreed upon, the woman keeps custody of the children and the man pays her aliment; and pretty stiff aliment too. I was told by a doctor in Russia (he thought it a good joke!) of a woman who quarrelled with her husband one morning. Off she went indignantly to Z.A.G.S. down the street for a divorce. She returned in a few minutes and waved the separation ticket in her (now ex-) husband's face. He retaliated by going out and fetching back another wife, so there were now three in the single apartment, the ex-wife, the new wife, and the husband. The ex-wife then, to balance matters, went out and fetched in a new husband! If any Communist commissar in Britain ever tried to impose this casual union upon the female proletariat here, I'd take long odds that he'd soon be running for his life.

For a contribution of 3 roubles I got certificates of marriage and divorce away with me, although the young registrar smilingly insisted upon defacing them, and I was presented gratis with a small four page booklet of quite unexceptionable injunctions as to moral behaviour, mostly extracts from the code of laws of the U.S.S.R., and winding up with a supplementary decree by the Plenum of the Supreme Court that (in English translation)

"The person who enters into registration of marriage for the purpose of utilising a woman for sexual reasons with the intention afterwards of breaking the marriage is to be sued according to the Code of Laws 153 section."

Thousands of marriages were afterwards solemnised by a religious ceremony, but the only marriage recognised by the State was the civil one at the registrar's office.

Then to Moscow. Outside the city could be seen men with bare feet, families housed in old railway carriages, and other evidences of the privations and struggles which the proletariat were undergoing. Inside the city I had a room at the National hotel with telephone and bath: was given a new interpreter, who turned out to be a smart talkative dame from Chicago; and was offered every assistance by Mr. Andrei Tchin (I hope I spell his name correctly), a director of Intourist, and whom I had met in London before he was expelled in M. Rokovsky's time. He struck me as a most sincere and capable citizen, and I was later grateful to him particularly for procuring me entry into the Kremlin. He had piloted Mr. H. G. Wells about just before I arrived, and he quite appreciated the fact that I wanted to see below stairs, and not merely front shop window stuff.

But in the end Intourist or O.G.P.U., or it may be some mischance, partially beat me. I had a good camera and had gone about quite openly photographing all sorts of interesting subjects—among others priests, slums, free markets and (to the undisguised horror of my guide) the Lubianka prison! Towards the end of my Moscow sojourn I had a visit from an Intourist agent who said it was a rule that all photographs taken in the Soviet Union must be developed in the country and that if I wanted to avoid delay on leaving I had better get my spools developed now. Intourist would do the developing gratis.

It looked reasonable enough and since I had nothing to hide I handed over about 12 spools which were lying readily available in a suitcase, but omitting to hand over a similar number of spools which were in a trunk, and not so readily available. I got back my 12 spools all right, stamped impressively as passed for export; and in due course passed by the customs people they were. But when I returned to Glasgow and sent my developed films for prints to the Kodak Company I got back some beautiful pictures of the Ural mountains and other show places in Russia where neither I nor my camera had ever been. The Urals had been substituted for my ragged priests and my Lubianka prisons and my slums. When I wrote about the substitution I was informed that an error had occurred, but I never got my original snaps back, and years later I heard that the same error had befallen other simple and ingenuous people with cameras.

From outside, the appearance of the Kremlin is most impressive, especially when at night it is floodlit, but inside it disappoints: Napoleon's bust, millions of pounds' worth of ancient junk, pearls, gold, old state carriages, swords, armour, the headgear of dead patriarchs in precious stones! The most beautiful exhibit, I thought, was the huge ivory eagle built from hundreds of thousands of separate parts and presented by the Mikado to the Tsar upon the occasion of his coronation. Ivan the Terrible was buried in the Kremlin and my guides were amused by my comment that he appeared to be smelling yet, until they suddenly remembered that, in another part of the Kremlin, the new hierarchy was installed. In Russia you don't joke about the gentlemen of the Presidium. I forbore to ask questions about how Captain Hill and Colonel Boyle during the early Bolshevik period had managed to steal the Rumanian Crown jewels. The jewels had been given by the Rumanian authorities to the Tsar for safe keeping, and had been retained by the Bolsheviki. Then at the instance of Queen Marie of Rumania, Hill and Boyle had purloined them from the Kremlin and had run them back to Rumania.[1]

I was taken to the Museum of the Revolution, where some incredible and revolting pictures are on view, e.g. of a peasant woman—said to be an authenticated case in old Tsarist days—giving suckle to her master's puppy dog while her own baby was thrown away. Another type of picture too, I was shown, a cinema one of high technical efficiency; the photography and music were first class and it had greatly impressed Mr. H. G. Wells. It was entitled " The Three Songs about Lenin " and was really a propaganda masterpiece.

And still a third special visit I remember: it was to the Soviet Hendon,

[1] See—still in some of our public libraries—Captain Hill's books *Go Spy the Land* and *Dreaded Hour*. Both these great " underground " narratives have disappeared from our book markets. I believe they were frowned upon when Russia became our ally during the war, and have not since been reprinted.

the great Russian air display, where I was piloted out by Mr. Maisky, who had arrived on holiday from London. There were about 200,000 spectators: a splendid parachute jumping exhibition, and the huge Maxim Gorki plane, said then to be the biggest in the world, with its printing machinery on board churning out propaganda literature as it circled the airfield.

Litvinoff I did not see. But with Vishinsky, then in the ascendant, after the Engineers' trial, I had a long *sederunt*. At that time he was the assistant Commissar for Justice, and I am certain he was convinced that the British engineers were guilty. He argued in favour of the Soviet system whereby two assessors from the Factory sat beside the Judge and had an equal vote in law, and on fact, with him, saying that they were there to defend the proletarian state. There was *habeas corpus* in Russia: accused persons must be tried within two months, and there was provision for bail except in danger to the State cases. Contrary to what is western public opinion of him today, I formed a high estimate of his forthrightness and his sincerity.

I had nearly two hours with old Bukharin, the editor of *Izvestia* with its two million circulation. He told me he could sell ten million copies if he could get the paper. He was one of Lenin's personal friends, talked 150 words to the minute, and never paused for breath: was small in stature, round-eyed, with a childlike face, almost bald, with a clear skin, slight pointed beard, and small moustache. He would consider any means to preserve peace, including an international police force, if it became a concrete proposal; but he did not think peace could be preserved under capitalism. Told me that Hitler's agents were trying to float an international loan, but he was sure they would fail; and if they failed the likelihood was that the German Communists would come in. Looking back upon that interview now with the little man in his clipped English, cocksurely zig-zagging to and fro across men and affairs in the world, he strikes me as being just about the last man to be standing in a dock, four years later, and publicly abasing himself, declaring that, " The crimes for which I have accepted political and juridicial responsibility are sufficient to justify my being shot ten times over."

In my interview with him he talked at length about the possibilities of a war between Russia and Japan over the ownership of the Chinese Eastern Railway in Manchukuo. He thought the Japanese had made " a first class blunder in leaving the League of Nations," and that Russia would have the moral support of the greater part of the world. When I asked him if the Soviets, in the event of an unprovoked attack and seizure of the railway by the Japanese, " would have more than moral support," he replied, " We would. But I cannot speak of that. For the moment it is enough that France will keep Germany and Poland off our rear. Mr. Roosevelt in America is our friend."

He was, however, completely cagey on one point about which I repeatedly pressed him. Why if Russia might soon be fighting for her existence in the Far East should she be irritating Labour opinion in Britain by her Communist interrupters at public meetings, and by the general vilification and abuse of the Labour movement industrially and politically in Britain, the which was about the sole stock-in-trade of the Communist Party in England and Scotland?

The utmost in reply he would say was that the Government of the U.S.S.R. had nothing to do with that. "International Communist proclivities and propaganda you must discuss with the Communist Party officials."

Though I told him I would publish his detailed views about the tactics of a Russo-Japanese war in the *Forward* (which I did) he expressly forbade me referring to him otherwise than as "a knowledgeable Russian." I honoured his stipulation at the time,[1] but he is dead and no harm can result from publication now.

In the ballroom of the Hall of the Nobles where Bukharin, and before him, the British engineers had been tried for sabotage and treason, I met Maxim Gorki. He was presiding that day over a congress of Soviet writers, and was obviously a very sick man; he was tall with a drooping moustache, and a twitching face. H. G. Wells I think had upset him somehow, for it was only Wells' iniquities I could get him to talk about.

The Kholkhozes (collective farms) were most interesting even although the ones I was first taken to were, I fancy, carefully selected for inspection, and the later ones I visited without guides or previous notice were not quite so good. One farm in particular was splendidly cropped. It was of 128 hectares (multiply by 2½ for acreage) and maintained 108 families, growing vegetables, cabbage, carrots, potatoes, tomatoes, and onions chiefly. It had a crèche, two schools (in one school room there were 58 pupils) and a common dining room; the 'propaganda' was carried to such an inordinate length that the only picture in the crèche for the babies to look at was a huge cromeolithograph of the Commissar for War, and in the kindergarten there was a banner display

"We are developing under the banner of Lenin and Stalin."

On the area covered by that particular Kholkhoz there had been at one time 13 Kulaks, or more prosperous peasant farmers. Most of them, who

[1] *Forward*, 29.9.34.

had opposed collectivist farming, were simply " sent away "—presumably to labour on the White Sea canal works. The collectivist farmers, so the chairman told me, could be divided into three types, slackers, good workers, and shock workers. The slacker was first warned, then for a second offence was fined up to 5 days' income, and for a third offence, expelled. Where he went to after that, deponent knew not.

It was reported that the individualist farmer in the neighbourhood was producing about 60 per cent less than the collectivist farmer, and was gradually and of his own volition joining up in the Kholkhoz; but when I went round the remaining individualists I could get no answer of any kind as to why they did not rush to join a Kholkhoz and reap their share of the 60 per cent increased production. In that year (1934) about 65 per cent of the peasants were in collective (Kholkhoz) farming, and from 12 per cent to 15 per cent engaged on State farms, none of which I found time to inspect. The remainder, 20 per cent, must therefore have still been individualist farmers.

If a Kholkhoz raised 40 tons of cabbage, 15 tons went to the Government at a fixed price, the remainder, 25 tons, was retained by the Kholkhoz and could be eaten or sold in any free market the farmers chose. Of potatoes, if 23-25 tons per hectare were grown, only 2 tons were taken by the State at the fixed price of 20 kopecks per kilo; this was one-third of the market price. The Government made no levy on crops of parsley, cauliflower, celery, etc.

There were other taxes of course. Some Kholkhozes had to pay a joint tax of 620 roubles per annum, although that was reduced by 15 per cent as a reward for larger production. In addition they had to pay 20 roubles per household; but I could not make head or tail of who paid for police or government inspectors or schools. The roads were awful, and the furniture in the houses, and the living conditions, betrayed a standard of living far below anything our agricultural labourers have had to put up with. On the other hand I was assured on all hands that no peasant left the collective farm of his own accord.

The figures I got going round Kholkhozes on the outskirts of Moscow in no case squared with the figures given me by Walter Duranty of the *New York Times*, who, with Wicksteed of the *Daily Telegraph*, appeared to be the only English speaking pressmen still stationed in Moscow. Duranty said bluntly that about half of the peasants' crop went off in taxation—25 per cent of a State tax, 20 per cent in a Traction tax, and 5 per cent in minor levies. These figures I must say were later questioned by high Soviet officers, but I think there is no doubt about it that M. Troyetzkey, chief of the Economic Institute of Gosplan, did not over-estimate when he said to me that one-third of the total income of Russia was going to the production of capital and two-thirds to the production of consumer goods. The proportion to capital was over high; it was too many guns and too little butter and the present generation was suffering.

Alexander Wicksteed, the *Daily Telegraph* man, had been a Quaker who had gone out to the Soviet Union I gathered, for sentimental reasons, and had decided to remain there and teach English at the University. His home was a tenement at Kostomavovski, Moscow, and his room 6 yards long by 3 yards broad was shared with a young Russian who was learning to speak English, and who had inclinations to serve as a religious missionary among the heathen somewhere. This particular tenement was built in 1923; there were 15 rooms to every flat: an average of 5 persons to every room, and there were only 2 w.c.s, and latrines, and 5 taps for washing for the 75 persons. The smell of the latrines pervaded the rooms; and the sight of the latrines was if anything worse than the smell; the heads of every household had to pay 16 kopeks per month for the cleansing of these offences against amenity and health.

Rental charges were based upon income (means testing clearly was carried to the nth degree in the Soviet Union) and Wicksteed, whose income was 200 roubles per month, had to pay

9 roubles 50 kopeks for rent
4 roubles 26 kopeks for heating
10 roubles for electricity.

This was because he had an electric kettle. If he had surrendered his kettle his electricity charge would have been only 3 roubles in winter and less in summer.

In the newer tenements there was a closet, a bathroom and a kitchen to every three rooms. Frequently there were two to three families in every three rooms. They might have to go short in sanitation, but 75 per cent of the families had a telephone.

The engineers at the A.M.O. works, 23,000 of them, typical of the *élite* of the new Russia, got good three course dinners. Also they had free dentistry, free spectacles (but if special lenses were required a charge was made) free library, shower baths, medical attention, rest houses, two weeks' holidays with pay, and longer paid holidays if they were engaged upon specially difficult or dangerous work, and they had free burial from a social insurance fund. There was in addition a voluntary personal insurance system.

In the Law Courts I found many interesting side lights upon the working of the Soviet system. But in one criminal court where I was a privileged spectator, I was bored stiff until a Chinese—or perhaps he was a Mongolian—was brought in as a witness. The Judge asked him a question, whereupon he broke out into a long oration, twenty-four minutes by the clock, waving his arms, and yelling his emphases. When he had finished, exhausted, I turned to my interpreter and asked:

" What did he say? "

" He say no! "

As a negative it had been somewhat on the longish side.

There was greater social attraction for me in the short cases in the Civil Court. Here I got a seat beside Judge Novikoff (a very fair Judge, I thought) and two assessors from the Factory who had equal voting rights with the Judge. The Judge, minus a waistcoat, with a soft white collar and a loose tie, his cap on the desk in front of him, was hearing a case of negligence at a crèche where 2000 roubles' worth of linen had gone amissing. Two women were being charged. The first witness for the prosecution arrived late and was promptly fined 25 roubles (equal to $1\frac{1}{2}$ days wages) for being late. No oaths were administered in the court, but each witness was warned to tell the truth, otherwise he or she would be imprisoned. The bookkeeper, under severe examination by the Judge, admitted that he had never told the women accused to take an inventory of the linen. So he was reprimanded, the women were found not guilty, and the Judge intimated that he would report the management for gross carelessness to a higher authority.

There were 13 Arboritaria in Moscow when I was there, and at one of them the doctor in charge told me that in 1934, out of 5677 operations to get rid of an unwanted baby none had resulted in a fatality. Some of the women made the sign of the cross prior to the operation, but in every case they were lectured and urged not to come back. If they did return within six months, a second operation was refused.

The Bolshovo Colony experiment has been well reported to the world, and I hope it has been impartially studied by our Home Offices. The Russians have got something here, and it ought not to be prejudiced by the fact that it was founded by M. M. Djerskinsky and Yagoda of the O.G.P.U. Bolshovo is a self-governing colony of criminals and waifs and strays. They marry and give in marriage, get wages for production, have holidays; after three years they may get a passport and can join a Trade Union and/or the Communist Party if they are acceptable.

Hundreds of the colonists who are free to leave the colony stay on. The general meeting elects its own officers—all except the manager, the doctor and the chief engineer, who must be Communists. The members are taught labour habits, but Bolshovo is not a prison reclamation scheme. The produce output of the colony was of the value of 30 million roubles, and showed a profit of five million roubles. The colonists were building a palace of culture, and were making tennis rackets, shoes, skis, golf clubs, textile goods, etc., for export. All government credits were repaid without interest. The mottoes in the colony are 'Nothing for Nothing' and ' Incurables do not exist '; but I noticed that they sent some brigadiers to stand outside the public drinking houses in the nearby villages to warn off the weaklings. There was a film *Pass to Life* which I thought particularly good on the Bolshovo, and it might be worth some enterprising British Cinema manager's while having a look at it.

Perhaps I should add that one of my most treasured photographs which I took in the colony was of the " Boss " of the murderers' section who was said to have no fewer than fourteen murders to his discredit, and who stood proudly to face the camera.

The one outstanding dispute at the time I was in Moscow between foreign concessionaires and the Soviet Government was over the Lena Goldfields Company. All the other properties which had been appropriated from foreign concessionaires, had (so the Soviet authorities declared) been compensated for, and Litvinoff when at the Foreign Office had struggled to get the Lena dispute out of his road too. The Assistant Commissar of Finance, M. Levine, told me they were making a fresh offer to the Lena Company, and M. Trifonoff, the Chairman of the Concessions Commission, declared they had offered £1,600,000, which was all the Company had ever put into Russia, but that sum had been refused. How the dispute ever ended—if in fact it has yet been ended—I know not.

CHAPTER XVI

THE YEARS THE LOCUST ATE

*Helgi the Lean was a Christian in name, but his faith was a very mixed
one, for though he was baptised and declared his belief in Christ he made
vows to Thor whenever he was engaged in sea-faring or any matters
that required hardihood.*

—' *Orkneyinga Saga* '—*The Saga of King Olaf Tryggwason*
(*Shepton's Translation, p. 170*)

THE PERIOD between the General Election of 1935 and the outbreak of
war in 1939 is not one during which many men on any side of public
life have earned enconiums from history. We all sensed the shame and
humiliation of Munich, but most part of us hoped secretly that Chamberlain was right and that Hitler could be bought off at the expense of our
acquiescence in his villainies towards the smaller nations. While all officially
gave lip service to the League, most citizens were appeasers of and sur-
renderists to the bludgeon and castor oil terrorists in Rome and Berlin.

Here and there a lone figure protested—a Churchill, a Maxim Litvinoff
(whose efforts for collective security have never had the recognition in this
country that they deserved!) or a Lord Davies, saw that appeasement simply
meant at once a cowardly surrender and an encouragement to further
aggression and terrorism; but the masses followed the Government appeasers,
and the Labour Opposition for years was satisfied to vote reductions in
military expenditure; men in high places like Lord Rothermere openly
proclaimed that Hitler was " a great gentleman " who " exudes good
fellowship ";[1] alas! only a year or two had to elapse ere his Lordship
was evacuating himself to America to escape his old friend's bombs. The
Rev. Dr. Knight, too, of the Scottish Bible Society in his Annual Report
for 1934 declared firmly that Mussolini " reads a chapter of the New
Testament every day " (omitting inadvertently any hint of the bayonet
exercise he provided in the evenings for his boy scouts, or the whiff of
poison gas he was storing up for the Abyssinians, with his succinct comment

[1] *Warnings and Predictions.* Lord Rothermere, 1939, Chapter VI.

that " niggers have no guns "!) And Lord Londonderry, our Secretary for Air, had got himself photographed with Hitler and Ribbentrop, and was so proud of the picture that he had it published in his book " Ourselves and Germany."

Almost it seemed as if we had reverted in our appeasements and obsequious *camaraderie* to the great days before the first world war when a First Lord of the Admiralty, Lord Tweedmouth, had " submitted to the Kaiser the naval estimates for the year before they had been submitted to the House of Commons."[1]

But Mussolini's defiance of the League over Abyssinia, and the Hoare-Laval pact, and the non-intervention farce over Spain, and the frank admission by Mr. Prime Minister Baldwin that he had been grievously misled in his previous optimistic estimates about aircraft production in Germany and Britain:

> " In my estimate I was mistaken. I was thoroughly mistaken on that point. I freely acknowledge it before the House—thoroughly mistaken, I repeat "—[2]

all created a revulsion to appeasement, and by September 1937 the National Council of Labour was declaring that

> " in the present state of the world a government must be strongly armed in order to defend the homeland."

A Welsh industrialist peer, Lord Davies, had founded a Commonwealth League to promote the idea of an international police force, and his propaganda had made considerable headway in public opinion. Mr. Eden and Lord Cranborne would have no more surrenderism and demanded oil sanctions on the Italian aggressor state, and upon it the Labour Party almost unanimously clamoured for an international economic boycott. This meant withdrawal of ambassadors and the use of every radio station outside Italy with incessant propaganda against the Italian Government and in the Italian language: it meant stoppage of postal arrangements, finance, chemicals, munitions, oil, everything, and as Sir Thomas Holland declared in his volume: *The Mineral Sanction As An Aid To International Security* :

> " Italy cannot supply from her own resources her requirements under war conditions, of chrome, coal, copper, iron ore, manganese ore, mica, nickel, petroleum, tin and tungsten."

Even a convinced pacifist like George Lansbury declared at Dumfries for an international police force. The United States, though not in the League,

[1] *Old Diplomacy*, by Lord Hardinge of Penshurst, p. 150.
[2] House of Commons 28.11.34.

intimated her willingness to co-operate. But international action there was not to be. Instead of League action on oil sanctions we got a Hoare-Laval surrender, and direct encouragement to Franco and Hitler, and a long step taken towards a second world war.

Meanwhile one of the supposed danger spots was Danzig, the Free City which Hitler was loudly threatening to overwhelm. Along with Major Milner, later to become deputy speaker in the House of Commons, I paid a visit to the threatened city in 1936, at the time when loud speakers were attached to the telephone poles in the Danzig streets, and every pro-Nazi stood respectfully to attention while Hitler's voice blared at them. Herr Greiser was then Nazi president; the Herr had leapt to fame for being the gentleman who had thumbed his nose at the League of Nations Council in solemn session, and he was supposed to be tormenting Mr. Sean Lester, the Free State Irishman who was then the Commissioner for the League of Nations. But when we had a long two hours' session with Greiser he was all affability and sweet reasonableness; he was a dove of peace, and assured us (we later found it to be true) that Jews were still participating in Stock Exchange business at the Artushof. When we pressed him about the disappearance of Social Democrat papers he became rather 'cagey' and finally he offered to send one Herr Frobuss, the chief of police, to our hotel to explain matters. When next day Frobuss arrived we found to our amusement that the interviewing room had been carefully 'arranged,' and as the interview proceeded, spies' heads bobbed up every five minutes over a curtain at the end of the room. We got just nothing out of that chief of police.

It was with difficulty that I could buy a copy of *Der Sturmer*, the German Nazi anti-Jew propaganda paper in Danzig, but finally I secured one in a shop down at the Docks. The line taken by the precious *Der Sturmer* was that at their ritual feasts the Jews suck the blood of Christian children, and Herr Streicher, one of Hitler's right hand men, who edited the rag, declared that Jewish butchers made their sausages from rats. The anti-semitic cartoons in the copy I got were savagely conceived and forcefully drawn, and much of the letter-press was devoted to the Protocols of the Elders of Zion— protocols which, by the way, had been proved in the Supreme Law Courts of Switzerland in 1935 to have been a deliberate forgery by an officer of the old Tsarist secret police. As propaganda I should think *Der Sturmer* must have had little effect, and some decent Germans in Danzig were thoroughly ashamed of it and openly denounced it as a low pornographic sheet. There was, however, in the streets, much marching and counter marching and heil Hitlering, and there was a general apprehension of a pogrom of some kind in the near future.

At home there was little artistry or *finesse* about the blatant propaganda falsehoods which were conceived necessary in these pre-war years. Of course once an audience was secured it was repetition and extravaganza, not delicacy of touch, that the practitioners employed. The *Vanguard* of Edinburgh (Protestant Action organ) in May 1935 did not hesitate to assure its faithful that

" The Pope is the cause of all the trouble in the world. Being the direct representative of the Devil . . . there is every kind of sin, iniquity, hypocrisy, sham, make-believe, delusion and immorality,"

but omitting, possibly for a subsequent catalogue, such clear evidences of papal responsibility for iniquity as the Colorado beetle, the high price of whisky and the B.B.C. depression " moving north from the Scilly isles."

The Burgos Spanish Insurgent Committee reported to the world that two of its women helpers at Baena were killed by Spanish Government forces through " having medals nailed to their eyes "; but as a general rule it was whenever Red Russia became the rag to the bull that the most memorable propaganda efforts were produced. There was a Count Castellane who published in 1934 a book entitled *One Crowded Hour*, in which the Chinese in the Moscow Cheka were described as skinning their victims and declaring " quite frankly that they were selling the meat on the market."

Sometimes the greatest masters slipped up, as when Sir Basil Thomson, our Director of Intelligence, got caught out in sending the forged copies of the Soviet paper, *Pravda*, to Riga. That story you can get in *Hansard* for May 1921. Some White Russians had arranged with a London printer to produce bogus copies of *Pravda*: the forged copies were to be sent to countries bordering upon the Soviet Union, and from these countries excerpts from the juicy falsehoods in the bogus *Pravdas* were to be telegraphed back across the world for the stiffening and encouragement of White forces everywhere. Unfortunately the British printer of the concoction had mistakenly adhibited his name and address on the back page of the *Pravdas*, and Sir Basil Thompson, so that the good work should not be wasted and thereby justifying his title as Director of Intelligence, had got the printer's name and address cut off before shipment. Mr. Shortt, the Home Secretary, rather denigrated Sir Basil's achievement, declaring it to be ' indiscreet,' and Sir Basil in his Memoirs, modestly omitted to make any mention of the matter.

Among the propagandists of the pre-war period who took high place was the late Dr. Knight, a distinguished scholar and archæologist who was director of the National Bible Society of Scotland. His reports were always of interest. Thus in 1933 he informed us that there had been 24 Baptists executed in January at Rostov by the Bolsheviki. Other 53 Baptists from the Caucasus had been taken to Rostov,

> "and in fulfilment of a sentence arranged at Moscow before their trial took place, they were put to death. They bore themselves with noble dignity. They accused nobody: they were silent while their Cheka judges yelled at them: they only prayed quietly and sang religious songs, O Lord, how long will this tyranny last?"

A challenge which, for a sport, I made demanding proof about these murdered Baptists, elicited only the reply that the authority for the murders was "the Rostov press." Upon being further publicly pressed Dr. Knight said his quotation was from a paper called *La Renaissance*, which in turn had been quoted by another paper called *The Alliance Weekly* in the United States. But the mystery further deepened when the *Alliance Weekly* was challenged and replied frankly that it knew nothing about *La Renaissance*. And when I got assurances from the Russian ambassador that there was no Rostov press, and it was now clear that there was neither *La Renaissance* nor Rostov press, we were left with the dark suspicion that the poor Baptists had been executed by some biblical enthusiast on a Scottish typewriter.

Of course the propaganda was by no means one-sided; indeed the Russians themselves are possibly the world's greatest experts at the business; and Sir Walter (now Lord) Citrine in his *I Search for Truth in Russia* relates how he copied from Russian school books in 1935 such delightful titbits about Great Britain as

> "Poison gas and machine guns are prepared by the bourgeoisie for the unemployed who demand bread."

And even today the Second Five Year Plan (1946-50) propaganda, published in English by the Soviet News (Illustrated Soviet Shilling Booklets) opens with the announcement to all who are likely to believe that,

> "As a result of the heroic efforts of the peoples of the Soviet Union and of its gallant Red Army an epoch making victory has been won— Hitler Germany has been smashed and Japanese imperialism defeated. The U.S.S.R. ended the war by completely vanquishing the enemy"—

but omits any mention whatever of British, American and other allied effort, and on page eight it repeats this kind of war "history":

> "Just as the Red Army fighting singlehanded in a long and arduous

I

struggle scored a military victory over the Fascist armies, so did the working people of the Soviet rear . . . score an economic victory."

That single-handed fight ought to be preserved among the greater mythologies of the world.

During the immediately pre-war years I found myself running a sort of private frontier war of my own against unscrupulous gangs of share pushers, bucket shop operators, bogus company promoters and the like, who, to the best of my calculations, were robbing simple minded investors of their savings to the extent of about £5,000,000 per annum. The *Daily Mail* and one or two weekly journals like *Truth* and the *Investors' Review* and the *Investors' Chronicle*, at great financial hazard of libel actions, sought to expose the rogues, but it was not until the Speaker of the House of Commons allowed me to expand the rules applicable to questions on the Order Paper and mention the swindlers and their efforts by name, that the Government wakened up to what was going on. It had cost the *Daily Mail* some £50,000 to root out a man called Jacob Factor. Jacob had been a barber in Chicago before he discovered that there was more money in peddling attractively printed but bogus stock than in cutting hair or shaving chins: and after he had skimmed the American market he and his associates descended upon London, where they had ' cleaned up ' about £1,000,000 before the *Daily Mail* very courageously had dragged Factor to the law courts and imprisonment, and his colleagues to deportation.

The bogus share pushers could not get at me for my House of Commons activities for libel: the best they could do, some of them, was in threats of physical violence; but Inspector Bell of Scotland Yard (a Hawick man, if I remember aright) was able to counter all the threats, and indeed was not averse to using me as a bait. On one occasion two swindlers sought an interview with me in the smoking room of the House of Commons. At that interview Inspector Bell posed as an M.P. and we both listened to great asseverations of innocence with reasons annexed as to why they of all men should not be harried in their honest business. Among other expostulations it appeared that the London Police and Scotland Yard were showing disgraceful favouritism, as for example in the way they were winking at the surreptitious return from deportation of Jacob Factor's chief lieutenants who were alleged to be again in active eruption and operating from a named, swagger hotel. At this piece of news, Bell kicked my ankle below the table to make no comment, and immediately our share pushing interviewers had gone, he hurried off to give instructions that a couple of detectives should proceed to that hotel disguised as waiters, white shirts, tails, *et al.*, and he arranged with the management of the hotel for the temporary employment of his men. That night three or four of the returned deportees were arrested during their soup course!

There was one rogue who specialised in floating companies with a capital of say £500,000 and allocating £499,900 of the shares to himself for considerations other than cash. These shares he then proceeded to sell to simple folk; his literature was most attractive and persuasive.

Another rogue would start a 'snowball' land or agricultural company; his speciality was aiding the townsman to promote agriculture; everybody in a city could own a fruit tree, or a hundred fruit trees, or a thousand fruit trees; and the fortunate purchasers would get their names upon particular trees and the company would nurture and cultivate the trees for their owners, paying them the profits, less a small commission for expenses, at the end of the year. Each tree would only cost £1. The first year's dividend might be perhaps 5s. (paid of course from the subscriptions of the investors) and the news of this great and prosperous concern spread rapidly. Widows, spinsters, clergymen, and lawyers, fell for the scheme, and money rolled in to the agricultural promoters. So long as the new investments vastly exceeded the bait money paid out as tree profits all was well.

One adventurer was caught out only because he made the mistake of going to a Labour Exchange and inducing two hundred happy beneficiaries there to sit in a group photograph (for payment to each sitter of a bottle of beer and a pie) holding spades and other agricultural implements, and with their trousers tied beneath their knees in proper rural labourer style. Above their heads in the photograph was the legend that these were the employees of such and such a company.

This photograph, widely distributed as share pushing propaganda, was held to be fraud, and the promoter forfeited bail and skipped the country.

Or you could invest in mushroom or soya bean plots. One mushroom company had taken almost £250,000 in subscriptions from the public. The Soya bean venture offered a sure return of 10 per cent, but it later transpired that the promoter, a gentleman called Smolensky, rather regarded the 10 per cent as a figure of speech. And I forget what interest the Federated Empire Bank promised its depositors, but its founder modestly hid the fact that he had served four terms of imprisonment. The splendidly designated Bank of London, after three years, had to be wound up with cash assets of £33 and a deficiency of £167,000.

After much exposuring of these rogueries the Government gave us a Committee of Enquiry under the chairmanship of Sir Archibald Bodkin, and following upon that, a Prevention of Fraud Investment Bill which to a considerable extent protected the gulls from the sharks. But I for one regretted that the opportunity was not at the time taken to stop a misuse of the Bank Nominees system under which share-holders in public companies could remain hidden beneath the all-embracing designation of Bank Nominees Limited. This practice was clearly an evasion of the Companies Act of 1929 which provided that public company share-holders had to be registered, and the register made open for inspection on payment of a small fee. And I, without avail, repeatedly drew attention to the fact that one of our largest aircraft manufacturing companies had among its share-holders Bank Nominees from an Italian Bank, from a Belgian Bank, and from a Swiss Bank, and that other five aircraft concerns in this country had substantial holdings of their stock held by Bank Nominees Limited, and that indeed one of these companies had two-thirds of its total stock so held.

All these financial trickeries on the home front, however, faded away in public interest before the rustlings of the coming storm of war. Mussolini had defied the League of Nations and had poison-gassed the Abyssinians; and an economic boycott of the declared aggressor in this case had been hamstrung (or more politely, frustrated) by timidity, and perhaps by treachery, among the nations; instead of a resolute shunning of the war-monger and a systematic bombardment of public opinion in Italy from all the wireless stations in Europe, some oil corporations were allowed to sell him oil, some financial houses continued to change his money, and we all kept our ambassadors in Rome, and our postal services, and our trains running to him; in other words we aided his aggression; we shared in his loot. But the Hoare-Laval pact behind the back of the League of Nations, and the agreement to let Mussolini get away with the major part of his conquest, when that secret pact was disclosed, really stunned and angered the British people, and Sir Samuel Hoare, who had acted for the Government, had to be thrown overboard.

In Paris—Mr. John Gunther[1] commits himself to the assertion—in 1939 there were 102 daily newspapers and only two of them completely honest, with their news columns not for private sale. The others would publish any kind of 'news' for money, and Gunther adds that in 1935 during his aggression in Abyssinia Mussolini spent 65 million francs in corrupting the press of Paris. In Britain on the other hand the press almost to a unit was pro-League of Nations and anti-Mussolini, and nearly 7 million citizens had signed the Peace Ballot, and had given an affirmative reply in favour of applying collective sanctions if necessary. How, under such circumstances, a British foreign secretary could involve himself in the conditions of the Hoare-Laval pact remains to me one of the great mysteries of the nineteen thirties.

Then too there was the cynical impudence of the Non-Intervention

[1] *Inside Europe*, pp. 142-3.

Committee over Spain—so impudent that a Duchess M.P.[1] sickened at the shame of it, and refused any longer to take the whips from a Government which would give the brazen farce any countenance. Almost everywhere in Europe the caveman arose and clubbed his neighbours; the lamps of liberty flickered and went out: the Jews ran hither and thither seeking escape; in Hitler's Germany the Trade Unions and Co-operative Societies were smashed, their funds plundered, their leaders exiled or driven to concentration camps. Appeasement, surrender, abasement, humiliation, dirt eating, were all offered to placate the Fascist leaders: in vain! President Roosevelt appealed publicly to Herr Hitler for a guarantee that he would not invade a list of specified nations. The appeal was treated with contempt.

No use now calling for international boycotts, or an international police to restrain the warmongers. Too late now; the League of Nations had been allowed to slither to decrepitude. The only alternatives left were a cowardly acquiescence in the death of democracy or a desperate resistance in a war for which we were unprepared with arms, until these arms could be procured.

---

[1] She, the Duchess of Athol, wrote a Penguin Special, *Searchlight on Spain*, and lost her seat in Parliament as a result of her breakaway from her Party allegiance.

CHAPTER XVII

WAR MEMORIES

*But I tell you my lord fool, out of this nettle danger we pluck this
flower safety.*

— Shakespeare, Henry IV, Act II, Scene III

*I must go and meet with danger there or it will seek me in another
place and find me worse provided.*

— Shakespeare, Henry IV, Part II, Act II, Scene III

*Take these men for your ensamples. Like them remember that pros-
perity can only be for the free, that freedom is the sure possession of
those who alone have the courage to defend it.*

— Lines on the soldiers' memorial tower on the campus of
the University of Toronto

THERE WAS little remnant of a passive (or non) resistance left in this
land when appeasement for very shame and futility could go no farther.
And when war ultimately came to our world there were no Quislings in
Scotland, and but few who carried pacifist surrenderism the length of
making no preparation for the relief of suffering among the civilian population. A stray peace-pledger or two may have continued to cry aloud that
A.R.P., and ambulance, water supplies, hospitals, food storage and transport,
shelters for homeless folks, and fire precautions were only capitalist war
propaganda. But these theories were never—so far as I know—carried to
the length of refusing to eat food that had been carried on a ship where the
crew had dared to protect themselves with life-belts and guns against
submarine attacks; and the most extreme peace-pledger drank his tea and
paid, therefore, a war tax like the rest of us.

In the spring of 1939 I was invited by the Government to become
Regional Commissioner for Civil Defence in Scotland, but I could not
readily bring myself to believe that the then administration would not do
another Munich upon us. Herbert Morrison was invited to be the Commissioner for London, but he shied off, I believe, for the same reason as
impressed me. Finally, however, after a meeting with Sir John Anderson

and Mr. Arthur Greenwood, the deputy chairman of the Labour Party, I agreed to co-operate with the then Lord Advocate (now Lord Cooper) in making arrangements for Civil Defence in Scotland, but I insisted that so far as I was concerned the appointment of a Commissioner for Scotland must be deferred, and I reserved my decision about acceptance of the Commissioner's task until (and if) we should actually be at war with the Fascist-Nazi assassins.

Some months afterwards the King when visiting Edinburgh asked me why I had refused to have myself announced as Regional Commissioner in the spring. It was almost on the tip of my tongue to quote to him one of Winston Churchill's quips—that Mr. Neville Chamberlain was the one British Prime Minister who, faced with the choice between war and dishonour, chose both—but I contented myself by explaining that I did not want to run the risk of being associated even indirectly with an administration capable of a second Czech humiliation.

If the Germans landed and if communications were cut with the central Government in London, the Regional Commissioners had to take charge of civil affairs. They were to be the civil authority until they were either shot or concentration camped by the enemy. Then their deputies and district commissioners were to take over control. When they in turn were liquidated, then presumably by that time German *gauleiters* would be in charge, although, as Mr. Churchill had speculated, there would be a British émigré government carrying on the war, perhaps from Canada.

In the meantime the Regional Commissioner was to supervise A.R.P. and Civil Defence arrangements generally: he was to persuade and convince the laggards among the local authorities: he had to remove difficulties and jarring edges: he had to keep up the civilian morale: he had to prepare for the worst and hope for the best. But I, for one, was given no guidance as to whether I was expected to stay at Edinburgh in the event of a German invasion in the east of Scotland, or whether I ought, like Bruce and Bonnie Prince Charlie, to skip to the islands of the west.

Meantime I was given Lord Airlie—a first rate friend to work with— presumably to keep me in good political face with political opponents who otherwise would have looked for my horns and my tail. Norman Duke (now Sir Norman Duke) was my Chief of Staff, and we had a splendid team of district commissioners and assistants; a war room equipped with all the latest news receiving apparatus; and we had great wall maps with pins and flags indicating where bombs were falling.

There was no limit to the urgent and sticky problems set me. Where, for example, were the elephants and lions and tigers from the zoos and circuses to be sent? And the Scottish Crown regalia and jewels? There were, I think, only four men who knew where the regalia and jewels were built into the castle wall in Edinburgh, and the hiding place had been skilfully covered up; I often wondered what would happen had a bomb hit the four of us. The chances were that the regalia might have been lost until judgment day. I know that Mr. Percy Rose, an under secretary at the Scottish Office and later King's Remembrancer, who was the officer primarily responsible, had taken the precaution of sending a plan of the treasure concealment to the High Commissioner in Canada in a sealed envelope, though whether accompanied by adequate descriptions and clues I know not. But there is one story of the burying of the regalia which I do not think has ever heretofore been told. Along with the Scottish crown and jewels there had been a bayonet, and somehow or other during the packing the then Lord Advocate, now The Lord President, Lord Cooper, had slipped and got the bayonet stuck in his leg, so badly that he had to go off to the infirmary and have his leg treated for tetanus.

Then too there were the whisky stocks. Where were they to be transferred? Mr. D. C. Thomson, owner of Dundee newspapers, kept harrying me with that one, and saying without being conscious of the *double entendre* that I was the only man who could shift the lot. Alas, I tried the disused lead mines at Wanlockhead, but Customs and Excise would not hear of it, and all other local authorities to whose areas I wanted to shift the inflammable liquids protested vehemently: finally a shipload of whisky worth £1,000,000 was sent off for safety to America, but the vessel (she was, by the way, called *The Politician*) ran ashore in a fog near Barra Head, and the Hebrideans regarded the wreck as a gift from Providence, remembered to this day with awe and gratitude and immortalised by Mr. Compton Mackenzie in his *Whisky Galore*.

We had to get arrangements made, too, for shifting the Banks and their valuables away to safety should the Germans land. But it was the evacuation of the mothers and children (and especially the mothers!) from our crowded industrial areas to billets in the country districts that gave us our greatest headache. In vain I had pled with London to be allowed to postpone our Scottish evacuation for say a month after the school holidays, so that the children would be back at school again and at least inspected by our medical, nursing, and sanitary services. After ' the clartier, the cosier' *interregnum* of the school holidays it was essential that the children be given a physical all-clear. But London decided upon a uniform evacuation date for the whole country and in three days we in Scotland transported and billeted over 170,000 mothers and children.

Upon the rural housewives in many a village there had descended what was thought to be the seven plagues of Egypt, and as one old lady put it: " Ah weel, they can get on wi' their war noo : we ken the warst! "

Many good stories of the evacuation came our way. There was one of the angry mother who arrived, and dragging her boy with her, at the Education Offices in Glasgow demanding to know if " that gulloot Hitler disna' ken that this is ma day at the steamie "; and the several times repeated account of the city children who would not take milk that did not come out of a tin or a bottle. Most of the remembered anecdotage relates to insanitation and is unprintable.

During the evenings our wardens went about blowing whistles whenever chinks of light were seen beneath the householders' blinds. But in the early stages of the war there was one exception to the blackout: a great prisoners'-of-war camp on the outskirts of Edinburgh. Do what we liked there was no blackout at that camp, the authorities declaring that since the time of Charles I or II or somebody it was an inflexible rule that prisoner camps should be lit at night to prevent escapes.

Politely at first, I explained that Charles I and II were both dead, and that we could not very well run a blackout system on the rest of Edinburgh if a huge fairy light system was to be permitted on the outskirts. No use! Charles I or II had laid down a rule. And in 1939 it took a prime minister's private secretary and a prime minister to get that fairy light system at Edinburgh shut down. But that was not the end. Immediately the blackout was in operation, for two nights hard running, prisoners escaped down the road to Peebles, and that had never happened until these crazy civilians interfered with the Charles I regulation!

At that same camp, on one occasion when I paid it a visit, there was a grim prisoner with folded arms walking about behind the barbed wire. He was speaking to nobody. I was told he was the captain of a large German merchant vessel which had been picked up as it was scurrying for Hamburg. I went in to speak to him. Had he any complaints? " Noddings to complain! " Was he being well treated? " Noddings to complain! " Well, I would be speaking on the wireless and I would tell the German people that he was quite happy and that he wanted for noddings!

" Von meenit," he cried. " I vant a chair! "

" What," I said, " have they not given you a chair? I'll see about that! "

Outside the barbed wire I asked the camp commandant why the old chap had not been given a chair.

" The scoundrel," said the commandant. " When he came to us he was very angry that his crew should have surrendered, and that they had also forced him to surrender. His crew surrendered to us with their clothes all packed up in suitcases, and the captain denounced them as traitors and Communists. And the first night he was here at this camp he broke the legs off his chair and was hammering his crew, and breaking their heads with his chair legs. Now he darned well sits on his hunkers." Only he didn't say darned or hunkers!

A wide variety of troubles came the way of the Regional Commissioner. Demands for deep shelters were clamant, and could only partially be countered with maps showing sewage and water mains underground, and by graphic descriptions of the kind of death one might die if a bomb penetrated to a sewage pipe running over a deep shelter. In Edinburgh we got more help against the deep shelterists from a canvas of householders with underground basements; from these householders we received promises of much emergency accommodation.

But these were days of grim, defiant, humour. After a bombing raid there would be a barber's shop with its windows blown in, and a notice posted up: "More open than ever!" A competitor down the street reported: "A close shave last night. Come in and get one." That was beaten by a London shopkeeper who announced: "Blown out, blasted out, but not sold out." And there is a Lancashire story of the boy who, after spending his first night in an Anderson shelter, declared: "By gum, Mum, my bum's numb!"; but I'm afraid I've forgotten the *locus* of the shop which, after a severe blitz, exhibited a placard: "You should just see our Berlin branch."

I liked best, however, the anecdote of the irate wardens who, during a complete blackout, saw a gleam of light in an Edinburgh tenement. Up the stairs they marched and knocked at a door. After some delay it was opened by a small frightened boy:

"Who is in here except yourself?" demanded a warden.

"Naebuddy, sur. A cam in when ma brither gaed oot, an ma brither cam in when ma faither went oot!"

"Come, come!" said the warden, "whose house is this?"

"This is no the hoose, sur: this is the cloaset!"

Quite a storm of protest arose in the early days of the war as a result of the Ministry of Food in London fixing retail prices for tomatoes graded according to the climatic conditions of Kent and Surrey, but quite inappropriate to our later ripened crops in the north. The prices were high when the first crop of south England tomatoes were ready (and when Scots tomatoes were not ripe enough to share the good price!) but low prices had been fixed for the period when the Scots tomatoes were due for the market. So growers in Lanarkshire declared they would be ruined, and we had great trouble in securing a readjustment of prices to suit our Scots climatic rates of growth; an illustration of how devolution—timeous devolution—was imperative if a sort of Scots Sinn Feinism was to be obviated.

There were tragedies too, which I was powerless to prevent. One I remember well. An Italian merchant in Edinburgh, whose family were serving in the British Forces, a man who had been all his adult life in Scotland, and who was known as a generous and public spirited citizen, and a great loather of Mussolini, was incarcerated in accordance with some formula about enemy aliens. The police knew it was a mistake; the then Lord Advocate (now Lord Cooper) did his utmost to secure the man's release and I bombarded the army authorities. But by the time we had convinced Security of the sheer injustice of its action the Italian had been ' lost.' We traced him from Saughton jail to camp after camp in England, but the trail failed us until it was announced that he had been drowned in the *Andorra Star* when that vessel was sunk by enemy torpedo as she was carrying prisoners and enemy aliens to Canada.

Unforgettable, too, the ghastly bombing of Clydebank when only twelve houses escaped damage, and the hospitals in the west were filled. In the March-May raids there, fifteen hundred people were killed and 2000 seriously injured. Of the population of 55,000 only 2000 could find any kind of habitation, however ramshackle, in the town, and poor, shivering, nerve-racked folk, bereft of their worldly goods and possessions and mourning some loved one torn to bloody rags by massed bombing, had to be sheltered and tended in widely scattered homes all over the West Country; and the stink of the burning oil from the great containers which had been hit: the smoke from the smouldering tenements: in the midst of all the chaos and destruction volunteer vans being driven by women from the Voluntary Services; the handing out cups of tea in the streets; the massed funerals of the victims—these memories abide!

But there is another, and one recalls it with pride, of the workers of John Brown & Company turning up next morning grim and purposeful at the work gates. Within 48 hours three-fourths of the industrial production of the neighbourhood was resumed, although the men had to be transported, some of them for long distances, morning and night to their employment. A tribute too is due to Lord Provost Dollan of Glasgow (a most capable and enthusiastic chairman of the Glasgow A.R.P. machine, although I think he sometimes had rather resented the co-ordinating pressure upon Glasgow by the Civil Defence organisation for the West of Scotland), to Sir Cecil Weir, the first District Commissioner, and after him to Sir Steven Bilsland and his deputies Sir Hector McNeill (later Lord Provost of Glasgow) and Joe Westwood (later Secretary of State for Scotland), and to the splendid array of Civil Defence volunteers, men and women, whom they had gathered together and trained for the great ordeal.

And north, south, east, and west in Scotland—how proud we were of the fact also that only one in every thirteen of the Civil Defence forces ever accepted payment for his or her services and sacrifices; in twenty counties in Scotland every warden was unpaid; all the district commissioners and their deputies set the example, taking no payment; film exhibitors gave free shows for evacuated children; the Wholesale Co-operative Society started my equipment as Scottish Santa Claus with 1000 toys; there was in 1939-1940 greater community of feeling and greater good-will among ourselves than probably at any time in our history.

But those were the hectic days and we had spy alarums in them. One alarum gave us considerable excitement behind the scenes. A German submarine had landed agents on the Morayshire coast. One pair of them, a man and a woman, had only a short run before being caught. They had gone to a railway station and asked for two third class single tickets to (if I remember rightly) Aberdeen! The station master, who was also booking clerk, supplied the tickets and said " One-eight-six," meaning of course, one pound, eight shillings and sixpence, but the contraction seemed to puzzle the ticket purchaser, who started to count out in pound notes— ' one, two, three, four, five, six, seven, eight,' and then the six confused him.

The station master said " No, only one-eight-six," whereat the puzzled purchaser began again his count of pound notes up to eight. By this time the station master surmised something was wrong, and said: " Wait a minute, and I'll get you change." He then slipped behind the office and sent his boy for the local policeman. When the policeman arrived he fortunately took the precaution of ' frisking ' the stranger and found a Luger pistol in his hip pocket. This settled the question of the price of tickets to Aberdeen, and the man and woman were taken to the police station to give a better account of themselves.

Meanwhile two farm workers going to their fields saw a man with a Homburg hat, a trench coat, and carrying a green suitcase wading in from the sea. They stood and gaped at this curiosity until the man disappeared along the road in a mist. When the two farm workers returned for food to the farm, all the talk was about a man and woman spy who had been arrested at the station.

" Oh," said one of the workers, " that would be the mannie we saw wadin' in frae the sea this mornin'."

" What! " cried the farmer. " Say that again! "

When the story of the sea-wader was repeated the farmer promptly phoned the County police, who were, when they arrived, anything but complimentary to the two witnesses. Hours passed, and the mannie with the green suitcase had disappeared completely. Every police station was warned: hotels were watched, but without avail.

Two days afterwards, on a Saturday night, a green suitcase was handed in to the left luggage office at Waverley Station, Edinburgh. Every green suitcase being under suspicion and possible examination, this one was privately searched, when it was discovered to contain a sending wireless set and a wizened apple, and a pistol.

The left luggage staff was reinforced by plain clothes police, and on the platform outside, a superintendent disguised as a porter paraded up and down with a luggage barrow, and several hefty looking policemen posing as idlers were stationed at nearby vantage points.

When later that night the ticket for the green suitcase was handed in a signal was given, the porter ran his barrow at the man's legs, and the idlers sprang to life and surrounded him. As they were rushing their captive to a waiting room, a group of women Co-operators returning to Fifeshire from a day's trip, thought they saw a poor inoffensive man being assaulted by a gang of ruffians, and they began shouting for help; they were loud in their denunciations of the uniformed police who stood by and let such outrages occur!

Meantime all the captive wanted was his apple, and he refused to be comforted by offers of newer and better ones, the reason being, as we learned later, that his wizened apple contained a sending code for use on his wireless. It was understood that effective use was made of this code by some of our bright Security Officers, and that, through it, well prepared bogus information was transmitted to Germany, leading two of their submarines into traps where they were destroyed.

There was another 'spy' story, but one in which I was an unwilling participant. I had fixed a Saturday upon which at every road block in Scotland every motorist would be required to produce his identity card, there being a suspicion that some enemy agents were careering about. All the arrangements having been made, I went away home and changed my clothes for an hour or two's fishing on a Perthshire loch. Returning late at night my car was stopped and a Home Guard stuck his face forward demanding my identity card. Horrors! In changing my clothes I had forgotten to transfer my identity papers, and I had not a scrap with which to establish myself. Excuses were of no avail, and just as I was on the point of being marched off to a police station for further questioning, a policeman emerged from the darkness with " Oh, it's you, Mr. Johnston." He had met me at some inspections, and now vouched for me. So I escaped.

But on the Monday when I was receiving police reports on the Saturday test, the Police Officer in charge said he regretted to have to report that one dubious character had been got in Perthshire, but that he had impudently passed himself off as the Regional Commissioner, and a stupid Home Guard and policeman had let him go!

Charitably I said these things would happen, and let it end at that!

And there was the incident of the *Cossack-Altmark*. The *Altmark* was a German vessel which had been denounced in our news as a ' Hell ship.' It was alleged that she was carrying large numbers of British seamen prisoners to Germany; they were starved and maltreated, and almost suffocated below decks, and there was a leper among them. H.M.S. *Cossack* had raided the *Altmark* inside Norwegian territorial waters, and had released the prisoners. And Mr. Churchill, then at the Admiralty, anticipating a howl of protest from Germany about the violation of the canons of international law, and being especially anxious not to embarrass President Roosevelt's following in America by any illegal action on the part of the British Navy, phoned me, earnestly urging that great preparations should be made to welcome the starved British prisoners when the *Cossack* arrived with them at Leith.

Pictures of the starved and emaciated British seamen being carried down the gangway on stretchers would take the edge off any German accusation about our violation of the Norwegian 3-mile limit. So the Admiral at Rosyth (who was cheerfully and affectionately nicknamed as " The Ocean Swell ") and I set about our preparations. We flew up from London all the American pressmen we could lay our hands upon: we had cinema cameramen in abundance; we had buses standing by for transport; we cleared an hospital for the reception of the victims; the Ministry of Food rose proudly to the occasion; we had bands with trumpeters, and great welcoming crowds surged round the docks.

Alas, when the *Cossack* came in she had upon her deck crowds of well-dressed, prosperous looking, cheerful ex-prisoners, cheering the British Navy, the cheers varied now and again by a huge buck negro in a straw hat crying " Are we downhearted? " And yelling a defiant " No." The negro was also at some pains between times to shout to observers on shore: " Me British! "

" Something funny here! " said the Rosyth Admiral, and when he was piped aboard he learned that the repeated messages from the First Lord of the Admiralty to the *Cossack* asking for particulars about the health of the emaciated prisoners had resulted in the Cossack's crew turning out their lockers to rig the prisoners in new clothes, and that the prisoners had hardly stopped eating since they had left Norwegian waters, and that the leper was no leper at all but an unfortunate who had suffered from a foul shave. The Navy had poshed up the prisoners and so killed a propaganda that Goebbels might have envied. The camera men had to fade silently away.

Another memory of these hectic times! Late one cold blacked-out winter evening a card was handed in to me. The owner, to judge by the degrees after his name, was evidently a person of some consequence. I was busy and asked that he be interviewed by a deputy. No use, back came the word that the visitor would await my personal convenience. Finally he was ushered in, with a little naval rating, my commissionaire, standing behind him in case he should prove an enemy agent or a half-wit with some grievance, or an inventor with a patent for disposal about freezing the clouds, or similar ingenious contrivance for destroying enemy aircraft.

I looked at the visitor's card again, and saw that he was an engineer with considerable experience in large constructions, here and in Canada.

" Well, sir," I asked. " What can I do for you? "

" Have you not been advised by the Minister of Home Security of my coming? " he replied.

" No, I have no word about you," I said.

" And you have no idea of why I am here? " he queried.

" No."

" Well, I'm your new regional works adviser."

" And what, may I ask, is that? "

" Don't you know? "

" No, I do not," I said.

" Well, no more do I," he commented.

And that was the rather unusual introduction of an old retired engineer who had been prised out of his retirement and sent north to me to keep us right about what to do if the Forth Bridge were bombed or some such major disaster as that had occurred. Mr. A. D. Swan proved himself a valuable public servant, and his painstaking efforts to keep London departments right about materials and constructions, interlarded frequently by ironies and cynicisms of great pungency, were a constant joy to us all.

About this time too, Lord Airlie, who was always fidgety about being confined to a civilian post, had managed to get himself into the Army, and Lord Rosebery, an active restless enemy of all bureaucracy, was installed in his place. If you wanted a thrill of excitement, equivalent to say parachute jumping, you could always invite Lord Rosebery to motor you along Princes Street and make a circular dive through the traffic, and head for home again without a mishap. Once I badly blotted my copy book with him. We were out at Dalmeny House, and he was proudly exhibiting a picture of a horse of his that had won the Derby. Almost with an air of reverence he ejaculated " Blue Peter! "

" Indeed! " I commented politely, not knowing anything about its pedigree, its points, or its achievements.

" Yes," he added. " I was offered a big sum of money for that horse from America."

" And why didn't you take it? " I innocently and courteously asked. But immediately I was aware I had said the wrong thing.

. " I would die in the poorshouse before I would part with that horse," declared his Lordship. " Not for all the money in the world would I part with that horse! "

Obviously I had roused not only the sportsman but the affectionate owner; his horse had given him what was perhaps one of the most memorable triumphs of his life.

In the memoirs of John Winant,[1] the great American war-time ambassador to London, and in the memoirs of Harry Hopkins[2] (Harry the Hop), President Roosevelt's confidential agent, there are references to an occurrence in Glasgow which, for some of us who were participants or spectators, will remain an indelible memory. Neither Winant's nor Hopkins' account is, however, quite correct. Here is my recollection of what transpired.

Lord Lothian, the British Ambassador at Washington, had died, and Lord Halifax had been appointed in his place. Meanwhile we knew that pressure was being exercised upon President Roosevelt not to engage the United States in the war, nor indeed to take any steps which however unwittingly might eventually land them in the war. On the other hand the British Prime Minister, Winston Churchill, was appealing direct to the President for cruisers and protection for the food supplies to Britain. Britain, he asserted, would never surrender.

Against that it was believed the United States Ambassador in London, Mr. Kennedy, was reporting to his government that Britain would go the road France had gone, and that she could not for long withstand the Wehrmacht. Roosevelt's position must have been difficult. He had great German, Italian, and Irish populations; he had a strong pacifist and isolationist electorate to handle, and here was his ambassador sending doleful prophecies of an imminent British collapse. Yet Roosevelt's sympathies as well as his national interests were all with the resisters to the armed gangsters who were riding rough over Europe. And what was he to do? He sent his confidential agent, Harry Hopkins, a frail, ailing man, over

[1] *A Letter from Grosvenor Square*, p. 20.
[2] *White House Papers I*, 246

here to enquire as to the facts and report to him direct. So Hopkins was going about in night shelters, in railway trains, and wherever people congregated in crowds, as well as to Government agencies, making estimates as to the probabilities, and as to the spirit of the people. But what he was advising his President to do, no man here could learn.

Then when Lord Halifax was leaving from Scapa Flow in the *George V* for his ambassadorial post in the States, Mr. Churchill conceived the idea that it would be worth while arranging a party to see him off, and inviting Harry Hopkins to be a member of the party, the real reason for the visit to Scapa being, of course, less to see Halifax off on his voyage than to show Hopkins the might and majesty of the British Fleet.

The party went by special train and ship to the Orkneys, whence I got a message from the Prime Minister to meet him at Waverley Station, Edinburgh, and accompany him over to Glasgow, where he had promised to inspect our Civil Defence forces. I duly awaited the train; when it arrived I jumped in and was taken to the P.M.'s private compartment. There I was told that nothing had been got out of Hopkins; he was poker faced and dumb as an oyster. We had lunch together, the P.M. and Mrs. Churchill, Hopkins and myself. When we got to Glasgow the P.M. received a rousing welcome; railway whistles, tramway gongs, cheering crowds; everywhere the greatest enthusiasm and affection for the national war-time leader were made manifest, and Hopkins I am sure was keenly observant of it all.

Meanwhile I had got Norman Duke to organise a dinner for the party in the North British Station Hotel, and when the inspections and public engagements were over we gathered together, the Lord Provost and Mrs. Dollan, Sir Steven and Lady Bilsland, and some other Civil Defence notabilities, and with the P.M.'s guests we adjourned to the hotel. During the dinner I had discovered from Harry Hopkins that his grandmother or his great-grandmother had been born at Auchterarder in Perthshire, and I had promised to get his pedigree hunted out for him. When the dinner was about over, the P.M. sidled up to me from the other end of the table and whispered an injunction to remember to propose the toast of the President of the United States immediately I had proposed the toast of the King.

Duly I did both, making no speech, but this did not suit the P.M. who, under the pretext of proposing my health, made a spirited and eloquent declaration about British determination to live free in the world at all costs, and how united as a nation we were against the gangs who were ruling by concentration camps and terrorising the subservient nations. After I had briefly replied, saying flippantly I had never dreamed I would ever be following Mr. Winston Churchill any more than he, no doubt, had ever envisaged having a character like me in his entourage, I called upon the Lord Provost, and after him, Sir Steven Bilsland, and then some impulse came to me to call upon Hopkins.

" We have tonight," I said, " with us, a friend from overseas. If he cares to say a word to us, we shall all be delighted. This is quite an informal gathering; no press representative is present. And more particularly do I welcome Mr. Hopkins for the sake of his old grandmother from Auchterarder."

And then, slowly, Harry Hopkins arose. I can see his white drawn face yet, but I cannot recollect the first half-dozen sentences he spoke, though I would give a great deal to be able to do so. Possibly they were mere banalities, mere courtesies. Then came from him something like this:

" Mr. Chairman, I am not making speeches over here. I am reporting what I see to Mr. Franklin Delano Roosevelt, my President, a great man, a very great man. But now that I am here and on my feet perhaps I might say in the language of the old book to which my grandmother from Auchterarder, and no doubt your grandmother too, Mr. Chairman, paid so much attention, that (and here Hopkins paused and looked straight down the table at Churchill) Wheresoever thou goest we go, and where thou lodgest we lodge, thy people shall be our people, thy God, our God, even unto the end."

That was all. He sat down in dead silence. Churchill's eyes welled up in tears. Here was the first news that the United States was throwing its weight upon the Allied side. Later when Churchill told Winant the story in London he was " overcome with emotion."

Hopkins' biographer says that " publication of the unprepared speech was censored, but word of it spread all over Britain, and it had an effect greater than Hopkins had dared to intend." I doubt whether that is accurate ; I am certain it was many months afterwards before any leakage occurred and then the story was only quarter told.

CHAPTER XVIII

SECRETARY OF STATE

Give me neither poverty nor riches; feed me with food convenient for me: lest I be full, and deny thee, and say, Who is the Lord? or lest I be poor, and steal.

—*The prayer of Agur, the son of Jakeh. Proverbs xxx, 8-9*

I want to tell you with a full sense of my responsibility that if you discuss the position as a whole, without prejudice or bias as to things that may or may not be irrelevant, to the great issue before us or otherwise as the case might be, I will not betray my duty in this emergency by dictating what I may or may not agree that what is right on the wrong side may be utterly wrong on the right side unless we stand shoulder to shoulder and see absolutely eye to eye as in this crisis we are logically compelled to believe the truth must ultimately win through, and we shall all come to recognise, you in the audience and me on the platform that whatever you or I may think individually and collectively, and I tell you this quite frankly, the whole must be greater than the part.

—*Obfuscatory political peroration, attributed by A. M. Thompson to the late Mr. J. H. Thomas*

TOWARDS THE close of the war year 1940, Mr. Winston Churchill had determined to reconstruct his cabinet, and I was among the new players he had evidently determined to sign on. In vain did I protest that I was doing a man's job where I was in Scotland as Regional Commissioner, and that I loathed London. He refused to take my noes for answers, and he even went the length of asking my wife if it were she who was preventing me from going to London to assist him. My wife, poor woman, knowing nothing about previous invitations and declinatures, and regarding the Prime Minister as the nation's last white hope, wanted to know from me why had I refused to help him; had I quarrelled with him in any way?

Finally in February 1941 the Prime Minister telephoned me and asked me to come down to London to see him about an important matter. At Downing Street I was not left long in doubt about the important matter! " What ails you about joining the National Government? "

"Well, for one thing I want to get out of partisan politics and write books!"

"Write books? What kind of books?"

"History books."

"History!" (a disdainful snort). "Good heavens, man, come in here and help me to make history!"

I suppose that a rabbit cornered by a boa constrictor would have had just about as much chance of escape, but I did at least manage to ward off being planted in a high but (for me) unsuitable English office, and before I was completely hypnotised into accepting the post of Secretary of State for Scotland I had mustered up sufficient sense to table prior conditions.

"What are they?" I was asked.

(Me): "First, I should want to try out a Council of State for Scotland —a council composed of all the living ex-Secretaries for Scotland, of all parties; and whenever we were all agreed upon a Scottish issue, I could look to you for backing!"

(The P.M.): "That seems a sort of national government of all parties idea, just like our Government here. All right, I'll look sympathetically upon anything about which Scotland is unanimous. And what next?"

(Me): "I don't want to take any money for office during the war. My resources are adequate to my needs, but I don't want to make a song and dance about it."

(The P.M.): "Right! Nobody can prevent you taking nothing!"

And in the end I was bundled out, a little bewildered, having signed on for two, and perhaps occasionally, for four nights' journeyings weekly in the train between London and Scotland—a most miserable prospect—but buoyed up with the knowledge that for so long as I could last it I would be at the centre of things during ' our finest hour ' and that I would be given a chance to inaugurate some large scale reforms under the umbrella of a Council of State, and which reforms, if we emerged intact as a nation at the end of the war, might mean Scotia Resurgent!

Coming down Whitehall, I ticked off in my mind several of the things I was certain I could do—even during a war. I could get an industrial parliament to begin attracting industries north, face up to the Whitehall departments, and stem the drift south of our Scots population. And I could have a jolly good try at a public corporation on a non-profit basis to harness Highland water power for electricity. And I would have a stab at teaching citizenship in the schools. And an attempt at altering the foolish rating system we had in Scotland—so foolish that as compared with England where the private builders between the years 1918 and 1939 had built 30

houses, our private builders had built only one; and that whereas in England
and Wales at the 1931 census there were only 4½ per cent of the houses
sized of one or two rooms, in poor old Scotland there were 46 per cent,
ten times worse! And I remembered too a letter from a clergyman at
Kirkmaiden in Wigtownshire during the evacuation period declaring that in
his parish 70 per cent of the houses had neither water nor sanitation, neither
outside nor inside, wet or dry, and that only two houses out of 400 in his
parish had been brought up to sanitary standards. And I wondered how far
their inadequate sleeping conditions pre-war were responsible for the fact
that the young recruits to the Argyll and Sutherland Highlanders were
adding 9 lb. to their weight in 16 weeks at Stirling Castle, as their officers
assured me they were. And I had ideas about hospitals and about afforestation, which I was certain might be operated without legislation, and I
might even try a convention of Scots M.P.s in Edinburgh and see what
would emerge politically from that.

Maybe I had condemned myself to many night journeys in the train,
but I promised myself some excitements as a recompense.

By the autumn of 1941 I had secured assents of co-operation in a Council
of State from all the survivors who had held office as Secretary for Scotland,
and although we were officially designated The Scottish Advisory Council
of ex-Secretaries, the Press had cottoned on to the label Council of State,
and Council of State we remained.[1] We all promised to collaborate in
surveying problems of post-war reconstruction in Scotland, and it was
understood that our one binding article of association was that when we
got unanimity we would each of us do our utmost with our political
associates outside to get concurrence from them too; where we could not
get unanimity among ourselves we would lay the problem aside—individuals
among us were free to take their own line upon disputed issues: as a Council
we would concentrate in securing results upon issues where we were agreed
about Scotland's interests.

There was a surprisingly large field of agreement. And none can say
but we acted promptly. By October we had set agoing an enquiry into
hydro-electric development in the Highlands under the energetic and competent chairmanship of Lord Cooper. In ten months the Cooper Committee
reported unanimously in favour of a public, non-profit making corporation
to generate and transmit electricity from Highland water power. By January
1943 a Bill based upon that report had received its first reading in the
House of Commons; and it sailed through both Commons and Lords
without a division, the few old Adamites who could not understand any-

[1] The Council consisted of Lord Alness, Sir Archibald Sinclair, Sir John Colville (now
Lord Clydesmuir), Mr. Walter Elliot, Mr. Ernest Brown, and myself.

thing outside faction fighting for faction fighting's sake being shocked and warded off by my threat that if this great chance of securing a use of water power for the nation was sabotaged, I would make it my personal business to inform the 51st Division when it returned after the war of the names and addresses of the saboteurs.

I knew most of the nests from which the corbies would operate; the colliery owners had retired from the struggle, and their shareholders wanted no notice taken of the pit bings and so stopped talking about how the Hydro Schemes would destroy amenity. A few shameless twelfth of August shooting tourists, who themselves took care to live in the electrified south for eleven months in the year, moaned about the possible disappearance in the Highlands of the picturesque cruisie; and I had one deputation whose spokesman was sure we were engaged in a conspiracy to clear Glen Affric of its crofters and its sheep; in response to enquiries he had not been up at Glen Affric himself, and he really was surprised to learn that there were neither crofters nor sheep in the Glen for these many years past.

But this time the Bill was outside partisan politics. I roped in the leading personalities in all parties, eight Cabinet Ministers, as its sponsors, and especially here I should like to pay a tribute to Sir Kingsley Wood, the Chancellor of the Exchequer, who not only allowed his name to go on the back of the bill, but, despite some Treasury hesitations, insisted upon supporting the provision under which Hydro Board stock to the extent of £30,000,000 was guaranteed by the Treasury on demand by the Hydro Board.

We escaped the legal obstructions which political and commercial interests in the United States had placed in the way of the Tennessee Valley Authority[1] and the savage opposition which the Ontario Power Commission had, in its early stages, to suffer.[2] For the first time since the Reform Bill of 1832, a major Scots measure had reached the Statute Book without a division, and for that memorable result the all-party Council of State can be largely thanked.

In February 1942 we had formed the Scottish Council on Industry. It was to be an independent body—a sort of industrial parliament; it was to draw its members and its funds from the Local Authorities, the Chambers of Commerce, the Scottish Trades Union Congress, the Development Council, and the Scottish Banks; its functions were the safeguarding, the stimulation, and the encouragement of Scottish industrial development, both during and after the war. And faith, but we had much need in Scotland

---

[1] The T.V.A. was challenged 41 times in the Law Courts of the U.S.A.

[2] Sir Adam Beck, the first chairman of the Commission, had to defend himself against no fewer than six attempts to land him in gaol. Now in Canada they are raising plaques to his memory.

for such a body, for at the Scottish Office there was no Board of Trade: no machinery of any kind for industrial contacts. We had seen our motor car industry and our calico printing go south; even the printing of our Scots telephone directories had gone to Harrow. We had seen the rearmament factories being started in England; all we got in Scotland was the storage capacity; we saw our girls (500 per week of them in the spring of 1942) being drafted away to work in the new factories in the south.

Unless drastic and immediate steps had been taken to correct these drifts to the land beyond the Cheviots, the outlook for Scottish industry and the Scottish nation post-war had been bleak indeed.

The first chairman of the new Council was the Lord Provost of Edinburgh, Sir Will Y. Darling, and among its most active members were the late Bailie Elger of Glasgow, the Secretary of the Scottish T.U.C., and Sir Steven (now Lord) Bilsland. Representatives of nine United Kingdom and three Scottish Departments of State attended the sittings of the Council as assessors. The facts were sifted, and Scotland's industrial case presented in the proper quarters with authority as it had never been presented before, with this result—and the following figures speak for themselves.

In three months Government production (not storage) space in Scottish factories and workshops jumped from 500,000 square feet to 1,000,000 square feet. By four months production space had leaped another 500,000 square feet; by six months another 350,000 square feet. Nine months after its inception the Council announced that there had been 119 new industrial units established in Scotland, and with a total employment personnel of 25,000, covering a wide range of industry including children's outerwear, uniforms, wood wool, utility clothing, bedding, etc.

Between the beginning of 1942 and the general election of 1945, over 700 new industrial enterprises (or substantial extensions of existing undertakings) had been authorised in Scotland, involving a labour force of 90,000. Three supply departments between them had been induced to expend in Scotland £12 millions on factories and plant.

There was one other noteworthy decision taken in 1942 which ought to be recorded. After a meeting between the Council of State and the Chairmen and General Managers of the eight Scottish Banks, the Banks held a special meeting in December at which they passed the following resolution:

" That this Committee of the eight Scottish Banks desires to meet the wishes of the Secretary of State and the Council of ex-Secretaries in doing everything possible to co-operate with the Advisory Council on Industry to promote Scottish industrial interests in the post-war years."

The drift north had begun, and probably at as great a rate as we could find housing accommodation for the newcomers.

In October 1941, I tried a meeting of Scots M.P.s in Edinburgh, toying for a time with the idea of getting the gathering staged in the old Scots Parliament House; but that might have stirred up much legal and some political trouble; there were several M.P.s whose Scottishness had but a tender stem, and it was desirable to provide as few pretexts for absenteeism as possible. Well, anyhow, 27 M.P.s of all parties turned up—the first ' occasion ' for 234 years—and although one or two newspapers started to shout at the absentees, I was really quite pleased to get an attendance of about 40 per cent, especially when the M.P.s who came had to pay their own rail fares, and give up their vacation in attending. They were introduced to all the departmental chiefs at St. Andrew's House, and informed of what was being done administratively in their constituencies. But it was clear that there was little purpose in a frequent repetition of the experiment—it had no teeth—and that I had better fall back upon the area group meetings in London during the time Parliament was sitting, as I had tried to do with some success during the period 1929-30 when I was under-Secretary at the Scottish Office.

While the going was good, the Council of State set afoot all sorts of enquiries—in number 32—and immediately we received the Committee reports we secured, in most cases, action *instanter*, sometimes by legislation, but mostly by administrative pressure. The Modernisation of Existing Houses report, however, still awaits a Government fiat. The report on the compulsory notification of V.D. ran us full tilt against the English Department of Health, who managed to get us staved off by securing a U.K. enquiry by Sir Henry Dale and a small committee under his chairmanship as to whether it was possible, or desirable, to have notification in Scotland and not in England. Later the Dale Joint Committee decided against the Scottish point of view.

But we got Crown Lands in Scotland handed over for administration to the Scottish Office from the English Ministry of Agriculture; we got equality rights in the Forestry Commission; we got away with the Clyde Basin experiment in the use of the splendid Civil Defence hospitals for free specialist examination, and, if necessary, treatment of the civilian war workers. It was obviously foolish to have the well-equipped hospitals often standing empty and their staffs awaiting Civil Defence casualties—which, thank God, never came—while war workers could not afford specialist diagnosis and treatment.

The success of the experiment—by April 1945 we had wiped out the waiting lists of 34,000 patients on the books of the voluntary hospitals—

was such that our scheme had been extended from the Clyde valley to all Scotland, and blazed a trail for the National Health Scheme of post-war years. In this experiment which started in the industrial west of Scotland, and thereafter spread over the country, the voluntary hospitals played up well on the question of waiting lists; no friction, no antagonism: indeed they made a small monetary payment for every patient taken off their hands, and a vast amount of preventable suffering and pain was simply obliterated.

These hospital waiting lists saddened me. I got one old chap in an East Coast hospital who had been on a waiting list for seven years suffering from hernia before he was treated. The average delay in treatment on Ear, Nose and Throat cases was about 70 days. It was not unusual for hernia cases to have a waiting period of two years. Chronic appendix cases had been known to wait six months, and minor cases sometimes had to suffer for twelve months before the insufficient hospital accommodation and staffing could work down to them.

After our Civil Defence hospitals had effectively drained off the waiting lists, we started a supplementary service to aid the general practitioner. We held meetings with the G.P.s and before anybody could think up hostile slogans we had the G.P.s enthusiastically sending their difficult cases of diagnosis to State Specialists, and, where thought necessary, to Civil Defence hospitals for treatment. Ten thousand patients were timeously treated that way.

We got too the swagger hotel at Gleneagles converted into a fitness centre, first for colliers, and then for war workers generally.

But I had a bad flop over the teaching of Citizenship in the schools. Despite backing from the Council of State—and especially from Lord Alness—I failed to make any serious headway in importing into our school system what I thought was, or should be, the first necessity of all education, a culture of good citizenship. True, we got an advisory council on education and recommendations about the prime necessity of turning out good citizens; we produced a splendid pamphlet on the subject; but the polite, although obviously reluctant, acquiescence, and then do-nothings, and the Petronella dance-like side-stepping of the pundits filled me with foreboding that we were not going to break far into the existing codes.

Some there were who vociferously claimed that it was the business of the Church to give any teaching involving ' morals '; others there were who declared it to be solely the duty of the parents at home; and there was a hard core of materialists among the teachers who didn't much care what they taught in school, so long as their students passed the examinations, and since the exam papers were set to the tune of the University preliminaries, and since the University preliminaries paid no attention to citizenship—well, why worry overmuch about the notions of this fellow at St. Andrew's House? And he might not be long there anyhow.

I tried every crack in every door—told some Inspectors of Schools that I was getting Harry Lauder, and Harry Gordon and Dave Willis, and every Scots comedian to ridicule at the Christmas pantomimes much of the rubbish that was being palmed off in the schools as education. I asked in public for support from agriculturalists against such examination questions in geography as:

" State what you know about either Chinese or Egyptian agriculture."

Fifteen marks for an answer to that one! But I knew not how many marks were accorded for a complete answer to the puzzle which Arthur Woodburn had fished out of an examination paper set in an Edinburgh school.

" What happened in 410, 563, 597, 1066, 1174, 1189, 1215, 1265, 1295, 1328? "

And any swollen personal *expertise* upon affairs historical over which I may have rather flattered myself, was amusingly punctured by an enquiry about King Henry VII. One Saturday night a wee lass at a Stirlingshire school came to me to assist her with her essay. She had to provide 1000 words by Monday morning upon the exciting and worth-while subject: " How did King Henry VII consolidate his position on the throne? "

After trying in vain to think out an appropriate ribald answer I got down from my shelves a Cambridge Medieval History, and, with the addition of what I knew in the rough about the feudal system, I dictated what I thought to be a letter-perfect thousand words. A fortnight or so later, meeting the wee lass again, I asked her how she had got on with her essay, and received the reply:

" Oh, fine. Got it back today and written across the corner was *Promising Work!* "

Perhaps the nearest examination question to good citizenship I was able to discover during the war years was:

" What attempts were made to solve the economic and social problems of Rome in the second century B.C.? "

but that at any rate would have a firmer classical backing than the scholastic puzzlers reported from America by Mr. O. Henry:

" How many teeth has a camel? "

and

" What is the number of bones in the human skeleton exclusive of the teeth? "

When I was taken to open new schools I would publicly declare that I was indifferent if the girl students knew nothing about the height of Mount Popocatepetl, provided they could cook a vegetable stew, and could beautify a home, and had been taught the rudiments of health and first aid and citizenship, and some of the arts and handicrafts.

I went about assuring the rank and file teachers that as a citizen I would vote with two hands for increases in their salaries and their status, if they would but put up an occasional side show fight for diesel engines in the schools on Clydeside[1] and motor cars for instruction purposes in the country generally. I did not know how many teachers were still earning their unduly low salaries disembowelling and contorting passages from Chaucer and Shakespeare, and passing the resultant boneless wonders on to their pupils as parsing, or whether they were still engaged, many of them, in compelling their hapless victims to memorise great chunks of meaningless gibberish in a dead language about Caesar's campaigns against the Nervii.

If they would not accept my mild descriptions of how their professional skill was being misdirected, well, how much less would they be pleased with the sort of commentary that George Bernard Shaw was making. " Our school slates," said he, " are not clean; they are scrawled over not only with sham Latin verses, but with fabulous history, barbarous superstitions, obsolete codes and slogans, and the accumulated nonsense and rubbish of centuries."

Maybe, however, I carried my campaign for realism in the school rooms much too far for good tactics when I told the House of Commons during the Scottish Education estimates debate in July 1943 that it was about time the drum and trumpet history and feudal fiction taught in our schools should be supplanted by something like this:

" In Plantaganet times lice, itch, and skin diseases were common afflictions of the aristocracy, and there was a great Queen who took a bath only under doctor's orders. Even more remarkable was the case of Louis XIV of France, who, so we are informed, bathed only once a year and apart from rare occasions did not wash his face. The great Cardinal Wolsey was wont to carry about with him an orange scooped out and filled with a vinegar soaked sponge to counteract the odour of his contemporaries."

[1] At that time neither in Glasgow, nor in Renfrew nor Dunbarton counties was there a day school with a motor car for engineering instruction purposes. Ayr County had three, Lanark had one.

That might indeed have served in an argument about the improvement which has taken place in sanitation since the time of Queen Bess, but dragged into a propaganda for citizenship, it showed only the sort of disgusting stuff that a Secretary of State was really contemplating for the school history prisoners.[1] Toleration could not be expected to go so far as that!

We did much better with a well staged Convention on Juvenile Delinquency, timed when the Scottish people were becoming alarmed at the increase in juvenile crime. In the year 1942 there were 19,000 cases in which the charges were proved, and half of the offences were *not* for swinging on the backs of vehicles in motion or bathing in canals, or other exuberances of which we were all guilty, if guilty be the appropriate word, and of which indeed, if we lived in a country parish, little notice was taken by anyone in authority; but they were for offences involving dishonesty; they were not for offences like loitering or playing football in the streets, but for such crimes as theft and housebreaking.

In one Ayrshire housing scheme there were 133 child delinquents in one year. In a single street in Ayr, out of 350 children 15 per cent had passed through the law courts in 1942. In Glasgow one boys' school with a roll of 543 had 101 offenders, and only one of the offences was for a triviality. On the other hand there were 140 schools in Glasgow where the record of delinquency was under 3 per cent, and in my own home town there was a headmaster with over 1000 pupils, half of them boys, and an average annual delinquency of 1 per cent; in over 20 years he had only 3 pupils sent to an approved school. Always there has been a natural effervescence and ebullience among the young of the human family; always a natural and understandable disinclination to accept irksome rules of good conduct imposed upon them by age and experience: and always, alas!— or nearly always and everywhere—a lack of facilities for blowing off steam in healthy recreation. But we had to face the stark ugly fact that housebreaking by juveniles had increased in Scotland during the previous ten years, although housebreaking by adults had hardly increased at all.

At the convention, which I regarded as a sort of substitute for a long drawn-out Committee of Enquiry, I hazarded a guess that " where the headmaster wills it, and his staff support him there is a perpetual raising of the school morale. There grows up a pride in school honour and tradition which has a decided influence on the conduct of the scholars outside of school hours." And I suggested that headmasters whose schools are kept

[1] Perhaps I should make it clear that these comments of mine on an absolete and foolish education paraphernalia may not be applicable to the tuition presently being given in our schools. The E.I.S. reports from its Reform Committee and the Department of Education's repeated appeals for a saner system must surely have had some effect.

clear, or almost clear, of delinquency convictions should be invited to appear before the local authority and be publicly thanked by the Provost on behalf of the community. We thank and reward a man who jumps off a bridge to save a child from drowning. How much more should we congratulate and reward a schoolmaster who, by forethought, exhortation, and organisation of a public school spirit, succeeds in saving perhaps hundreds of pupils from acquiring criminal records and habits and our whole social organism from grave perils!

Out of that Convention we certainly got some results in youth service, in child guidance clinics, and in the probation system. But the emphases I thought were somewhat wrongly placed; they were laid more upon dealing with the delinquent boy after his fault had been committed, and not upon giving him timely guidance in good citizenship, and in co-operation with his fellows for worthy and inspiring ends and purposes.

But I explored another side-line in citizenship during these war years, making a large scale effort at linking up our education system in the schools to a better nutrition in the households of the people, and to a better distribution of the surplus produce of our agriculture and our fisheries.

We had already arranged that milk should be provided for the scholars in the schools to their manifest nutritional benefit, as well as to the benefit of milk farmers. And now it appeared mere child's play to use the domestic science classes in the schools for the proper cooking and popularisation of our primary Scots products, among the finest foods in the world—oatmeal, herring, and Scotch broth. In pre-war years our average consumpt of oatmeal was only one-fifth of an ounce per person per day. To our nutritional advantage it could have been ten times that. It had an energy value of one-third over that of white bread. Its vegetable fat (not its fattening) content was four times that of white flour. But it should be properly cooked, and not served up like a dog's breakfast, a sad, saltless, pasty mess, such as is commonly offered you under the label of porridge in many London, and I regret to say in some Scots, hotels. If it be the case that there are 94 different ways of cooking a potato, about 80 of them are bad, and I'll swear all the bad ones are undergoing commercial test in one public restaurant or another I have sampled.

Nutrition in many schools was one of the unknown sciences; there were in the year 1939 actually 27 girls' secondary schools in Scotland—nearly 12 per cent of the total—where no cookery lesson of any kind was given; in some schools the emphasis appeared to be upon icing cakes and chocolate biscuits. Some of the newer schools had no equipment for domestic science whatever; and in general cookery was regarded as a sort of badge of domestic servitude, and something to do with ' slaveys ' below stairs.

Tests in three counties showed that just under 20 per cent of girls were leaving school without having received any instruction in cooking, or, to give it a designation more acceptable in the best ' code ' circles, nutrition. My own daughters left the Girls' High School in Glasgow without having had any lessons in nutrition, although they received the customary dose of Chaucer. It was not that the science was unknown outside the schools— Miss Marion McNeill's " The Scots Kitchen," for attractive dishes compared favourably with the pick of the *chefs d'art* of the European masters!—it was simply that nutrition was an inferior subject in most schools, and was crowded out altogether in many. As a corollary, a crazy custom existent to this day, if you ran a restaurant and wanted your menus thought well of, you must have them printed in French, and the vast majority of your customers, being gamblers by instinct, stick a hopeful finger upon a line on the menu and announce to the waiter that they will have some of that, even if unwittingly they should be pointing to the date, or toothpicks extra.[1]

Well, side by side with such a state of affairs, I had, during the war years, the Oatmeal Millers' Association explaining to me that they could not sell anything like the quantities of meal they produced, whereupon I induced them to hand me over a sum of money (if I recollect aright it was about £200): then I got the National Farmers' Union of Scotland to give me another £200, and the balance of what I wanted—I think £400—I screwed out of the Chancellor of the Exchequer for an experiment in the better nutrition of the people of Scotland, explaining hopefully to him that he would save his donation on public health because there would be fewer stomach ulcers! No doubt he thought he was getting me off his doorstep cheaply compared with the requests made to him by other callers.

Fortified then with £800, Dr. Jardine of the Department of Education got me printed some beautiful and impressive coloured certificates, guaranteeing that Miss So-and-So was the best cook of Scots domestic produce in her school for the year x. The local school winners we took to a County Competition and gave the winners there a still more impressive engrossed certificate of merit, plus 10 savings certificates; and the County winners we took to a cookery jamboree in Edinburgh, and presented the national winners there with still more handsome testimonials and prizes.

In the year 1943 over 20,000 girls in Scots schools entered the competition; that was 20,000 consumers with many of their mothers and sisters and aunts at home testing their skill and assisting in the tuition. The scheme had an immediate economic effect on the oatmeal market, and licked up the sur-

---

[1] The Railway Hotels are the worst practitioners in this obsolete and foolish snobbery-inspired food menu system.

plus;[1] its effect upon nutritional standards in the homes could not be measured, but it must have been appreciable; and it indicated one important method by which a stabilised and guaranteed market could be secured for a primary product in Scots agriculture.

The King and Queen came to Edinburgh to present prizes to the all-Scottish winners among the school girls, the King being welcomed with the statement that the last occasion upon which a Sovereign had interested himself in oatcakes, he had allowed them to be burned; and when the Queen was presented with a book of the winning recipes there was publicly added the hope that it might be a means of improving the culinary arrangements at Buckingham Palace—a pious wish which obviously afforded the King some amusement!

Next year, 1944, I tried to include the cooking of herring among the subjects of the competition, but this was manifestly too much for the classical wee-frees and in some areas they managed to get the competition stopped altogether; the odour of fried herring, it was thought, might distract other scholars engaged in important mental memory work about the wars of the Austrian succession, or in mental gymnastics about how the sum of two numbers equals the sum of their squares plus twice their product. There were, it is true, other arguments advanced against the poor herring: for example, it had so many bones in its make-up that it was not safe for children. The very obvious retort that children had to be taught to avoid bones, just as they had to be taught to use a knife at table—both valuable stages in any worth while education system—fell upon deaf scholastic ears. And unavailingly I offered a handsome prize for any inventor who could produce a simple gadget which the housewife might use in boning a herring. A machine suitable for operation by a fishmonger had been devised and was in the market, but a cheap and easily operable herring boner suitable for the home was not then, nor is it now, available—a hint there for the Herring Industry Board! But between the smells and bones, and school time-tables, and the terror of classicalists that their traditions were in mortal danger, after the break up of the war-time government in 1945, the attempt to use the schools for the popularisation of our primary products was allowed to peter out.

Our Scots Ancestry Research Council, another form of marketing a native product, was, from its beginning, a popular venture. It started with a handsome donation of £1000 from Lord Rosebery in commemoration of his Derby victory in the previous year with his horse Ocean Swell. The

[1] Indeed the statement was made later in 1944 on behalf of the Oatmeal Millers that their output had gone up 4½ times since the outbreak of war. Some part of that increase was undoubtedly attributable to the School Competition.

Registrar General, Mr. Kyd, was Chairman of the Council, which included University History Professors, the Lyon King at Arms, the Keeper of the Records, the Historiographer Royal, and the leading librarians in the country; and for a modest fee all the known Scottish records would be searched for particulars of an applicant's pedigree. From the Dominions and the United States especially, people who had, or who believed they had, Scots ancestry wrote for information, and in the first twenty months some 2000 enquirers were supplied with historical data about their progenitors, and occasionally were placed in contact with existing relatives in the old country. Here was an effective agent for the British Commonwealth as a race-binder; it was a family uniter, and a stimulator of a homeward bound tourist traffic.

I got the idea of this Council from seeing a young woman searcher sitting at Borthwick Castle (where our Records had to be stored for safety during the war) and going through old parish records of Inverness-shire with a magnifying glass. Also she had as I remember a hot-water bottle, for the day was bitterly cold, and the castle built before the discovery of central heating. My visit of inspection was a purely formal one, but I became intrigued by the spectacle of this solitary searcher.

"May I ask, Miss, what you are looking for?"

"Yes, Sir, I am tracing out the ancestors of people now in the Mormon community in the State of Utah."

And there she was hunting back our parish registers on commission from the Mormon church, hunting back for the pedigrees of citizens of the United States whose ancestors had left Scotland possibly a century or two centuries ago. There was a religious motive in the quest. Apparently any present day member of the community of Saints can get his ancestors into eternal bliss by proxy, but to succeed he must first know who these ancestors are. Hence the young lady's research work.

She told me she was getting 50 per cent successes; that she had been at the task for several years, and that one 'ancestor' she was commissioned to trace was a Reverend Gilbert Snowball who in times past had been not a Mormon but an incumbent of the Barony Parish of Glasgow.

Our Scots Council, in its early stages, had to survive the humorists— every second writer-up remembering an anecdote about a family tree that was traced back to the assizes, after which the family asked no questions —but we got the benediction of the United States Ambassador, and the High Commissioners from Canada, Australia, New Zealand and South Africa, and the demand for the Council's service had so grown that by 1950 it was reporting it had search requests sufficient in number on hand to engage the staff for a year ahead.

During the war, agriculture in England and Wales was led by a forceful and energetic minister, Mr. Bob Hudson. Most certainly he did not fall asleep upon his job, and he carried on a number of small frontier wars with other government departments whose activities appeared to impinge upon the preserves of his ministry. These wars kept him so engaged that he had only time for an occasional wary keek round the corner at me; and he acquiesced latterly with more or less good grace to the crown lands in Scotland being disjoined from his control as English Minister of Agriculture, and handed over by Statute to the Secretary of State for Scotland, who was Scotland's Agricultural Minister.

But he resisted, and in this he had Treasury backing, my plea for a uniform milk price in Great Britain. There existed a disparity of almost 1*d.* to the gallon between the average price paid by the Ministry of Food in England and Wales to milk producers, and the price paid to Scots milk producers. That seemed most unreasonable, and over it there was considerable irritation in Scotland. So much so that round about 1944, when I would be addressing farmer audiences, I had to make the best shift I could at disarming critics by reminding them that I represented in Parliament the sacred field of Bannockburn, the Wallace Monument on the Abbey Craig, and one side of the bonnie banks of Loch Lomond; any *bona fide* Scots grievance therefore had in me a most sensitive listener; one had, however, to admit that there was substance in the contention of English ministers that there were areas south of the border where the price was actually lower than the Scots price: that all these disparities were of long standing and reflected at least to some extent transport charges to markets: and that anyhow (less substance in this however!) the middle of a life and death war was not the time to engage in costly arithmetical adjustments!

Though that medicine did not always work, it was generally felt improper to throw too many Scottish stones at the M.P. for Bannockburn, and I escaped when many another would have been hounded and kicked about and his life made a misery.

Our agriculture *vis-à-vis* England's was sturdy and efficient. Professor Ashby had proved to the Society of Arts in 1942 that farming in Great Britain as a whole, and measured by output per worker employed, was on top of the world. But when I came to split up the British figures I discovered that Scotland was well ahead of England. Between 1941 and 1944 our grade A quality beef had risen from 82 per cent to 89 per cent: England's figure was stationary. Whereas our proportion of T.T. milk was 25 per cent, in England it was 3 per cent; or if measured by percentage of supply, in England and Wales 6 per cent: in Scotland 33 per cent.

Our wheat yield per acre was almost 2 cwt. better than south of the border: our barley the same percentage better: our potatoes one-fifth of a ton better: our oats equal; and we appeared to be beaten only in beet sugar. On oats, beef, sheep, and potatoes, we fed ourselves and exported a surplus of nearly 1,000,000 tons, and for good measure we exported 150,000 tons of fish.

We had, of course, our black spots. Sheep farming for years had been in the doldrums; drainage bad, bracken surging forward like an inland sea; above all a crazy marketing system, a gamble: wool in one year would fetch 12⅞*d.* per lb.: next year 5¾*d.*; and the upland sheep farmers without wintering for their flocks could not withhold them or regulate the sales, but were compelled to crush forward *en bloc* to the autumn markets, with fantastic price results; store sheep of the first quality varied in price from 91*s.* 11*d.* per head in 1920 to 29*s.* 4*d.* per head twelve years later; the store lamb from the hill was an unfinished product; it had to be sold to the feeders upon a competitive basis: the more prolific the crop of lambs in any one year, the greater the pressure upon the feeder grounds, and the lower the price paid to the man who raised the lambs.

The hill sheep farmer carried on his industry under unnecessarily difficult conditions. To the hazards of nature and climate there was added the uncertainties of a competitive home market, a limited amount of fattening land, and the imports of canned mutton and lamb, which, in 1938, had amounted to £333,000 in value.

We got a committee of enquiry under the chairmanship of Lord Balfour of Burleigh which *inter alia* had recommended that surplus stocks should be taken by the Government to hill grazings specially retained and reserved for the purpose, and the lambs there fed until a more profitable market could be found later in the season, or until the lambs—if wedders—became two or three years old, and could be sold at the higher weight.

The National Farmers' Union put up an alternative proposition; it was that a subsidy should be given to farmers who could retain their own wedder lambs and feed them. This, they believed, would result in some easement at the markets in time of glut, would tend to raise prices at the markets for all store lambs, and would in any case result in an economic gain of mutton to the country later on. Since the war, the demands of the Ministry of Food and regulated prices have eased the position.

The shepherd's house was, as a rule, appalling: the amenities of civilisation had passed it by. The subsidies under the rural workers' cottages had been seriously misused in some areas, but I always thought the remedy was to tighten up the administration of the Acts, and not to cancel them outright. Cancellation, I am afraid, has prevented thousands of farm workers and their wives in the remoter areas from sharing, in this generation, something in the way of sanitation and internal water supplies. The modernisation of existing dwellings is not only an urban necessity.

Hopefully in the war years I cast loose what propaganda I could in favour of a flat rate, irrespective of distance, for haulage of goods by road or rail. Had not the principle been accepted by the Post Office? It was the same charge for franking a letter for one mile as for five hundred miles. The stamp fee for carrying postcards and letters for two street lengths in London or Edinburgh was precisely the same as the fee from Cornwall to Stornoway. More noteworthy still, the parcels delivery charge per lb. weight by the Royal Mail was the same whether for carriage along two streets, or across two counties, or from Land's End to John o' Groat's. If the Post Office delivery service could carry and deliver fifteen pounds, weight upon that all-Britain uniform charge basis, why not sixteen pounds, or sixty pounds, or six hundred pounds?

But more than that, was it not the case that all controlled price foodstuffs had to be sold at the same retail price commodity by commodity wherever they were sold? Basic slag and sulphate of ammonia for use upon agricultural land had a uniform price per ton at every railway station in the country. Live stock had a standard price at all Ministry of Food collecting centres. Seaborne coal had a uniform basic freight charge, and the adoption of the principle there had meant reductions to island consumers by from 6s. to (at Lerwick) 19s. per ton. If we could have got the Post Office and the Ministry of Transport further committed to an all-British freight rate, the cultivation of much marginal land might have been secured without heavy subsidies, as well as a re-peopling of the countryside. But a universal transport rate was too big a mouthful for the public to swallow during a war, and there were many interests affected. So, as the Americans say, the proposition had to be put upon ice.

I know not if Lord Boyd Orr ever visited the sea fish farming experiments, inaugurated during the war years at two small enclosed sea lochs, arms of Loch Sween, near the Crinan Canal. Here would be something after his own heart—a team of research workers operating from a little laboratory near Lochs Craiglinn and Kyle Scotnish, under the joint auspices of the Zoological Department of the University of Edinburgh and Imperial Chemical Industries Limited, and trying out a theory of increased sea fish cultivation with immense possibilities. When I visited these researchers they were feeding the plankton in sea water with sodium nitrate and superphosphate, and they claimed that they had succeeded in multiplying the normal rate of growth of plaice and flounders by over 300 per cent and up to 500 per cent.

Flounders under this chemical feeding had grown four times as fast in length and between sixteen and nineteen times as fast in weight as they did normally.[1] At Craiglinn too they were feeding oysters and telling me how it was possible to start, or restart, oyster cultivation on the West Coast of Scotland; and I've forgotten what astronomical number of millions of eels they thought could be produced, but I went away hot foot to Mr. Amery to interest him in the potentialities of a vast increase in food supply to India by dropping quantities of eels and eel food in the rivers there.

Eels may be a cultivated taste: in Lancashire yes, in Lanarkshire, no: but the plaice, the flounder, the oyster, are of common succulence to practically all our population. So on with multiple fish farming, immediately the scientists are able to leap their last obstacle! That last obstacle is the fact that indiscriminate feeding of the sea feeds dog fish and sharks, and cuttle-fish as well as the edibles. When selective feeding of the edibles, and of the edibles alone, becomes possible, Lord Boyd Orr's finger-posts to a starved world can be taken down.

And as for the brown trout and its propagation, the first chance I had of interference with nature was when as chairman of the Hydro-Electric Board I could encourage the inauguration of a trout laboratory at Loch Faskally in Perthshire. There, with the aid of grants from the Development Commissioners, the Board[2] has fathered the setting up of a station where the scientists can test out what species of trout and what kind of feeding will be most suitable for the great number of dams being created all over the north of Scotland for hydro-electric purposes. In Canada the Fishery Research Board declares that creel censuses taken of eight unfertilised lochs show an average annual yield of only 1 lb. of fish to the acre, whereas in properly fertilised lochs the yield is between 40 and 41 lb. per acre, and at Blue Lake in the Laurentians fertilisation by crushed limestone and " Gardenite " is said to have doubled the average trout weight in one year. The United States Fish and Wild Life service declares that fish farming can yield from £200 to £300 in value of edible fish per acre of water every year, and that fertilisation only costs from 11 to 20 dollars per surface acre.

Meanwhile, and emanating from the activities being stirred up under what was the Council of State umbrella, there was arising a new spirit of independence and hope in our national life. You could sense it everywhere, and not least in the Civil Service. We met England now without any inferiority complex. Our tails were up. We were a nation once again.

One example among many! Reports would come in of ruthless exploitation in lettings of furnished apartments. Occasionally an old chair,

[1] See the account in the Journal of Marine Research for December 1947—A Sea Farming Experiment in Scottish Sea Lochs, by J. E. G. Raymond.

[2] The Scottish Home Department has been most co-operative and helpful.

a bed, a strip of linoleum, and a picture of Moses in the bulrushes, would jump a room rent to £100 per annum; furnished dwellings were not under the Rent Restriction Acts, and the worst sufferers from this conscienceless plunder were the poor folk who had lost their all—furniture and home— through aerial bombardment. But when we sought legislation to enable impartial tribunals to be set up here, there and everywhere, to assess fair rents for furnished dwellings, the English Ministry of Health thought there was insufficient evidence to warrant the innovation, and that tribunals would only result in furnished apartments being withheld from offer, and all the rest of it.

In the old days that would have killed the proposal for legislation stone dead. Scotland, although perhaps with a growl, would have yielded; the big brother's decision would have been regarded as final. But not so during the war. Now we were fortified by a Scottish Council of State, and I went forward to the Cabinet for legislation, backed by the members of the Council, and despite England's refusal to come in, we got our legislation, and relieved thousands of poor folk from onerous and unjust burdens. Years afterwards England and Wales elected to follow our lead.

And we held on desperately in Scotland to whatever skilled building trade workmen we had in the country, explaining volubly to whomsoever came forward for a fresh combing-out for war service that we had 405,000 houses without separate w.c., or sanitary convenience, and that our pre-war building performance ran from 21,000 to 26,000 houses per annum.[1] We explained that many of our skilled tradesmen had already gone to shipbuilding and would be unlikely to return, and that we simply dared not assent to farther diminutions. Our stand assisted the Local Authorities, the Special Housing Association, and private builders, to complete in Scotland during the war 36,200 houses, in addition to repairing 75,000 houses damaged slightly or seriously by aerial bombardment:[2] it enabled us also to secure the erection of civil defence hostels in such manner as would enable their rapid conversion after the war to separate dwelling houses: it gave us labour too for the restoration and rehabilitation in suitable cases of dwellings previously condemned, and for the conversion of empty shops and offices into dwelling houses. To these latter remedial expedients, for which we got 100 per cent grants to the local authorities, there were people who—themselves sanitarily housed—rather looked down the side of their noses at what were admittedly sub-standard, albeit temporary,

[1] England and Wales built about 340,000 houses per annum in pre-war years.

[2] In England and Wales there was no housebuilding during the war. On the other hand their seriously damaged (545,000) and slightly damaged (3,150,000) houses vastly exceeded ours numerically and in their Goschen proportion. During the war England went in for first aid repairs.

reliefs to the homeless. But, and I gratefully record it, the most vigorous supporters we had at that time were the Communists.

And when the war ended we had sites approved for 112,000 houses, and sites where the servicing was either completed or in progress of completion for 14,000 houses.

Then there were the Planners, the post-war planners. Who was going to plan the planners? Every now and again some ingenious gentleman in London would exude a plan for a centralised planning of our industries, our housing, our roads, rails, canals, airports, our shops, our churches— yes, the location of our churches!—and our beer shops. And you never knew in what rapturous moment some persuasive hierarchy at a ministry might have been authorised to so plan and blueprint us. Before any such dark night fell, and to ward off the menace, it was essential that we had in Scotland a *fait accompli*, a regional association of local authorities in the East and one in the West, each appointing, at Government expense, a distinguished planning consultant, and authorising major outline plans into which all the plans of the governing bodies in the area could be dovetailed. In the spring of 1943 we got these regional planning bodies set agoing with Sir Patrick Abercrombie as consultant in the West and Sir Frank Mears in the East, and thereafter, when centralised planning boiled up in London, I could always point to the prior existence of my regional associations and say that centralisation must stop south of the Cheviots.

Heaven knows there was great need for co-operation among local authorities for planning upon a regional basis. Down one valley would run two sets of water mains; in another area contiguous local authorities had scrambled for water from the same hill gathering grounds and had built duplicate reservoirs within a mile or so of each other; in other areas roads had been sited and planned without reference to the continuing roads in a neighbouring county; the absence of any joint action in drainage schemes had cost vast sums in public money; rivers had been, and still were being, polluted in the area of one local authority and the filth run through the areas of several other local authorities before being discharged into the sea. There was indeed abundance of room for voluntary agreements and plannings between adjacent or nearby local authorities; federal action, yes, for common ends and purposes, and every urgency for propaganda to the securing of them; but the big centralised stick, no; the very threat of it aroused antagonism and frustrated achievement.

The local authorities rather fear the planners; they fear invasion of their sovereignty and autonomy; they fear the costs, and they are bewildered by the jargon which the planners have developed among themselves. Here for example is an excerpt from the West of Scotland Planners' report:

"In the case of the towns lying on the fringe of the conurbation, decentralisation will largely be met by additional peripheral development in a direction away from the centre."

That should be set to music!

Unfortunately these East and West regional associations among Scottish authorities have been disbanded, so that each local governing body now plans upon its own footrule, subject always to a growing guidance and control and dictation from central authority at Edinburgh. A great pity, I think, and the sooner the local bodies co-operate again in regions the better.[1]

At anyrate, while these regional bodies lasted in Scotland they acted as sure and sufficient buffers against the planners from London, and once when a ministry was set up with Lord Reith in charge it perforce had to be decreed that he was only Planning Minister for England and Wales, and that the Secretary of State for Scotland was Planning Minister North of the Tweed. But we, the two ministers, were to act in co-operation; most certainly, and in cordial co-operation at that; only there was the chalk line at the Cheviots! And we were to act in co-operation with the Minister of Health in England and Wales—a triumvirate in fact!

But the whistle had hardly blown for planning when Lord Reith had sent a letter of some kind to Coventry City Council about rebuilding, and since building and local authority contacts in England and Wales were the statutory duty of the Ministry of Health, there developed at once what might be described as an iceberg atmosphere in the planning area south of the Cheviots. In fact the meetings of the planning potentates could not be held either at the Ministry of Planning or at the Ministry of Health, so they had to be held on neutral and impartial territory, which was Fielden House, the Scottish Office, with the Secretary of State holding the bonnets. And—report had it—a speculative gentleman at the Treasury had started a betting book upon how long the planning set-up would last. But only dates within six months were accepted, so as to keep the betting within bounds of probability; the holder of a very short dated security won!

Of course our Council of State did not always pick winners out of the hat. Sometimes we were beaten, and our only reward was the knowledge that we had put up the best fight in our power. We failed to get compulsory notification of V.D., though we did our best after Sir John Fraser's committee had reported that during the four years 1939-1942, no fewer than 29,000 people in Scotland had contracted a major venereal disease.

[1] Reasons why even a large city cannot plan by and for itself alone are fully well set out in *The First Planning Report*, March 1945, by the City Engineer of Glasgow, Mr. Robert Bruce, pp. 80-81.

Nor did we manage to get Prestwick designated as an international airport. Lord Rosebery as Secretary of State for Scotland in the succeeding Government, the Caretaker Government as it was called, managed to secure that. But we both of us failed to get a share of aircraft orders for Scotland; and although the Scottish Aviation Company at Prestwick agreed at my request to convert themselves into a public utility company, limited dividends *et al.*, we never got any satisfaction to our demands from the Government for feeder services emanating from Prestwick to other parts of Britain after the transatlantic passengers had landed there.

What worried us particularly was that the new and vital aircraft construction industry should be passing us by. The motor industry had gone south, and now here from a race of skilled engineers and craftsmen, among the finest in the world, was going also aircraft production. And five years afterwards, in January 1950, when I got from the Minister of Supply via my friend Adam McKinlay, M.P., the figures for 1949, they disclosed an even more alarming picture than even the one we had contemplated in 1944. For the year 1949 the Government's expenditure upon aircraft production and repair was £96,000,000. Of that sum Scottish industry got only £4,000,000. There were 37 firms in England engaged: in Scotland only two. The English firms employed a labour force of 103,000; Scotland's labour force employed was 5000.

By 1945 the National or Coalition Government was disintegrating. No doubt several leaders on all three parties would have much preferred to co-operate for some time in cleaning up the mess of war. But the Old Adam of sectional groupings and party strife had only hibernated while the fear of Hitler was over our world; and now that the Allies were in Berlin the pressure from the extremer rights and the extremer lefts for a renewal of the wars at the hustings became almost irresistible. Mr. Churchill might indeed have drawn upon the bank of his wartime prestige and preserved a political unity in the country for some time longer; but he had become chairman of the Unionist Party. So the tom-toms were beaten, the dervishes danced, and even Mr. Churchill, who during the war had actually entrusted the supervision of the police forces in England and Wales to Mr. Herbert Morrison, and their supervision in Scotland to myself as Secretary of State, was constrained to start the hare that a Labour Government would be compelled to accept a Gestapo police! Deep called to deep.

For my part I insisted upon going out, although offered entry to another House, first by Mr. Churchill, and later by Mr. Attlee. But I had served twenty of the best years of my life trailing down to London town, and I had long ago made up my mind that what energies were left to me would be used in my own country; indeed I thought of trying to form a band of kindred spirits drawn from all groupings and from all the arts, sciences, and administrations, private and public, who would refuse to travel south for residence, would fight it out in Scotland, and who would dedicate themselves somewhat on the lines of the Gokhale-Joshi servants of India.

Well, with the end of the National Government came also the end of our experiment in political co-operation for Scottish national ends. Into that experiment of the Council of State had gone four years of effort, and in it I had sunk many of my own energies and hopes. As we parted at our last meeting we knew our experiment had worked; we were now no longer representatives of an old nation in decay, but of a young virile people lit up with the assurance that whatever men dare in unison they can do.

And what, pray, was the alternative to co-operative action upon matters where we were agreed? It was disintegration, strife, chaos. We simply got nowhere. Now at least by our united effort we had got somewhere. We had got Scotland's wishes and opinions respected and listened to, as they had not been respected or listened to since the Union, and that was the considered conclusion of a body of men who had each of them tried to operate under the old dispensation.

For a certainty there are considerable achievements in housing, in health, and in the right to work, which could be rapidly secured for this generation if they were taken outside the realm of party strife. The number of issues upon which any given community or nation is, or classes in a nation are, in fundamental concurrence, is very much larger than is generally supposed. Begin with the common cold and the infectious diseases, and work right up to the complete absence of Quislings in Scotland at the time of Dunkirk and you become surprised at the vital territories where by tacit consent the armies on both sides can fraternise.

Far, far am I from suggesting that anyone should surrender any tenet or principle about which he is convinced. Not in the slightest. Certainly I propose to hold on to mine; but surely a firmly held principle is not weakened—indeed it is strengthened—if it be not tied to some irrational stupidity that we must refuse to co-operate with the opponents of that principle, upon entirely other matters about which in fact we are agreed.

I came across the other day a press cutting wherein is reported a speech I made at the Thanksgiving in the Usher Hall of Edinburgh when the war was over; it recorded my conviction then: it records it still: perhaps it expresses the feelings of many others of my countrymen:

" Their dominant emotion that night was of thankfulness and pride; regret and sorrow too for the premature loss of loved ones who have gone for ever from our friendships and our lives. But above all—thankfulness; thankfulness that we have been spared the horrors, the humiliations, the bestialities of the concentration camps; thankfulness that our free institutions and democratic systems survived, and that when there was a knocking at our door of an evening we need not fear it was an immediate summons to a Brown torture house of the Gestapo. Pride too we feel—justifiable pride—at the bravery and courage of our kith and kin in the Armed Forces everywhere in air, on land and sea; in the immediate and instinctive rally of all the nations in the British Commonwealth to the cause of freedom. Pride in our Merchant Mariners who defied the U-boats and kept our food lines on the ocean; in our civilian population who so imperturbably and with such grim determination withstood for these long years the bloody terrors from the skies.

" Pride too in that when the dark days of Dunkirk came there was not one quisling or surrenderist in the Government. Not one. And pride in that we had the sound instinct and the sanity to close our ranks in a common front against the Hitlerite terror and submerge what partisan differences had hitherto divided us.

" It was this unity of purpose that saved us, that took us from the brink of destruction and gave us the strength to achieve victory. It was this corporate all-in national effort, each for all, that enabled us to match the hour, and to withstand—at one period entirely alone in the world—the organised fury of the Fascist and Nazi powers of darkness. If we could only recapture part of that enthusiasm, *élan* and common purpose, recapture it for the much-needed reconstruction and betterment of our world—if only we could lift great social crusades like better housing and health from the arena of partisan strife, what magnificent achievements might yet be ours.

" In unity lies strength: in concurrence, the possibility of great achievement in better housing, better health, better education, better use of leisure, greater security in income, and employment. In barking at each other's heels; in faction fighting and strife over non-essentials lie frustration and defeat for everybody. Let the multiplicity of partisan groups in France be a warning to us all. Yet be that as it may, and whatever fate may have in store for this, our generation, tonight we have common share in the proud sentiment that rings through the St. Crispin speech of Shakespeare's *Henry V*:

> ' *He that outlives this day and comes safe home*
> *Will stand on tip-toe when this day is named.*' "

CHAPTER XIX

AFTER THE WAR

Ye fearful saints, fresh courage take :
The clouds ye so much dread
Are charged with mercy and shall break
In blessings on your head.

—*Cowper. Olney Hymns*

The Lord Lyttleton who flourished at the time of the Reform Act of
1867 handed in an amendment in the House of Lords " to the effect that
a condition of the franchise should be that an elector must be able to
write. Nobody at or near the table could read what the noble lord had
written and the matter was referred to his lordship, who withdrew his
amendment."

—*Mr. Harold Rylett, letter in ' The Times' 11.2.29*

ALMOST EVERY second man of my generation has had a memorable war experience. Most of my experiences were neither very dramatic nor romantic; and I certainly could not claim a civil defence medal for smashing my right arm twice, the first occasion when I was engaged in demonstrating how easy it was to operate a second-hand motor cycle, and the second in falling down some rocks while fishing on a Saturday night on a hill loch above Loch Awe. And, since we all got rather callous about our near misses from Hitler's bombs, our sympathies were perforce reserved for the near relatives of the people whom the bombs unfortunately did not miss.

But occasionally an ' experience ' would have its humorous facet. One morning—it was the day the Germans hit the Law Courts in London— I had arrived from Glasgow at Euston Station: got into a taxi, and was propelled in almost solitary state down Southampton Row, not knowing that the siren warnings of a coming air raid had sounded. My cockney driver must have known, but possibly the frequency of the raids had rendered him indifferent, and he said nothing on the subject to me. Everything was preternaturally quiet, and then, just when we were at the foot of Kingsway, there came a sudden flash, a shrieking whistle and a deafening roar, and amid the crashing of office windows and masonry and by a blast which got under the chassis, my taxi was lifted bodily in the air as if it had been a magic carpet in an Arabian Night's Dream, or a small boat on a heavy sea, and then set down with a savage jerk on the pavement. The driver looked round:

" Are y'urt, sir? "

Rather foolishly I ran my hands over my legs.

" No, I don't think so. And you? "

" Oh, *Ah'm* orl right."

And then, after a pause in which he was evidently searching for the *mot juste*, " The bastids! "

And taking the stub of a cigarette from over his ear he lit it, started up his engine, and drove calmly away through the broken glass, the debris and the billowing acrid fumes, the while I speculated on the strains that had gone to the making of our merchant seamen and our cockney drivers.

And I have a memory of the aerial Battle of Britain. It was the Sunday morning, and I had travelled down from Scotland to see what damage had been done, and what lessons in protective civil defence we in Scotland could learn from what had happened at Croydon. It was a beautiful sun-lit morning, and I took the air leisurely on a bus top to the Croydon terminus. Just on the stroke of one o'clock we arrived, while the sirens were sounding again. A police inspector, who had awaited my arrival, refused to allow me to wait above ground and see operations by the enemy planes which were coming over in arrow formation, glistening silver fish in the sky: so I was herded down to a hall-like shelter under a public house; and as I live by bread, there was a bookmaker with a straw hat, standing on a chair and taking bets upon how many of these enemy aircraft we would get down today! Ere we came away I wanted my police *aide* to get the bookie's name and address, and charge him the next day in the law courts, telling the bookie privately that if he were fined his fine would be paid for him, and all his expenses met. My idea was that the prosecution would be good 'news' in America, where it would probably do as much to dispel any fears that Britain was going down and out as any amount of official protestation by our statesmen could do.

But the police inspector refused to oblige, waving the prosecution suggestion aside as under the circumstances ridiculous. Next day when Winston Churchill was told of the police officer's declinature to co-operate, he ejaculated—" What a b——y fool! "

Perhaps the most impressive and appealing propaganda we had in the States was a press photograph of a little fellow of five holding his younger sister by the hand. The background was the family home in ruins. If I remember aright the mother had been killed, and the little fellow was telling his sister not to cry because the King said we all had to be brave. Later when a team of American doctors came over to help, their chairman told me that when he had seen that picture on a cinema screen he had straightway walked out with a sob in his throat and volunteered for service in London!

Even to those of us who escaped physical dismemberment or loss of close relatives, five years of war must have taken nervous toll. Personally I would never leave the Endrick valley early of a Monday morning but I would halt by the Gonachan Bridge and take a long look at a vista I might never see again. I leave to others more competent, to make an estimate of how far the stomachic scars inflicted by some war-time diets afflicted more permanently our nerves. But the war-time dietaries off the ration in hotels were frequently repellent and nauseous. And a week's diet of war-time bread, half kippers, the terrible London porridge, and the synthetic concoctions that blushed and discoloured the plate when the waiter produced them and introduced them as sausages, made one yearn for the dietetic glories and succulencies of convict fare which I had seen (at an official inspection) in Peterhead or Barlinnie. Life off the ration during war-time was hard!

At last in 1945 the war was over. We could go back to our civilian occupations, our insurance managerships, journalisms, and what not, like the G.I. in one of Mr. Bill Maulden's brilliant cartoons (and like my friend Dr. Hugh Dalton), with a song in our hearts! My one time daydream of inaugurating an evening paper in Scotland had been abandoned partly because of rising costs, partly because it was a long task ahead for a young man, and I was no longer that, and partly because I wanted to complete my *History of the Working Classes in Scotland*, with a companion volume for this century. But just as I had retired from public life, voluntarily and in good array, and was preparing to engage myself in the writing and research work that I loved, did I not go and get myself inveigled in a series of public appointments which *in cumulo* tied me up for at least time and half, and left me no leisure at all!

HYDRO-ELECTRICITY

*No longer do men look upon poverty as inevitable, nor think that
drudgery, disease, filth, famine, floods and physical exhaustion are
visitations of the devil or punishment by a deity. Here is the central
fact with which statesmanship tomorrow must contend.*

—David Lilienthal, chairman Tennessee Valley Authority

*It doesn't matter what I think any more. You can't tear those dams
down.*

—Wendell Wilkie—Chief Opponent of
the Tennessee Valley Authority.

ONE OF these appointments was as chairman of the North Scotland Hydro
Electric Board. That Board was at the time encountering heavy weather.
It had lost one scheme at a public enquiry, Duntchelcraig; its great Tummel-
Garry projects were under ceaseless bombardment as being supposed
potential destroyers of amenity; many newspapers had opened their
columns to strings of vituperation from the letters-to-the-editor brigade;
fantastic and ridiculous imaginations from beauty lovers, some of whom
saw in their visions the Highlands being converted into an amalgam of a
Black Country, a rubbish heap and a desolation; commercial salmon
interests, anglers, and *hôteliers*, whose business they foretold would be
ruined, all cried aloud in protest. Then there were the assured ones who
knew that the Hydro Board was a deep-laid plot to sell Highland water
power cheaply to England (was not that why an English parliament had
passed the Act?), and there were the worthies who had it from a man who
heard it on good authority that there were secret arrangements to set up
electro metallurgical plants in the Highlands which were to be supplied
with great blocs of Hydro power at cost, and the domestic consumers in
the Highlands were to scramble for the meagre supplies that were to be
left, and the said Highland domestic users were to pay through the nose for
what they were able to get.

Sir Alexander McKenzie Livingstone, ex-Liberal M.P. for the Western
Isles, forthrightly called upon " all lovers of the Highlands " to protest.
" It would," he declared, " be a sorry reward to the Highland soldiers
fighting abroad to find on their return that their homeland had been
irreparably disfigured."

The antagonism of the *New Statesman* expanded to the length of asserting
that the Hydro Scheme " involved the denial of electricity to the Highlanders," and (better still) that the provision in the Bill that each Hydro
Scheme was to be laid upon the table of both houses of Parliament for 40

174

days was but " a safe device used for legislation for subject races." A vigorous protest by Mr. George Mathers, M.P., against these crazy perversions—a protest which the *New Statesman* had the grace to publish— rather slammed the door there; but my old paper the *Forward* seemed to find hospitality (without be it said footnotes of correction) for some sad, indeed inexcusable, attempts at sabotaging a great national effort in public ownership.

In its columns a well-known publicist kept at it week after week. One week he wanted to know:

" If more and more of Scotland's electric power is to be generated from water resources what will happen to the electric generating stations and the coal industries in the Lowlands."

He wanted an assurance:

" that new industries are not to be established in the North at the expense of existing industries."

He did not want a separate Board for the Highlands.

" Why not give the C.E.B. authority to develop the Hydro power resources in the Highlands and bring the results into the national grid."

And as if that were insufficient prejudice for one issue he added the bright suggestion that the Hydro Board would be paying 4 per cent or 6 per cent as against the $2\frac{1}{2}$ per cent paid on war loans or 3 per cent on municipal loans.

Another week it would be:

" Why the hurry? "

" The 51st Division would not want to dig tunnels and construct transmission lines in the Highlands after the war for the benefit of the combines without knowing the reason why."

But his main thesis, despite the clear and specific injunctions in the Bill as to first priority to the Highland consumers, was regularly that:

" The main purpose of the Bill is to provide power for electro-chemical and metallurgical plants."

All this and other perverse and fatuous antagonisms I must say rather distressed me at the time; but fortunately Mr. Neil Beaton, then chairman of the Scottish Co-operative Wholesale Society, had been a signatory to the Cooper Committee report upon which the Act was based, and was a vigorous and capable exponent of the New Deal for the Highlands; moreover there was Bailie Elger of Glasgow, the competent Secretary to the Scottish T.U.C.; there was the Lochaber Labour Party, the Scottish Council of the Labour Party; there were practically all the Scottish Labour M.P.s; there were in fact the cream of the Labour and Socialist forces in Scotland, its organisers and propagandists, who were united in support of public ownership of our water power for electricity as embodied in the Act which had passed both Houses of Parliament.

But the sniping went on from left and right and centre. That the arguments were often contradictory did not matter a hoot. Great landlords and sporting *gentrice* who lived in London or the Riviera most part of the year, and saw amenity in the Highlands only along the barrel of a sporting rifle, joined glad hands with a half-baked Celticism which objected to selling any water power to the southern counties of Scotland, even at a profit. And the economists, who did not want any public money spent on anything very much, linked up with the speculators who thought that splitting the atom would give us in time all the power we needed, while the Scottish Nationalists in a convention foolishly declared that

" The most serious objection to the scheme is that power development by public enterprise is to be handed over to private concerns."

Much virtue of course in the words " handed over "; but it is a bright idea, isn't it, that the G.P.O. should refuse to carry letters, telegrams, or parcels for private business concerns?: and the nationalised railway refuse to carry private business merchandise?

The Hydro Board's collection of press cuttings during the *furore* over the Tummel-Garry project today makes entertaining reading. One Scottish editor allowed a correspondent, who bravely gave his name and address, the hospitality of his columns for an outright assertion that the town of Pitlochry was to be " practically obliterated "; another newspaper actually permitted a man who boasted a scientific degree to assert that " the Sloy Scheme would cost £250 per unit."

But the laurel wreath for the best effort in irrelevant blatherskite was surely that offered during the debate on third reading of the Bill in May 1943. It was delivered by a Welsh University member, Professor Gruffydd. I have no earthly idea of where in the Celtic firmament our Lord Lyon King at Arms would place the Gruffydds, or whether the good professor had ever been in Scotland, but he worked himself up thus in antagonism to the Bill.

" A deadlier method of destroying what remains of Highland life I cannot conceive. It is a method which will end for ever the life and civilisation of the Highlands, and substitute for them not even the life and civilisation of the Connemara cabin; it will be the life and civilisation of the Dublin slum."

Were that piece set to music one would love to hear it sung to the 20,000 new consumers who every year in the Highland area are being added to the numbers enjoying, for the first time, the benefits of electricity. Between January 1948 and July 1950 there were 47,000 new consumers connected up and three-fourths of them in rural territory.

Nevertheless, looking back upon the struggle with the Luddites we can say we got off lightly, although their combined incitements certainly managed to impede the initiation of schemes under the Act—an impediment for which some of them have since gracefully expressed regret (and in view of the power shortages which have in post-war years afflicted our world, well they might!) But Graham's *Social History* rather encourages by reminding us of the opposition encountered by General Wade in his road building in the Highlands.

". . . the Highlanders angrily grumbled at the change; complaining bitterly that the gravel wore away the unshod horses' hoofs, which hitherto had gone so lightly over the springy heather."

And as for planting hedges:

". . . alarmists declared that hedges would harbour birds which would utterly devour their grain, and that they would prevent circulation of the air necessary to winnow the grain for the harvest."

In 1710 when James Meikle introduced fanners to winnow the grain the innovation was denounced as not being God's wind,[1] and the potato, not being mentioned in the Bible, made slow progress in the Highlands. The Post Office engineers too must have had a lively time with their telegraph poles and wires when they first faced the amenity defenders. But it was not the peasant or his wife who gave Hydro Electricity the obstructive trouble in the late forties of this century. It was—in the main—the people who wanted a solitude for themselves during the summer and autumn months of each year; and the cumulative effects of all their propaganda and mischief making boiled up to a serious crisis when the impartial Amenity Committee, appointed by the Secretary of State, was persuaded by 3 votes to 2, to recommend that the Pitlochry dam and the Pitlochry power station should be taken out of the Tummel-Garry project altogether, thus rendering the scheme completely uneconomic and useless. Fortunately at

[1] See Scott's *Old Mortality*: Mause's protest to Lady Bellenden.

the public enquiry which was subsequently held this majority recommendation was overturned, and the scheme was proceeded with, no harm whatever being done in the result to any amenity in the district, as passers by can today see for themselves.[1] Indeed coloured photographs of Loch Faskally are now being selected as attractive headpieces for commercial calendars by a printing firm in Perth, and the Association for the Preservation of Rural Scotland has generously paid tribute to the amenity preservation and indeed improvement work of the Hydro Electric Board.

Nevertheless the abuse to which Lord Airlie, the then chairman of the Hydro Board, had been subjected rather got under his skin. His was a sensitive nature and he had not been hardened to public controversy interlaced with personal malediction; he had never developed the pachydermatous hide, and when the abuse began to be spread over his relatives (his son was blackballed from membership of the Perth hunt) he felt he had had enough. He and his colleagues on the Board then looked around for some new figure whom they could recommend to the Secretary of State as willing to attract the forked lightning from the vested interests, while the Board as a whole, and its engineers, hurriedly got on with the dams and the power stations.

And after some persuasion from Mr. Neil Beaton, Sir Hugh McKenzie, Sir Duncan Watson, and the Secretary of State (with the Deputy Chairman, Sir Edward MacColl blandly assuring me with—for him—unusual statistical recklessness, that the duties of chairman would only occupy me about one day per month, meaning perhaps that, as I told him later, I would have one day clear per month from these duties!), when Lord Airlie resigned I was immediately fitted into his shoes.

Someone no doubt some day will submit to the public a complete chronicle of the teething troubles of the Hydro Board—a Board which is by statute not only a generator of electricity, but is a distributor of it over 74 per cent of the land area of Scotland; and, which is more than that: it is a Board enjoined to promote and encourage the economic and social welfare of the Highlands. When that forecasted chronicle is compiled it will be found that a public-spirited group of men had interpreted their duties on wide canvases: an experiment in wind power in the Orkneys: the closed gas cycle turbine: the encouragement of native industries, e.g. stone quarrying: the trout laboratory: the pleasure boats on the Pitlochry dam: the encouragement of a new electrical generating plant industry in Scotland, and other major efforts.

---

[1] I ought here to pay tribute to Walter Elliot, M.P. When the Tummel-Garry Scheme was in danger, and some of his own party looked like bolting, he wrote a courageous and steadying letter to *The Times*.

After the War

The Board's first loan with the aid and participation of the Scottish Banks was an unqualified success, although some London finance writers and money marketeers publicly denounced it as undercutting and as not sufficiently attractive to the professional lenders and finance houses.

There are many pegs for anecdotage. There were the early struggles for camp hutments; timber was simply impossible to get; yet as we travelled over the land we saw war-time camps, some of them in splendid condition with baths, wash basins, and so forth, all complete, but abandoned. When we offered to purchase the best of these camps we had first to find the appropriate sub-department in charge: then that sub-department would have difficulties in discovering who could give any authority for disposal: then it would be discovered that the camp had not yet been ' declared redundant' or ' de-requisitioned,' or some other evasive mouth filler like that. Meanwhile the camps would be in process of cannibalisation: builders' lorries would be seen departing with perhaps a fine free load of rain water pipes, or plumbing, and enterprising tinkers might have—surprisingly?—doors or baths for sale. So there was nothing else for it but that the Board must serve notice to all whom it might concern, that with or without permission, we were sending contractors to lift a camp *holus bolus*: that we would keep careful tab of every bolt and nut taken away, and that we would be ready to pay cash whenever proper and arbitrated demand was made of us.

Technically perhaps it was larceny, and there are some kinds of larceny for which you can get penal servitude, but at that time we had on the Board two knights and a privy councillor, and once everybody on the Board was assured that there was no hamesucken involved, and that we would be defended if need be by an ex-Lord Advocate, we decided gaily that the risk of prosecution was worth the taking.

From one camp and two abandoned hospitals down at Wig Bay near Stranraer we got, just in the nick of time, hutment accommodation for some 3000 men, accommodation which was forthwith transported by road and rail to our Glen Affric scheme in Inverness-shire. During these operations and on others of a like kind later on, I must say there was little difficulty in negotiating an equitable settlement price with the Ministry of Works. But there were, alas, valuable structures and equipments dotted all over Scotland—in Tiree for notable example—which simply were allowed to go to unmerited wreck and ruin, through lack of a Disposals Board with powers to seize and sell abandoned property. No service department which had deserted, or had forsaken, a property in the earlier and more hilarious days of the peace, should have been permitted to stand in the way of the beneficial use of that property in the national interest.

When electricity was in process of being nationalised in Great Britain by the Act of 1947 there was serious danger that our Hydro Schemes would be swallowed up in the new mammoth organisation. Already successfully socialised ownerships like municipal Glasgow's or municipal Edinburgh's, it was announced, were not to be regionalised with neighbouring company and municipal ventures, but were to be swept up into an all-British net with, so far as generation was concerned, the directives vested in London. And there *were* well-grounded fears that the Hydro Board was also for the tumbrils: its identity to be lost: its economic development and social improvement purposes for the Highlands submerged or cancelled outright, and possibly the last hope of stemming the depopulation of the crofting counties shattered. There were people at the Ministry of Fuel and Power who could conceive of nothing but a unified centralised control by some gigantic machine covering the whole country from the Shetlands to the Isle of Wight, something perhaps on the model of the National Coal Board.

But the Scottish Office had not exactly come up after the last shower of rain and it well knew what would be at stake were the North of Scotland Hydro Board to be administratively disembowelled. I was convinced too that if I could but get up Mr. Shinwell (then Minister of Fuel and Power) and Mr. Herbert Morrison—both, as I knew, competent administrators— I could make them aware of the tragic blunder that would be committed were the water power assets of our northern counties to be torn from their native economy and made to serve not reinvigorated straths and glens, but already overpopulated industrial areas in the South. Fortunate it was for Scotland that both ministers were in time able to come North. When they arrived—separately—and saw and listened they both had the vision to declare forthrightly for the retention of our autonomy, and Mr. Shinwell was so determined to let it be known where he stood on the matter that, after a lunch at Pitlochry, when the press representatives whom I had ready in an adjacent room were summoned in to hear the Minister's views, he repeated with emphasis his intention of seeing that our Hydro powers would not be impaired in any way by the new Bill. Some of his *entourage* from the Ministry were not so pleased.

Mr. Morrison at Sloy, though with greater native caution not broadcasting his conversion, left me in no doubt whatever but that we could count on his support.

Our relations with the British Electricity Authority were on the whole not bad. I could always rub along harmoniously enough with its chairman, Lord Citrine, and the memory of some old campaigns in which we had co-operated gave us both a restraining influence sometimes upon our respective *aides de camp*, but there was for some time one large sized bone of contention between the two organisations. Prior to the nationalisation of electricity in 1947 all our Hydro Schemes for distribution and generation in the North of Scotland had to be submitted for technical vetting by the Electricity Commissioners. Over a long period of years these Commissioners had acquired a vast background knowledge which enabled them to know exactly what information to solicit before they approved of a scheme. But now the Electricity Commissioners had gone, and Parliament rather hastily looking round for some alternative body to vet our Hydro Schemes had, if you please, fixed upon the British Electricity Authority as the appropriate approver. It mattered nothing that the B.E.A.'s officers might have been experts in steam stations but have no experience in hydro dams and plants; nevertheless there we were, handed over by an Act of Parliament, so far as approval of our new generation schemes was concerned, to the officers of our chief customer. That customer fortunately had no entitlement to concern himself with our distribution schemes; our distribution schemes had to secure only the approval of the Secretary of State for Scotland, and of him alone.

But very speedily difficulties inherent in the approval arrangements of our new generation schemes began to arise. The B.E.A. wanted information about our finances, about our engineers' reports, and other matters which never had been demanded by the old Electricity Commissioners, and which appeared to us to be but the beginnings of a long reach out to London control of the North of Scotland Hydro Board's affairs by the B.E.A.

We offered to supply, and did in fact supply, precisely the same volume and type of information which we had previously tendered on other schemes to the now defunct Commissioners. But that, insisted the B.E.A., was not good enough for the B.E.A. So long, it declared, as the responsibility was placed upon it by Act of Parliament, for approving of our schemes, so long would it only pass our schemes with a qualified and limited approval in view of the " limited " information we were supplying. True, we had a panel of the most reputable outside civil engineering experts in the country at our disposal: our high level staff had, many of them, a lifetime's experience in hydro construction works; but the Act of Parliament now said that it was the B.E.A. which must approve our generating schemes, and the B.E.A. would only approve our schemes upon its own terms.

We had of course any number of first class debating points in our favour; we could prove that it never was the intention of Ministers when the Act was being fashioned in Parliament that these ' approval ' powers should be interpreted otherwise than as the Electricity Commissioners had done in the past, and we could have offered with quite as much reason (and quite as much annoyance) to vet the B.E.A.'s Welsh Hydro Schemes before they, the B.E.A., were permitted to put a spade in the ground—perhaps indeed with much more reason and justification, for at anyrate we had daily experience of the types of construction we would be vetting, and that was more than could be said of their vetting of our schemes!

But what was the use of debating points? There was an Act of Parliament and it was left to the Secretary of State and the Minister of Fuel and Power to accept (or not) the limited approval tags which the B.E.A. were adhibiting to our schemes—tags just as if the B.E.A. were auditors giving a limited certificate to a company balance sheet! Fortunately after hearing all the pros and the cons of the matter ministers decided to accept the B.E.A.'s limited formula as adequate warranty for passing our schemes.

As some erudite philosopher has said: " It's a great life if you don't weaken! "

There were other rockings of our boat. Barely had we started operations ere there came upon us pressure—great pressure—to apportion and docket large blocks of power for gigantic electro-metallurgical and chemical corporations at cost price, or even at less than cost price. It was forcibly impressed upon us that some of these concerns must have cheap power if they were to compete with Norway, or Central Africa, or the United States, and that if we failed to supply the power at the low prices desired the great corporations would go elsewhere and the nation would be disadvantaged. But firmly and unanimously we replied that if the corporations aforesaid were of such great national importance, and if they must be subsidised, then the subsidy should be a straight one from the national Exchequer, all British taxpayers sharing in the burden, as *ex-hypothesi* they were to share in at least some of the benefits; but for any sake do not expect us to acquiesce in the scrapping of our Act of Parliament, or evade our social obligations to the Highland population, or connive at placing on the the Highland consumer alone burdens which ought to be carried by the nation as a whole. If corporation A had to get 1000 million units at or under cost then clearly there was going to be no fund available from which we could carry, or assist to carry, electricity to the remote consumer, or to the small (and as we hoped growing) industries in the remote areas. And if to corporation A, why not also to corporations B and C already on our doorstep? So we dug our toes in the ground.

There was another occasion when our independence was justified. It was when we were fortunately able to prove that the special three months winter surcharge imposed upon domestic users of electricity throughout the rest of the country in the winter of 1948 would be a surcharge entirely inappropriate—indeed ridiculous—in our area.

The idea of the winter surcharge—with reimbursements through lowered tariffs in the summer months—was of course to induce consumers to limit their consumption of electricity during the winter. But clearly there were vital distinctions between our water power, which was naturally in greatest abundance during the winter, and steam generated power in the south country, which, owing to the demand for coal, was in precarious supply during the winter.

Our coal (water) came from the heavens; and since during the winter months we had spill over or surplus water surely it would have been a stark lunacy to impose upon our consumers a surcharge deterrent to the use of an abundance which would otherwise run to waste. Moreover to reduce prices in the summer time in our area and therefore to encourage a greater use in the summer, would have meant a risk of danger in periods of exceptional summer drought. For these and other reasons we escaped the winter surcharge in our area.

Our first loan, floated for £5 millions in July 1947, completely upset the astrologers on the London money market. The week prior to our issue the government of Southern Rhodesia had issued stock at 2½ per cent at 99, and the money market thought the terms so unattractive that all but 17 per cent of the issue was left in the hands of the underwriters. But we were certain that the people of Scotland would respond to an even less financially attractive offer—2½ per cent at par, for a great Scottish public purpose. And that, despite the dismal prognostications of the financial scribes, is what in fact did happen.

The *Investors' Chronicle* declared our issue was " almost certainly doomed to heavy under-subscription "; but the result, as the *Economist* (26.7.47) admitted, had succeeded in " confounding all market prophets, no less than 71 per cent was taken up—all but a fraction by subscribers north of the border."

And for the first time in a Treasury guaranteed issue the Bank of England appeared on a prospectus only on an equal basis with the Scottish Banks, and we had an Edinburgh firm and a Glasgow firm of brokers handling the issue on an equal basis with the Government's London brokers. So far as lay in our power we made a Scottish issue of our first loan issue, and we got £1 per £100 better terms than the London money market would have conceded us. Issues since that time have all been subscribed for by the National Debt Commissioners as a matter of Treasury policy, so that remeasurements of how Hydro Board stocks stand *vis-à-vis* other public stocks are not available, but on the one public test we were enabled to make we beat the money market.

For whatever success has attended the efforts of the Hydro Board in establishing the foundations of great national power assets in the Highlands, the Scottish press as a whole deserves considerable credit. When once the press editors were convinced that a real purposeful attempt was being made to build up a prosperous economy in the Highlands, and that this possibly was the last chance of several counties for survival, they played up splendidly. Especially in the north a word of commendation is due Dr. Barron of the the *Inverness Courier* for chasing away any prowling saboteurs who in critical hours might have houghed our heels. The politicians too—of all parties—frowned upon the few incorrigible partisans who were occasionally tempted to seize upon and magnify any mischance in our wide array—for example unavoidable delays in giving supplies of electricity to everybody all at once, or the obstreperous voter at the back of beyond who claimed that he should be promoted in the queue; these were and still are common sores, and liable to much inflammation!

Our Fisheries Advisory Committee no doubt had its own difficulties and, very properly, it was vigilant in protecting a great economic interest in salmon, although sometimes we felt we were being rather squeezed in swollen compensation for hypothetical damage; indeed there were occasions when the compensation urged upon us, had it been acceded to, would simply have wrecked the finances of a water power scheme; and upon these occasions, when we failed to persuade the Committee, and after we had fortified ourselves with the best fishery expert advice available to us, we had no other recourse but to refer the facts *simpliciter* to the Secretary of State for his decision. One such case was of a river in Kintyre where we were recommended to give compensation water to the equivalent of 3.7 million gallons per day throughout the year. This would have meant a loss of output in electrical power of one and a half million units per annum, or about £3000 in money. In addition we were invited to provide a water watcher or bailiff for all time coming. And what, think you, was the annual valuation of the total fishings on the roll? Only £7 per annum!

But we did honestly and sincerely endeavour to protect and indeed to develop every *bona fide* salmon food interest; and on one Perthshire series of schemes alone, I am sure upon fish ladders and one thing after another, we must have spent nearly a quarter of a million sterling in ensuring that damage to salmon was avoided. More than that, we promoted, along with the Development Commissioners, a trout laboratory at Faskally, hoping to learn from the researchers the type of trout fry and feeding which would best suit our dams and provide a great sport for thousands of people, as the T.V.A. had done in the United States.

FORESTRY

*Jock, when ye hae naething else to do, ye may be aye sticking in
a tree ; it will be growing, Jock, when ye're sleeping.*
                                   —*Scott.* ' *The Heart of Midlothian* '

IN THE YEAR 1943 the Forestry Commissioners under the guidance of their
energetic, forceful, and Napoleonic chairman, Sir Roy (now Lord) Robinson, produced their plan for post-war forest policy. Down to that year
any questions about afforestation which were asked in Parliament had to
be answered not by a Minister of the Crown, but by a Conservative back-
bencher, Sir George Courthope, and that even when a Labour Government was in office. Sir George himself was personally popular, but the
idea that a great public service operating with public funds should have its
own representative in Parliament and be apparently outwith the control
of the Government of the day, used to excite amazement, and sometimes,
derision.

Yet in their post-war proposals the Forestry Commissioners rather
flattered themselves that, like Jeeves the butler, they had given every satisfaction, but (as they reluctantly said) if there had to be a change which
" we do not recommend," then they did not want to be answered for in
the Commons by any other minister than the Lord President of the Council.

They stretched themselves farther. Quite understandably they wanted
control of the vast forest parks, but they also wanted control of water
supplies for campers and sanitation (that was the public health authorities
being politely elbowed out) and they wanted what they vaguely described
as " adequate contact " with the local education committees. They proposed to take care of the planning even of land other than planting land
for timber upon estates which they purchased. Of land for holdings,
cottages and " working space for future industries " they themselves would
do the planning. They designated as " forest regions "—" the country
round the Moray Firth and the Scottish English Border country."

But they forbore saying anything about their elaborate agricultural
operations; already they had made extensive incursions in sheep farm
owning, and, as I knew, they had already under their own direct management 29 sheep farms in Scotland alone.

In the next five years they proposed to acquire a further 3,000,000 acres,
but they offered no estimate of the farms they would acquire in the process;
and they generally conveyed the impression that without much encouragement they would be prepared to run agriculture, road making, the meteoro-

logical office, and take command of the Channel Fleet in their spare time!

Afforestation was to be a United Kingdom service, but there would be devolution, oh yes! That would be provided for. There would be an executive commissioner, instead of only an assistant executive commissioner as hitherto for England, Wales, and Scotland respectively. That showed how far it was their intention to travel. There would be consultative councils and there would be committees of the commissioners themselves who would deal with executive business, but, lest there be any mistake or misapprehension, the British Commissioners at headquarters reserved to themselves questions of policy, finance, personnel, research, education, and publications. All acquisition and disposal of land had to be brought before the Commissioners at headquarters for approval. At headquarters also they would deal with Estates and Holdings, Technical matters and National Forest Parks.

Whatever was left could be ' devolved ' without anybody losing much sleep.

But this rather foolhardy sticking out of the totalitarian chin not unnaturally evoked challenge from other departments of state, particularly agriculture, and rather obscured the really splendid sections of the Forest Policy Report. On afforestation the Commissioners had built up proposals for a carefully calculated programme, decade by decade, until between replanting and planting there would be in fifty years' time an effective forest service covering in Britain some 5,000,000 acres. Even that acreage, however, would only provide 35 per cent of our timber requirements, but it would be a most substantial improvement on the figures for 1933 when our home production only met 4.2 per cent of our needs.[1] These five million acres would provide full time employment in forest industries to the number of 250,000 and almost half of that employment would be located in Scotland.

In the end, and after a lot of hullabaloo in private, the Government decided against the (almost) separate Kingdom proposed for themselves by the Forestry Commissioners; the two agricultural ministers—he for England and Wales and the Secretary of State in Scotland respectively—were to be answerable for the Forestry service in Parliament; four out of nine Forestry Commissioners were to be Scots; of the first Commission under the new regime, four were Scots, one Welsh, three English, and one, the chairman, an Australian.

The four Scots were to form the basis of the Scottish National Forestry Committee which would sit in Edinburgh; the Scottish Committee was

[1] It is not generally appreciated that Britain is now the largest timber importing country in the world.

to be given wide powers. The Commissioners as a whole were to be guaranteed their Treasury money for five years ahead, so there would be no recurrence of the crazy 'economy' that compelled the Commissioners to destroy no fewer than 70,000 young trees, a destruction which was surely one of the most wasteful and indeed criminal decisions ever taken in the name of economy.[1] In the new set-up the chairman of the Commission was to have direct access—and not *via* the Departments of Agriculture—to the Minister for Agriculture and the Secretary of State for Scotland.

The post-war programme of the Commission provides for about 45 per cent of the plantation being in Scotland, and when the (almost) $2\frac{1}{2}$ million acres are in full development we shall, taking account of present staffs, have direct and indirect employment north of the Tweed for some 150,000 workers—an employment more extensive than in either agriculture or coal mining. Our Scottish collieries require nearly 14 million cubic feet of pit props per annum; this year we can only provide half the supply, the other half being imported at a cost of £1,750,000. We are so starved in softwoods of all kinds that we literally are at the mercy of the timber growing countries, and it was all but in vain that during the past two decades our great Scots foresters dinned into our ears the perils that a timber famine would bring to us.[2]

Had these men been hearkened to, many millions of pounds which this country has spent upon (insufficient) unemployment relief and for which no return was ever secured in public assets, might have been used in a forestry service, and have yielded considerable economic benefits to the nation.

And so, when the National Government fell at the end of the war, and I was invited to fill in some of my spare time as Forestry Commissioner, and to take the chairmanship of the Scottish National Committee, I leapt at the chance and stuck to the task for a couple of years. Unfortunately our efforts, certainly our efforts in persuading large numbers of estate owners to dedicate portions of their territories to planned timber growing, were rather bedevilled by an inadequate price schedule which the Board of Trade and the Treasury had fixed for home grown timber. Private timber growers complained that owing to rising costs of estate management and housing, timber felling at the scheduled rates was a losing proposition, and it was

[1] After the May Committee had reported in 1930 the Forestry Commissioners' income was ruthlessly cut, and they had no other course open to them but shut down their nurseries.

[2] Wiser than their generations in this respect were men like the late Lord Lovat, Sir John Stirling Maxwell, Sir John Sutherland, an active and enthusiastic forestry lecturer at the West of Scotland Agricultural College, Mr. Gordon, and Lord Mansfield. I trust Lord Mansfield does not feel embarrassed by a word of commendation from the Left; but it may surprise him to know that on Forestry propaganda he has often been an inspiration to thousands who otherwise differ widely from him on other political questions.

made no more acceptable to them when they learned that imports from abroad were being paid for at higher rates. Moreover they blamed the Forestry Commissioners for not standing up firmly enough to the Treasury and helping the timber growers to prove their case, from the Commission's own estate records. If I remember aright the Treasury argument for its schedule of prices was that the timber now ready for felling was planted and thinned and managed many years ago when costs were very much lower than they were in 1945. But the dispute, while it lasted, and it lasted for years, was the major reason why the dedication scheme of planned forestry on private estates made such tardy progress in the post-war years.

We in Scotland, however, pressed in season and out for more plantation upon peat land, and now one rejoices to note in the Report on Forestry Research (March 1949) that of the total area planted by the Commission in Scotland about 35 per cent is of one type of peat land or another, and that in particular the planting at the Lon Mor bog at Inchnacardoch, Fort Augustus, " has been most encouraging."

There have been many successful experiments in raising timber on low grade peat land, notably by Sir John Stirling Maxwell at Currour on the wild and desolate moor of Rannoch, and vouched for by Lord Robinson, the present chairman of the Commission, as " the most valuable ever done in Britain, and an inspiration to subsequent developments." Varying success had attended the attempts at Borgie in Sutherlandshire, at Onich near Ben Nevis, at Bennan on the Kirkcudbright Dee, at Tiendland near Elgin, and at Achnashellach in Ross-shire. But at the Lon Mor (Gaelic for Big Waste) at Inchnacardoch on peat eight to ten feet deep covered with a matting of scirpus reindeer moss and poor heather, the experts of the Forestry Commission have, for the past twenty years, been carefully controlling experiments with results which may well be of momentous consequence not only to the Highlands but, through the pit prop requirements of the coal industry, to the nation as a whole. On this most inhospitable waste in 1949 there were growing pine trees (species, *pinus contorta*, a Canadian importation) which reached a height of 25 feet in 20 years. This *pinus contorta* is the timber chiefly used for telephone transmission purposes in Western Canada, and there would not appear to be the slightest reason why, with our great stretches of bog in Perth, Argyll, Caithness, Sutherland, and Ross, our coal industry should for ever resign itself to a purchase of pit props from abroad at extravagant prices.

In the offices of the Forestry Commission at Edinburgh there were in my day, two photographs displayed upon a mantelpiece: the first of five employees, all who were engaged on the 9000 acre estate of Inchnacardoch in November 1919 when it was a sheep farm: the second photograph was of the seventy men who were employed as forestry workers on precisely the same land area in May 1926 when it was in the possession of the Forestry Commissioners. The contrast in employment, from 5 to 70 gives some indication of what is possible in the repopulation of our countrysides. And Sir John Stirling Maxwell has published valuable evidence from the 10,000 acre German forest of Spessart, showing that when an area little larger than Inchnacardoch is in full forestry production, and counting ancillary industries, there is provided constant employment for 303 men, and partial employment for 80 men and 70 women and juveniles.

I am far from suggesting that other and better types of land should not also be planted, and most certainly it is the case that timber grown upon poor peat grows less rapidly to commercial maturity than does timber reared upon good quality soil. Possibly thinnings for pit wood may be got from good soil in 15 years as against thinnings from poor quality peat in 25 years. Nevertheless, from every point of view, world timber shortage, rising prices against our basic coal industry, difficulties of foreign exchange, importance of a more rational use of our land surface, a better distribution of our population, it appears to me to be sheer lunacy that we should be importing £10,000,000 worth of pit wood from abroad when demonstrably we can raise that timber at home. With modern methods of Cuthbertson plough draining, and chemical fertilisation, land hitherto scheduled as waste can be converted into a profitable national asset. Moreover, under the new *régime* the Forestry Commissioners cannot override the Department of Agriculture and at their own hand insist upon planting land which Agriculture thinks might be used more profitably in the national interest. So there is every urge now to a more rapid planting of our peat wastes. When there is dispute as to the best use to which some estate can be put, both disputants, Agriculture and Forestry, have equal access to the Secretary of State, and he decides.

TOURISM

Let torrents pour then, let the great winds rally
Snow silence fall, or lightning blast the pine
That light of Home shines warmly in the valley
And, exiled son of Scotland, it is thine.

Love strength and tempest—oh come back and share them.
Here's the old cottage, here the open door.
Fond are our hearts, although we do not bare them
They're yours and you are ours for evermore.
                                    —Neil Munro. *The Exiles*

IN THE year 1930 when I was Under Secretary at the Scottish Office, there existed in London an active organisation, presided over by Lord Derby and called the British Travel Association. It was in receipt of annual subventions from the Treasury for propaganda in foreign lands. There also existed—just existed and no more—a Come to Scotland Association which received no Treasury subvention.

This differential against Scotland I conceived to be unfair and I began to bombard the Prime Minister, the Chancellor, and other important personages, with memoranda regarding the economic possibilities of Scotland as a tourist attraction, hoping that as a result of my importuning a share of the Treasury money would be directed to the Scots Association.

In due course, and to my delight (for I was then much more innocent and more easily imposed upon than I hope I am now!) I was authorised to get a Scottish Tourist Development Association formed, incorporating, as far as possible, the Come to Scotlanders. The new organisation would receive its Goschen proportion (eleven ninety-firsts) of the Treasury grant. But—and this is where my innocence was imposed upon—there was a string attached to the Scottish share of the grant. The new Scottish organisation had to hand over 25 per cent of whatever money it raised by subscription and donation, to the British organisation, allegedly as a contribution to the general British propaganda abroad, nobody being observant of the fact that Scotland already was paying her share of the British Treasury money through her taxation.

Well, well, I sweat cold when I think how I fell for that one, and my only consolation is that Mr. Walter Elliot and Sir Archibald Sinclair fell for it too; we all three united in promoting this supposed new tourist deal for Scotland. By the end of the first year as a result of the ingenious shuffle Scotland received the magnificent sum of £345 18s. 7d. (remember the odd coppers!) from the British Treasury for the development of her tourist trade, and the grant went down gradually year by year until in 1939 it was only £250.

At every annual meeting of the poor Scottish Travel Association its chairman, the Duke of Montrose, used to don his kilt and wave his claymore, and protest against the inadequacy of the Government dole-in-aid. Had it not been for the Hitler war, which stopped the tourist business and much else besides, the Scottish Association might have been induced to return its cheque in disgust to London, and the country thereafter might have been entertained by the spectacle of prominent personages exposing the farce by standing at the Waverley steps with explanatory placards, and with their hats out a-begging.[1] I am sure they would have got more money in that way for Scots tourism than was provided by the percentage of the grant with strings attached, which I have just described.

Finally the Scottish Council on Industry in planning Scotland's economic future set up a Committee of Enquiry on Tourism under the chairmanship of Dr. T. J. Honeyman. In May 1945 that Committee produced an interim report asking for an autonomous Scottish Tourist Board. By December 1945 the Board had been constituted, and I had accepted the Chairmanship, upon one firm and inflexible condition—that we would raise all our funds inside Scotland.

> " *Wha fules me aince, shame fa' him*
> *Wha fules me twice, shame fa' me.*"

No more handing over to London any share of the moneys we raised in Scotland for Scottish tourism. We would be independent in name and in reality. The United Kingdom organisation, controlled in London, could spend its Treasury money abroad as it thought fit and proper (although of course we would do our best to see that since the money was raised from Scotland, as well as from England and Wales, Scotland would receive its due apportionment of the foreign publicity!).

The new Scottish Tourist Board started off with an impressive personnel. It had two good treasurers and money raisers, the late Sir William Thomson of the S.M.T., and Sir Alex. King, both of whom were as resolute as I was against taking the English shilling with its subservient consequences. We got a first class secretary in Mr. Bill Nicholson, whom we lifted from an editorial post in the Scottish *Daily Mail*. We had the editor of a Scots Daily as our publicity convener, and we had County Conveners, County Clerks, Lords Provost, University Professors, Secretaries to Chambers of Commerce, and Conventions of Burghs, among our members. We had two stalwarts to represent us in London at meetings of the British organisa-

---

[1] That was Lord Alness's proposal.

tion—Tom Honeyman and Willie Ferris. Scotland never had a better watch-dog for its affairs than Willie Ferris. Mr. Roger Orr, a Writer to the Signet, took over the building up of a great organisation of tourist minded citizens who would get our literature. Mr. Wotherspoon, a lawyer, acted as Vice-Chairman of the Board.

It was not of course always an easy matter explaining to our local authorities when they were called upon for subscriptions to a drive for incoming tourists, that while the British Tourist and Holidays Board receive (year 1950) grants for foreign publicity from the Treasury to the extent of over £400,000 we in Scotland should take nothing, beyond insisting that the public money spent abroad shall be fairly spent upon Come to *Britain*, and not only upon Come to London or Stratford on Avon or the Isle of Wight.

But the vast majority of our Town and County Councils have long ago grasped the idea that if we are going to fight for the restoration of a passenger shipping service between New York and the Clyde, we cannot well expect Southampton, Liverpool, or London, to be enthusiasts on the restoration. (One English shipping magnate indeed upon whom I once spent two hours in New York endeavouring to convince him of the economic importance of the Clyde as a transatlantic passenger service waterway was good enough to say at the end that I had made a splendid case, but please not to forget that he was chairman of an English harbour board!)

Our local authorities in Scotland too are not blind to the fact that if we are going to attract great volumes of bus tourists from the south, we cannot in reason expect the hotel managements in the Lake District or Devon to spend a penny upon the matter, or that if we are ever going to get a big railway holiday camp like the one at Prestatyn in Wales or as projected for the Isle of Wight, it is really futile to expect predominantly southern interests to urge the expenditure of the necessary money in Scotland.

And he is a *naïve* Scots *hotelier* indeed who expects the Isle of Wight to co-operate in advertising the undoubted facts (1) that in the average year the sunniest region in the British Isles is to be found in the southern portion of the Inner Hebrides instead of as is generally supposed on the south-east coast of England,[1] or (2) that Wick has fewer days with fog each winter than any place in England and Wales, or (3) that the south-east coast of Scotland and the Moray Firth have an annual rainfall as low as London, or (4) that the Shetlands have two hours more daylight in summer than has Cornwall, for which last fact I have a vouchment from the superintendent of the Meteorological Office at the Air Ministry.

And any Scots *hotelier* or Scots hotel employee who in his innocence

[1] The Climate of the British Isles.—Bilham, p. 189

still credits southern hotel interests with anxiety about getting Business or Holiday Conventions organised to the Clyde or Perthshire, or Aberdeen, or Oban, should have himself photographed as a museum piece.

At anyrate it was not long before our Scots rural and seasonal licensed *hoteliers* understood what centralised and long distance control meant to them in the regulations imposed under the Catering Act. There was, for example, the spread-over period of the working day for hotel employees, after which double wages had to be paid. This might be all right and feasible in a three shift employment hotel service in London, but utterly inapplicable and impossible in a one shift system in Arran or the Hebrides, where the arrival and departure of guests is regulated by the tides and the vicissitudes of weather. Duplicate staffs too might be easily arranged for in the large cities, but in the rural areas, no! And even in the cities and larger centres sometimes employers and employees in Scotland had to connive at a simple arrangement for swopping staffs after the permitted hours, so that the business could be carried on at all![1]

These crazy attempts at imposing factory hotel regulations upon an essentially domestic and home-from-home service of course rallied the entire brigade of Scottish *hoteliers* to the support of the disinterested but vigorous protests of the Scottish Tourist Board, who, from a consumer's point of view, sought to rouse public opinion on the matter. And each time belated travellers had to be refused a cup of coffee or a hot-water bottle after hours, or a bus load of tourists any refreshment on a customary holiday because the managerial staff were under penalty if they served without payment of double wages: and each time a train load of trippers arrived to find a dining-room closed because it was an August Bank Holiday (perhaps a day in the year when the service should be doubled and not curtailed), the storm of protest grew in intensity![2]

But we could not get either the Trade Union most concerned or the official organisation of hotel proprietors to assent to our plea for an independent Scottish Catering Wages Board, officered and manned by people who knew the facts of the industry in which they were endeavouring to regulate the conditions of employment. We tried everything to get a Scottish Board—even offering to pay the expenses of a plebiscite conducted by the Government, of the employers and employees in the hotel industry in Scotland to ascertain their views. Always, however, we were simply fobbed off with the bland assertion that the British official employers and

[1] The Ministry of Labour figures for Unemployment among insured workers in the Hotel, Restaurant and Catering Industry as between January 1949 and January 1950 show an increase of 15 per cent.

[2] The *hotelier* was fined double time and an extra day's holiday allowance if he served upon " a customary holiday."

employees organisation were opposed to a separate Board for Scotland, as if that were any conclusive answer to what the *Scots* wanted.

The constitution of our Tourist Board, drafted for us by Mr. Gibson Kerr, the then Secretary to the Convention of Burghs, provided that our members retired by rotation, and that their reappointment, or the appointment of new members, should be at the discretion of the Council of Industry and the Secretary of State for Scotland. But right from the time our whistles of appointment blew we had hotel associations and other interested parties rather bewildered and resentful when their applications for membership of the Board were politely but firmly declined. It was apparently all but in vain that we explained how membership representation by employers entailed membership representation by employees: that if we had hotels, we must also have shipping and road transport, and rail transport, and air transport, to say nothing about catering, automobile, travel agents, brewers, distillers, soft drink manufacturers, coast landladies, and other interests, and that when we totted up the numbers of employers and employees involved we should require to take a public hall for our meetings and become a Donnybrook clash.

We preferred to be predominantly a consumers' organisation, taking whatever qualified advice we could get and as occasion required; we would set up a widespread Travel organisation; we would publish guide books, anglers' guides, registers of accommodation for all Scotland; we would publicise Scotland's scenic and historical attractions at home and abroad; we would establish close contact with all Scots societies overseas; we would pester shipping magnates and Ministers of State about the absence of a passenger shipping service between New York and the Clyde; and about lack of official encouragement to a Scots aircraft manufacturing industry; we would do everything in our power to assist Scots airports and terminals; we would assist in organising annual festas like the Edinburgh Festival of Music and Drama, and the Skye Week; we would assist motoring tests and sports like that of the Automobile Association's on the Rest and Be Thankful road; we would attract more bus tours to Scotland and co-operate in securing adequate accommodation for the tourists; we would endeavour to convince industrial local authorities that they had a vital interest in securing decent holiday facilities in coastal regions for their constituents,[1] especially now that there are $14\frac{1}{2}$ million people enjoying holidays with pay, many of them for the first time; we would run information *bureaux* for travellers, establish a photographic department, train guides, see that our hotels and hostels got a fair share of what furnishings

[1] Both Lanarkshire and Glasgow Councils have responded well to this phase of their public duties.

were available; be at some pains to advertise effective midge lotions at reasonable prices; encourage improved cookery of our native produce; do what we could through the local authorities to improve the sanitary facilities and the amenity standards of the dwellings in rural Scotland where summer boarders were entertained; attract and organise conventions; and raise a determined clamour and *furore* if there were any more closing of inns like Shiel—the only hostelry on a route of 50 miles!

Of course in the process we would trample on many toes and dissipate some delusions—such delusions for example as that there was anything derogatory or sub-standard in hotel employment, delusions which still persisted in another form, for example in the epithet ' slavey ' attached to domestic service. On the contrary this tourist industry measured in terms of employment was already (as at July 1949) our sixth largest industry, it was an essential part of our economy, and over large areas the main part. Other countries had made a huge success of their holiday industry. Canada for example drew more from her tourists than from her wheat, and we in Scotland had almost unparalleled resources and attractions in pipe music, in legend and romance, in scenic loveliness and grandeur, besides having some twenty million Scots born, or their descendants, overseas, in St. Andrew's Societies, Burns Clubs, Caledonian Societies, Orders of Scottish Clans, Daughters of Scotia, and what not, singing the old songs and proud of their ancestry. Folly beyond words not to do all in our power to tighten the bands of racial fraternity and to attract the exiles back to holiday in the land of their birth or whence their forebears sprang!

What can they know of Scotland who only Scotland know? The greater Scotland beyond the seas with its nostalgia for the old birth-place is a fact of some importance in the world, and who having experienced it, can ever forget the overpowering intensity of the Scottishness in the gatherings of our folk from Calcutta to Chicago? The singing of the Road to the Isles, Hail Caledonia, Scots Wha Hae, the Bonnie Banks of Loch Lomond, and the Tammie Wi' the Wee Toorie On It. When the last great war broke it was a MacKenzie King who was Prime Minister in Canada, a Menzies in Australia, and a Peter Fraser in New Zealand.

In our view tourism did not mean catching a few foreign plutocrats, bribing them north with a deer forest and then skinning them. We had wide aims; we wanted to develop the country and open up the show places for the proletariat and the bourgeois and the plutocrats as well. Even today eight miles of the bonnie banks of Loch Lomond from Rowardennan to Inversnaid are barred through absence of a road: and there are surprisingly few summer hotel-chalets like that one erected by an enterprising *hotelier* beside the Mousa and the Druidic standing stones in Orkney. That particular chalet enterprise long before the war was a great success, its 40 or 50 guest rooms in the season being eagerly booked up by anglers, antiquarians and artists.

And on the heights above Rothesay the United Co-operative Baking Society had established a number of simple, clean, attractive cottage huts, with altogether 400 beds for individuals and families; by the season 1928 they had over 3000 separate boarders. Then too, the Secretary of State owns 15 hotels in the Gretna district, and in the Cromarty Firth area 19.[1] There is no reason that I can see why these and other enterprises cannot be duplicated and multiplied, to the great and abiding advantage of the nation.

THE FESTA 1951

THE YEAR 1951 was not one which, given a free choice, the nation would have selected for its festivals. There was too much Korea-Rearmament lying about, and there were many citizens who considered amusement parks and fun fairs inappropriate simultaneously with a calling up of the Z class recruits. But when Herbert Morrison launched the idea of exhibiting the British way of life on the centenary of the great London exhibition of 1851 there was general acceptance among the political parties, and Lord Ismay, Mr. Churchill's friend, was induced to become chairman of the Central Committee.

Later, a Scottish Committee was set up, a good responsible Committee, and I was levered into the chair by the Scottish Office, Sir David Milne assuring me that the duties would be purely nominal.

At first, so we gathered from London, Scotland was intended to be given a fair share at the great London Festival. We would get a pavilion all to ourselves with a Scottish flag flying over it. And what could be fairer than that? Any Raeburn portraits or other art treasures we would collect and send down would be carefully tended, and—as sure as death! —returned to us.

But that was far from being our conception of the part Scotland would play in the Festival. We had no intention of sending our art treasures, or our engineering achievements away in crates to London for the summer of 1951, and witnessing our tourists go south *en masse* after them. Our idea was a Festival of Britain 1951, and not an economic disaster Scotland 1951.

---

[1] By the way, between 1921 and 1928 the Liquor Control Board (State Management) reduced its Gretna area licences from 29 to 15 and its Cromarty Firth licences from 39 to 19. This reduction (which is about 40 per cent) is in remarkable contrast with what has been secured in the rest of the country under the operations of the Scottish Temperance Act.

And so, lest there should be any misapprehension on the matter, we had
to let it be known to whom it might concern that the Burns Cottage, the
Wallace Monument, the Borestone at Bannockburn, the Arbroath
Declaration, and such like were remaining *in situ.*

From that it was an easy stage to a declaration that the appropriate stance
for any exhibition about shipbuilding and heavy engineering was on Clydeside, and that we did not require to build a new pavilion to house such an
exhibition but had in fact one erected and most suitable for the purpose—
the Kelvin Hall. We already had a great annual international festa of music
and drama in our capital city of Edinburgh, but we should be most happy
to have a share of what was going in the dissemination of the arts to the
provinces; we should welcome a visit from the exhibition ship, the
Campania: organise a clan gathering at Murrayfield in Edinburgh and a
march of massed pipers along Princes Street:[1] run all sorts of exhibitions
on books and crafts: encourage the planting of commemoration trees and
shrubs by local authorities, and by private citizens; and assist in every
possible way in the promotion of sporting events.

And so it was in the end. Everybody in agreement, and all achieved by
kindness.

[1] That march past was too much of a success. Over a quarter of a million people congregated in Princes Street to see it, and the police guard were swept away like chaff in a storm.
Fortunately no one was killed.

CHAPTER XX

AN INTERLUDE IN AMERICA

That we here highly resolve that these dead shall not have died in vain; that this nation under God, shall have a new birth of freedom: and that government of the people, by the people, for the people, shall not perish from the earth.

—*Abraham Lincoln. The Gettysburg Speech* 1864

IN THE autumn of 1947, being importuned from the United States by St. Andrew's Societies, Caledonian Societies, Burns Clubs, the Daughters of Scotia, and the Scots Clans Association (the last named organisation alone, having, it is claimed, a membership of 50,000, and a hierarchy of Royal Chiefs and Deputy Royal Chiefs, all entitled to musical honours!) to cross the Atlantic and tell America something of the projects afoot in the old Motherland, I set forth accompanied by my wife and Mr. Bill Nicholson, the Secretary to the Scottish Tourist Board. Thereupon the British Information Service muscled in to claim " a few meetings with Chambers of Commerce and the like." And what with one thing and another I found myself starting from New York on a tour of oratory, with four, and on occasion six, speeches or press conferences or radio talks per day.

It was more strenuous than a General Election campaign, and as I rocketed from New York as far west as Chicago and up into Canada, and back to New York again, the pace just about finished me.

And then there was the diet, fried Maryland chicken at every meal, so that I have not since looked an honest cockerel in the face, nor its remains upon a plate; and there was as an extra course at swell joints like the Waldorf Astoria in New York, a minute steak of the size and thickness of an elephant's foot. And everywhere pipers meeting you at railway stations, and old timers from Scotland shaking hands, and young timers with autograph albums, and cameras, and the awful night journeys in sweltering heat on a railway sleeper service that is many years behind ours at home.

There was great and nostalgic singing of Sailin' up the Clyde Whaur the Auld Folks Bide—tremendous enthusiasm for everything Scots, and for Scotland, and there was a band at Pittsburg—Andrew Carnegie's town—which had got kilts but not bagpipes, and so kilted and tartaned and sporraned they blew trumpets.

Even so we had better get rid of any idea that the United States is peopled today chiefly by evictees from the Highlands of Scotland and descendants of the Pilgrim Fathers. One American in every ten is a negro; there are nearly 5 million Jews, over $5\frac{1}{4}$ million Germans, $4\frac{1}{2}$ million Italians, 3 million Poles, nearly $2\frac{1}{2}$ million Southern Irish, and $2\frac{1}{2}$ million Russians; and while English is the official language there are 200 newspapers in New York State alone not published in the English language.

The America of which I had a fleeting glimpse is a *congeries* of racial clans and settlements being slowly fused in a great crucible into something unique, into some unpredictable amalgam, but vital, generous, friendly, alive: the races always trying something new, eager for gadgets and labour savers, and experiments, and living in a great continent with abundant food resources and raw materials. Their drug stores sell everything, even ironmongery, and are filled with customers sitting on counter stools, drinking sundaes, splendid T.T. drinks with ice. One Washington drug store advertises:

> " Food for the Hungry
> Refreshment for the Thirsty
> Rest for the Weary
> Medicine for the Sick.

Even in the smaller towns they have collective domestic refrigeration stores, where the citizen hires a locker, gets his own key, and keeps his own foodstuffs under refrigeration. The central railway stations are extremely good, but the sleeping car arrangements are primitive. In few places are there free public hospitals and the charges for treatment of the sick are atrocious, so that two maternity cases in two years mean ruin for a worker and his wife. But that cheerful, enterprising, generous people will sooner rather than later fill up these and other leaks in their boat.

Remember too that America has attracted the pick of the European basket, the adventurous, the courageous, the type that has taken risks in emigration, and that the immigrants are marrying into other immigrant groups.[1] So far, however, the races have largely been congregated in particular areas. In New York there are nearly two million Jews; and the Jew leaders had a lot to say about Palestine. While I was there some of the

[1] Professor Graham Wallas in *Our Social Heritage* declares that the white U.S.A. has a higher biological average than any nation in history, other than a few thousand Athenians in the age of Pericles, or the population of Iceland in the Xth century.

great dailies ran full page appeals for money to finance the running of illegal immigrants through the British blockade. Chicago has the largest Polish population of any city in the world outside Warsaw, and when you arrive at Buffalo railway station you see a monster poster: " Welcome to Buffalo, the heart of every Polish home."

The Milwaukee area is German, peopled by descendants of the social democrats who were hunted from the Fatherland in the Kaiser's time. Southern Irish have settled in large numbers in the industrial towns on the eastern seaboard, Philadelphia, Boston, New York. The Scots—though this does not apply to Canada—are more diffused, and exert less combined political influence. In a book I picked up at Brentano's stores in New York, *The Campbells are Coming*, there was quoted a study of the American census papers by one Walter McDowall who said that 166 out of every 100,000 of population in the U.S.A. bears the name of Campbell. The total population was 144 millions, so that the Campbells numbered 239,000. And that was male stock only: if account were taken of descendants in a female line the Campbell clan probably reached a figure of half a million.

And one night—though this occurred over the Canadian border—I was addressing a huge gathering, when I asked anyone in the hall who had not a Scots grandmother to hold up his or her hand. Not a hand went up. But from the end of the platform, where the chief of police sat, came the comment: " Sir, in an audience like this, is that question not an intimidation? "

And I have a memory of making my way one day along Madison Avenue in New York to a lunch organised by the St. Andrew's Society, when I spied a tall Highland chieftain in full regalia. He had his nose glued to a bookshop window. Later on I learned of him and spoke to him. He was chief of the Clan Fheargus with its headquarters on Loch Lomond side: spoke 18 languages, and was reputed to be the only white man living who had complete command over the dialects of six American Indian tribes. He spent some time—although without success—in endeavouring to persuade me to reply in Gaelic to the St. Andrew's Society vote of thanks.

Another Scots ' character ' I ran across was Mayor Welsh of Grand Rapids, chairman of the Association of Municipal Corporations in the United States. He was Glasgow born, and oh, so intensely proud of the Kilmarnock bonnet and the Sutherlandshire shepherd's crook which Sir Hector McNeill, the Lord Provost of Glasgow, had bidden me present to him. I know he wore that bonnet at public meetings and explained to audiences that it was the same kind of bonnet that Robert Burns wore, and that it was a minister called Welsh who had married John Knox's daughter, and that it was a Jane Welsh who had married Thomas Carlyle, and that a James Welsh had recently been Lord Provost of Glasgow, and if only the Ancestry Research Council could prove his common lineage with all three I am certain his cup of happiness would over-flow!

I had transported a lot of Kilmarnock bonnets and shepherd's crooks and clan badges and souvenirs for presentation purposes. Alas, however, they lay at New York while the Customs authorities speculated upon the value of each item; and for aught I know to the contrary there they may be lying still. Even the conjoined resources of the British Consulate and the New York Mayor's office failed to get my Scottish trinkets released for distribution during the eight weeks I was parading America.

While in New York I made up my mind to see, if possible, Father Divine, the worthy who had acquired such an ascendancy over the negroes in Harlem that it was alleged he had nearly half a million followers. In a land of crazy religions he had far outstripped the Billy Sundays and the Aimee Macphersons. His real name was Baker, size about four feet six inches; his speciality was that since the beginning of time there had been four thousand million billion folks on the earth (and if you doubted the figure you could produce your own calculations!); now obviously there wasn't a goin' to be even standing room in Heaven for all these people on resurrection morning and big crowds would sure require to be left outside. So if you wanted to fix your seat you must book it *now* and make your booking snappy.

The way to book was through the Divine organisation and its recog-nised agents—Faithful Mary, Hallelujah Dan, Pearly Gates, Sunshine Bright, Holy Shinelight and others.

The precise financial charges for the service were difficult to discover, but as they all went to the head man, Father Divine (alias Baker) that worthy was enabled to purchase for ready money an estate adjacent to the one owned by President Roosevelt at Hyde Park, just outside of New York. Down to this estate purchase point nobody had interfered with Father Divine. It was a free country and there was no law against booking seats in Paradise through any regular Celestial Travel Agency (Inc.). But it was another matter altogether when the takings were invested in an estate near the President, and with a black brother—and such a black brother! —installed as owner. Besides, there had been some censorious talk about Father Divine's marriage to a young white girl out West.

So an investigation of Father Divine's financial affairs was called for, and he was sentenced to a year's imprisonment, and a fine of 500 dollars, by Judge Lewis J. Smith in the supreme court of Nassau County. A week afterwards, however, the Judge died suddenly, and all Harlem saw the finger of God. During an appeal, Divine got out on bail, and the case against him apparently was quietly dropped.

Then there was some further investigation, but Divine produced no books, and kept blandly repeating a formula that,

" God don't keep no books! "

So the investigation got nowhere.

That was round one to his Reverence!

Then some young attorneys in New York State service contrived a scheme for rushing privately prepared claims against Father Divine into court upon a date when he would be well away on the Pacific coast; decree was to be secured against him *in absentia* with powers of search and seizure. And all this as plotted came to pass.

Round two to the Attorney for the State of New York.

But the Father was a long way off being finished yet, and I was told—with great glee and appreciation—how the Father kept dodging service of the decree of court. Sunday in New York State is a *dies non*: there is no legal service of documents that day, so all his Reverence had to do was to wait outside the boundaries of the State until one minute past twelve on the Saturday night, and see that his car left New York State no later than 11.55 p.m. on the Sunday night, and the process servers were baffled. All day on Sunday he could rabble-razzle the crowds in Harlem, but he was safe so long as he was careful about his times of arrival and departure.

" Ain't he cute? " said Mayor O'Dwyer of New York to me. " Ain't he just cute? "

To which, coming from a law and order country like Scotland, I replied that surely the State of New York was not so easily beaten. Couldn't the Mayor get a couple of his armed policemen to fillet the tyres of the holy one's car with bullets, so that he would be prevented from making his getaway on the scheduled time?

" Ah," said the Mayor. " But that would be illegal! "

And as I laughed outright at the jest the Mayor first put on an act simulating offended dignity.

But then he too laughed, for he was Irish.

And so far as I know Father Divine still flourishes. As side lines he runs with great profit a Central Peace Mission, a Father Divine Delicatessen and Grocery, a Peace Beauty Parlour, a Peace Radio Shop, and a Peace Coal Company. He is reputed to enjoy an annual income of 20,000 dollars, and to have made a convert of the widow of a manufacturer of a nationally advertised dentifrice; she has become one of his angels and has produced her bank book.

Boston as a city I liked—the tended graves of the martyrs of the war of independence: the home of one of the best and most honestly conducted newspapers in the States, the *Christian Science Monitor*: the home of a great university, Harvard: the town itself said to be the most anti-English city in America; it was controlled municipally by Southern Irish, and when I was there I couldn't see the mayor, Jim Curley, for he was in gaol serving a sentence for some income tax intransigence; during the mayor's enforced absence his mayoral salary was paid into his banking account.

The radio stations were all Irish controlled, and how it was arranged that I should be given a hearing on the air I do not know, but in the end it must have been considered safe enough, for besides being Scots I was only to be allowed to answer questions—put me without previous notice!—by a clever Irish attorney. And rather nippy questions they turned out to be, about how Britain was down and out, wasn't she? and how the value of our pound sterling had sunk to a few shillings, and such-like.

But my attorney friend did not get so much change out of his questions as I am sure he anticipated, especially when I got off in the air with a flying start about how during the war we in Britain had one house in every four blitzed or damaged; how we had tightened our belts, and stood alone in the world against Nazi brutality, while America slept until Pearl Harbour; and how although we ourselves were short of food we were not beggars but donors to needier people in Europe, and how Mr. Lemass, the Minister for Industry and Commerce in Eire, had publicly declared (14.9.47) his government's intention of doing everything in its power to maintain the stability of the pound sterling.

Perhaps it was these and other similar expository broadsides to the effect that Scotland was not begging, and that I was not in the States upon any cadging mission that had a rather surprising sequel in the *Eucadia* food ship. On the night of my return to Scotland I was rung up on the Transatlantic Line and asked if I would personally accept the delivery of a food ship on behalf of Scotland—"The only country in the world," as Mr. Michael Kellerhan, the President of the Boston Chamber of Commerce put it, "too b——y proud to beg!"

In due course the *Eucadia* from Boston sailed up the Clyde and the Scottish Tourist Board went busy distributing thousands of parcels through the local authorities; but I had some salty trouble with the Customs over half a dozen fur coats that some generous Boston manufacturer had added to the food stores. The Customs people would only allow the coats in free of duty if I would see them distributed as charity, and I had to seek the columns of the *Sunday Times* to convince Whitehall of the difficulty I would experience in selecting half a dozen needy ladies from the slums, and providing them with fur coats: also it was obvious when the ladies were selected that they could immediately, for cash, dispose of the coats! So in the end I got my own way. We secured an attractive mannequin to show off the garments, and a first class auctioneer to sell them to the highest bidders; the proceeds of course were used for general distribution among the aged poor.

In 1920 when Prohibition was the law in the United States a Chicago gangster called Johnny Torrio invited a bullet headed young ruffian of 23 to come up from New York and act as his lieutenant, organise his thugs, terrorise his competitors and monopolise the sale of illegal liquor in Chicago.

So Al Capone arrived from New York, got business cards printed:

Alphonse Capone,
Second Hand Furniture Dealer,
2220 South Wabash Avenue

and put a family Bible on his counter for luck.

Then the fun began; customers who bought their wholesale liquor supplies from firms other than Torrio's (remember this was under Prohibition!) were beaten up and their shops smashed. Within three years Al Capone had 700 men at his disposal, some of them armed with shot guns and Thomson sub-machine guns: the others, less well armed, were content with pistols and revolvers, knives and knuckledusters. Capone had complete control of the suburb of Cicero, installed his own mayor and controlled 161 bars (always remember this was under Prohibition!). Between 1920 and 1930 there were over 500 gang murders; witnesses and juries were intimidated. In the year 1927, according to Mr. Fred D. Pasley, Capone's biographer, the gang had a revenue of 60 million dollars, say £12 million sterling. By 1930 there were in Chicago 10,000 speakeasies or liquor shops: and Capone's fortune was estimated by the police to have reached 20 million dollars.

Beer trucks with armed men at front and in the rear ran openly past the chief police station; in one year there were 367 murders and not an execution for one of them; 30 million dollars a year spent in graft and bribery; at one gangster banquet the guest of honour was a detective who later became Chief of the Police!

Capone was finally got, not for murder, but for swindling the Federal income tax, which meant a trial outside Chicago. When he was released, suffering from tuberculosis, he started a new protection or insurance racket, guaranteeing, for a premium, shopkeepers and merchants against injury and destruction. But he died not long afterwards, and was buried in a 10,000 dollar casket and surrounded with 26 truck loads of flowers.

Chicago must have been a ' hot ' city at one time. It had a mayor who, when he was district sanitary engineer, forgot to pay income tax on 450,000 dollars earned in the two years 1926-1928. What may have confused him somewhat was the fact that his legitimate salary was only 15,000 dollars per annum.

While in Chicago I had a long and friendly interview with Colonel ' Bertie ' McCormick of the *Tribune*—a friendly relationship re-established when later the Colonel and his wife flew over to Scotland. The Colonel has his strong anti-English complexes, or, if you like it better, his crochets. His newspapers, for example, were instructed to make a point of referring to a British Ambassador not as Lord Halifax, but as Mr. Halifax, as if that mattered two straws anyway.

The Colonel's general working hypothesis is that Uncle Sam is a poor dupe, being swindled and pocket picked by the smart diplomatists in Europe. Occasionally he has a cartoon about The British Empire, and he had one where Mr. Attlee, with flag in hand, is addressing a half-witted Uncle Sam in the following words:

" Let's bribe Stalin with your two billion dollar atomic bomb, so Russia will let England rule Europe with the five billions you're going to lend us without interest."

This was the *Chicago Tribune's* idea of Marshall Aid—and Clement Attlee!

Colonel McCormick's history goes back a long way to the period after the battle of the Boyne when an ancestor who had fought for King William was refused the right to trade in Derry by an English governor; and the Colonel is going to take jolly good care that the old imperialist nobility of London do not slip fetters upon the U.S.A. The affront to his Derry ancestor is as real as if it had happened last week. But he is friendly to the Scots. He knows all about Bannockburn.

I found him as reasonable, as courteous and as widely read as any large scale newspaper proprietor I ever met. He certainly loathed Roosevelt, and he was busy building a bomb proof shelter beneath the *Tribune* office for the safety of his employees during the next war with (as he thought) the Russians. And although he was anti-English government, he was always willing that Britain should join the United States as the 49th State.

But he was most highly esteemed by his staff, and there was nothing of the Mayor Big Bill Thompson of Chicago about him, the gentleman who whenever he felt the necessity for a little more notoriety would announce to all whom it might interest that he was able and willing to give King George V of England a good poke in the snoot!

Of Washington my most abiding memory is neither of the White House nor the British Embassy; it is of being escorted one Sabbath morning to the most sacred seat in the North Avenue Presbyterian Church—Abraham Lincoln's seat. The preacher was the eloquent Dr. Peter Marshall, ex-boilermaker from Coatbridge in Scotland, and at that time chaplain to Congress.[1] A large proportion of the vast congregation were Scots or of Scots descent. And who, being himself from the Highland foothills and seated in the cordoned off Lincoln seat, and hearing " The Lord's My Shepherd " to the undulating strains of Crimond, just as if they were borne on the wind over the Scots moors, could be without a lump in his throat?

Amusing experiences too I had. Once when I was being motored out from Washington to address the Hood Women's College at Frederick in Maryland, I elected to sit beside the chauffeur so that I could get the crack of the countryside. The chauffeur may have been the college chauffeur, but he was not a very knowledgeable expositor of the ways and history of the inhabitants of the villages and towns through which we passed. When we came to Frederick, the historic town immortalised in Whittier's " Barbara Fritchie," I metaphorically took off my hat, and began:

" A world famous place this!

> ' Shoot if you must this old grey head
> But spare your country's flag,' she said.

Is there a monument to Barbara Fritchie? "
    To which came the reply:
" Yaas, sir, he's sure doin' well! "
    That I pondered in silence for a while: then tried again:

> " Up the street came the rebel tread
> Stonewall Jackson riding ahead
>
> .   .   .   .
>
> ' Who touches a hair of your old grey head
> Dies like a dog. March on,' he said.

[1]He died suddenly in 1950.

An Interlude in America

"Stop please when we come to Barbara Fretchie's house! It's sure to have been preserved."

To this plea came the reply:

"Yaas, sir, he's sure doin' a great trade." That bamboozled and silenced me until, on rounding a corner, I saw a huge poster:

BARBARA FRETCHIE CANDY

It was a key industry in Frederick; the candy, not the history.

But over at the Hood College a thousand young women students gave me the most appreciative hearing and the most intelligent questioning I received in the States! When I told that Barbara Fritchie story to Lord Inverchapel, our ambassador at the time in Washington, he capped it with another about Primo Carnera, once a heavy weight boxer and later a professional wrestler. When Primo arrived on the coast he was asked by a newspaper reporter:

"How do you like Los Angeles?"

Primo flexed his muscles and boasted: "I pin him to de mat in two minutes."

And there is an even better story about the diffusion of high standards of cultural knowledge in the States, as told by Mr. Franklin P. Adams. While his car was being filled up with petrol at a wayside garage, Adams had conversed with the garageman and had quoted Byron and Shakespeare.

"Who are they?" asked the garageman.

"Poets," replied Adams.

"I see," said the garageman. "So there's two of them!"

"There are five or six poets," declared Adams coldly.

"Well, I'll be durned," said the garageman.

Detroit is the Henry Ford car town. The Ford Company—all the shares, estimated to be valued at 800 million dollars, are held in the family—had sold 20 million cars by the time I was there, and were throwing thousands off the line every week. Old Henry had been a firm believer in the policy of high wages. Away back in 1914 he had startled the world and greatly annoyed some of his fellow capitalists in America by paying a minimum wage of 5 dollars (£1) per day; but he, and his automatic machinery, made his workers skip lively at their tasks for their higher wages.

There were arguments and allegations, for as well as against, the taskmastership of the Ford system, but I must say that judging by the appearance of the workers I saw and the Trade Union Committee men I interviewed, the critical allegations—mostly from outside Detroit—were grossly exaggerated. Costs of living however were high in Detroit, 20 per cent to 40 per cent higher than across the river in Canada: and I saw thousands of Detroit citizens over in Windsor on the Canadian side on a Saturday queueing up at grocery shops with pillow slips and sacks buying a week's provision.[1]

Old Henry Ford was no commonplace citizen. He was the son of an Ulster immigrant: a Methodist, a prohibitionist, a non-smoker; was fiercely anti-Jew and anti-Wall Street and anti-Banker, and anti-Trade Unionist for many years: made thousands of patents free to anyone in the world who would use them; was a 33rd degree freemason: ran a ' peace ' ship to Europe: once threatened never to build another automobile if Prohibition were repealed in the U.S.A.; could at a glance at a brick wall compute how many bricks it contained to a maximum of one or two per cent error!

Some commentators, Mr. D. N. Pritt, K.C., for example,[2] ascribe to these great Yankee capitalists a malign desire to dominate the world. It may be so. But you can see the things Ford at anyrate really treasured, in his Greenwich museum: the building re-erected stone by stone where Lincoln practised law, Edison's entire laboratory, and the original hawker's basket from which as a boy Edison sold papers and bananas; I should imagine that anyone who hero-worshipped Abraham Lincoln must have had other motive ideas in life than of dominating the world.

We may well suppose that to the end of time men will dispute about the success or failure in particular areas of the 18th amendment to the Constitution, that is, of Prohibition. After the end of the 1914-18 war all the States in the Union had officially endorsed the prohibition law, but now, I think only three States, Oklahoma, Mississippi, and Kansas, are officially dry; and even there, as John Gunther affirms, over 1000 local dealers in Mississippi hold federal liquor licences, and the State actually levies a black market tax on illegal liquor, this tax yielding nearly half a million dollars. Will Rogers, the humorist, has a wise-crack that " Mississippi will drink wet and vote dry so long as any citizen can stagger to the polls."

In Kansas during 1946 the United States Treasury started to prosecute Kansas bootleggers for tax evasion, and bonuses were given Kansas County attorneys for bringing violators into court. In one Kansas case an operator who had been robbed by a liquor syndicate proved that he had paid the police for protection; negotiations for the return of the booty to the victim took place in the county gaol, the County paying the expense of a long distance telephone call to ensure repayment.

---

[1] At Windsor, by the way, there is a plaque erected by the riverside to show the spot where slaves fleeing from the United States became free immediately they had landed on British soil.

[2] *The Star Spangled Shadow.*

Still there is local option in the States, and by all accounts a nearly genuine prohibition of retail sale of liquor in many working class and middle class districts in the larger cities. In Kentucky I was assured 88 out of 120 counties in the States were " dry " by local option. What had happened to national prohibition was that the production side of the liquor business had fallen into the hands of the rogues of the underworld, the Capones and such-like. Corruption on a mass scale followed, and the very foundations of law and order had been shaken in such cities as Chicago. To the inevitable difficulties of enforcement without direct local propaganda and democratic support there had been a widespread repugnance to obeying Federal laws and being regimented in matters of personal habit and taste, while young people who normally would have been ' dry ' of their own volition began to regard it as a matter of defiant citizenship and bravado to carry a flask. In the end all over the country (except in three States) the prohibition amendment to the constitution was repealed and in effect local option has been substituted.

Over such wide tracts of North America as are fertilised every week by the *Saturday Evening Post* of Philadelphia the most famous whisky in the world is Duggan's Dew. Nobody outside week-end fiction has either seen or tasted it, but some journalist had given its place of manufacture as Kirkintilloch in Scotland. And upon it being announced that Kirkintilloch was my habitat I immediately acquired distinction, and there were many direct enquiries with some rather broad hints about samples.

I am afraid, however, that I lost caste and was labelled mean, stingy, and non-co-operative every time I explained that Kirkintilloch was a dry town, and that there was no manufacture there of Dew, Duggan's or any other, certainly within living memory, and that the concoction was imaginary, and, like the story of the empty box, had nothing in it. I could see that even Lord Inverchapel, our Ambassador, had difficulty in accepting my denials about Duggan's Dew.

Nevertheless, when groups of tourists with wide awake Stetson hats and garish neckwear, and with cigar butts between their teeth are seen parading old Kirkintilloch town, the magistrates can be assured that the tourists are not searching for Roman remains.

Out of its abundance America is prodigal, sometimes in sheer waste of food, but often in her generosity to other parts of the world. Her waste in paper is really scandalous. Here was the *New York Times* for the first Sunday in December 1948 with an issue of 364 pages, and at a cost in our money of 7½d. In New York Scots grouse packed in heather were being advertised at 12 dollars, or £3 a brace. In Detroit hand-painted neckties with heads of Red Indians and the like were being sold in the stores at 60 dollars each, say £15, but in New York I was offered garish neckties at 120 dollars, or £30. As Mr. Churchill might say: " Some neck! "

One most interesting experience I had; it was of being taken to Wall Street and given a special permit to see from a gallery the apparently crazy operations in the central Stock Exchange chamber. Here was the nerve centre of the world of finance, and stocks and shares, with a frenzied mob of say 1000 brokers and assistants yelling and shouting as they watched the electric tickers going up, indicating the price movements of Chicago wheat, or Automobile stock, or Shipping or Steel shares, cheering at a rise, groaning at a fall, the floor littered with paper. It must have been a moving spectacle in October 1929 when 16 million shares were sold at disastrous prices, when speculative credit crashed, and stocks fell by half, and millions of people were ruined!

And where but in the United States would any architect or planning authority have had the daring to erect hundred-storey high buildings? The Empire State building, one of them in New York, was said to sway a yard in the wind.

Then there was the Tennessee Valley Authority which John Gunther describes as " the greatest single American invention of this century." When I was in the States the T.V.A. had saved 3,000,000 acres from erosion; it had become the largest power producing agency in the Union, it had built villages, become the inspiration of great increases in produce from the soil; it had stocked dams and rivers with fish and issued 247,000 angling licences; converted a wilderness, a desolation, and a despair, into a land of thriving prosperity.

David Lilienthal, the Chairman of the T.V.A., was later soured and sickened because of the shameful treatment (he was of Hungarian Jewish ancestry) he had received in a witness chair before the Committee on Unamerican Activities. Mrs. Lilienthal told me that when her husband left that witness chair she had said to him: " Now, David, that's the last of public service from you! " But nothing can detract from the great T.V.A. achievement itself, one of the most courageous and lasting memorials of the New Deal: a tribute for all time coming to pioneers like Senator Norris of Nebraska, to administrators like David Lilienthal, the chairman of the Authority, and to far-sighted backers like Franklin Delano Roosevelt, the President of the United States.

In my hurry scurry through the States I did not get much time to study the counterparts to our Labour and Co-operative movements, or to assess their leaders. But the Co-operative movement was very weak—in some cities completely non-existent. There was no Labour Party, the Unions urging their members to vote the Democratic ticket. Most of the industrial unions were strong numerically, and so far as I was able to judge, efficiently led. But I was not able to contact John L. Lewis of the Miners, or Philip Murray (a Scot) of the Steel workers. I had, however, a long talk with Murray's able chief of staff, Macdonald, and one of the brothers Reuther, Victor Reuther, a leader of the Automobile Workers (said to be the largest union in the world—it had a membership of 1¼ millions during the war) addressed a college conference with me at Kenyon University. Both the Reuthers had worked for a time under the Bolsheviks, training Soviet workers in an auto plant at Gorki, and Victor had a concise story of why he was not a Bolshevik. If that story has not been published it ought to be. But there were many allegations of hired gangsters, thugs, dynamitards, forged membership cards, and bribery, in and about the Unions, none of which I was able to check. Let's hope they were grossly exaggerated.

PART THREE

Thumbnails

I

RAMSAY MACDONALD

THE CLASSIC instance of the man who lingered overlong in public affairs is Ramsay MacDonald. For the last six or seven years of his life he had lost his grip: become woolly, evasive, and liable to enmesh himself in a jumble of words. He could work off without a blush such drivelling rhodomontade as:

"We must go on and on, and on, and up and up and up."

and:

"What we have to do is to pile up, and pile up and pile up the income of this industry in this way and that way and the other way."

When Lady Astor wanted him to put a woman M.P. on his front bench she was told:

"I should be very glad not only to have one in the Administration, but half a dozen, and if my Noble Friend will find that there are not quite so many, or even perhaps worse than that, I having made that statement to her, and given her that assurance, am perfectly certain she will not blame me for the result."

Lady Astor: "Arising out of that answer, may I say that I cannot understand it?"

Prime Minister: "I plead guilty. I did not mean that the Noble Lady should understand it. But I promise her this, that what I have said this afternoon will enlighten her tomorrow morning when she looks up her newspaper. I have nothing farther to add except to say this, that I believe the House, unique as it is, can perform a unique work for the restoration of this country."[1]

And to those who had known Ramsay MacDonald at his best it was a tragedy to hear him emit such blather as in his reply to Mr. Lloyd George on Unemployment:

"He thinks he is the only impatient man in this House to get things done. I will beat him fifty per cent any day he likes. Let us go ahead,

[1] Hansard 10.11.1931, pp. 70-71.

215

let us go on. In November the change of Government came in America. No doubt he has a hawk-like desire for action without bridle and without saddle across the Atlantic. It is quite possible in the right honourable gentleman's dreams that that should happen."[1]

In Mr. Churchill's vocabulary Ramsay MacDonald became "a boneless wonder." Mr. Malcolm Muggeridge wrote of him that he had reached a state of "doddering incoherency." He had become a target for some of Low's most devastating cartoons.

Instead of persuading him to retire not only from the Premiership, but from all public life, and go off on a long holiday, Mr. Baldwin and his associates retained him as Lord President of the Council, and he was actually put up in the House of Commons to answer questions about arrangements for the Royal Coronation—about precedence in the procession: about how many seats were to be allotted at the ceremony to deserving classes: about the lavatory arrangements, and other humiliations of a like kind. Perhaps it is unfair to suggest that Mr. Baldwin and his cabinet associates arranged he should give the answers; probably they were as ashamed as were the rest of the members of the House at the spectacle he was presenting.

In his heyday Ramsay MacDonald was a great force. Possessed of a resonant voice, great gifts of imagery, skill in exposition, and tireless energy, he carried on campaigns for an evolutionary, as distinct from a revolutionary, approach to Socialism, and he had collected an enormous following among the politically minded working class. He was one of the greatest descriptive journalists of his generation and had the gift of prose poetry in him. He had a wide acquaintance among the "key" leaders of political opinion in Europe. His great lack was of the saving grace of humour, and of being able to laugh at himself. Apart altogether from his economic writings, where humour could not be expected, I search in vain his volumes on my shelves, for example his *Wanderings and Excursions* and his *Margaret Ethel MacDonald, a Memoir* ("perhaps," estimates Lord Elton, "the most moving tribute in our language from a husband to a wife"), and I cast my mind back over the years during which he contributed weekly articles to my paper *Forward*, and I cannot anywhere see a glint of laughter. Not anywhere. Not once.

Occasions there were when his lack of humour became an embarrassment not only to himself but to his friends. There was a twenty-first birthday dinner to *Forward's* staff and contributors. And at it I remember Tom Dickson, a born mimic, was delighting the audience with exaggerated characterisations of platform mannerisms of, and perorations by, prominent

---

[1] Hansard 16.2.1933, p. 1312.

figures in the Labour movement. After he had mimed Snowden, Smillie, Maxton, myself, and others, I saw what was coming, a rather cruel mounte-banking of J.R.M., who was present—" Ah, my friends, my dear friends, we must go on, and on, and on, this way, that way, and the other way," and so forth. The victim unfortunately took it badly and a damper was placed upon the evening's entertainment!

Some of us had begged him at the time of the crisis in 1931 to resign along with the others of his Labour colleagues, and lead us in opposition, but he had evidently convinced himself that his duty lay in cutting his connection with his party and in joining the national safety combination, swallowing much of his past, e.g. in the taxation of co-operative society reserves and tariff reform. He had even in his first administration accepted, nay had insisted upon, adherence to the court dress traditions, knee breeches, buckles on the shoes, cocked hat, and toy sword, and all the rest of it. But he had resolutely declined to accept for himself what he called ' tinsel honours,' and to that declinature he resolutely adhered to the day he died.

His treatment of Mr. E. D. Morel was inexplicable, and his dismissal of Lady Snowden from the B.B.C. Board of Governors after his quarrel with Lord Snowden was beneath his dignity, but worst of all was the manner of his leaving the party whose General he was, and who had trusted him so. Silently, furtively, and without consulting his army, or explaining himself to them, he had gone over in a night to their opponents.

Yet no reasonable assessment of the man should be concentrated upon his later years. Earlier he had rendered memorable service to social democracy. He was one of the main architects of the Labour Party, and for at least a decade and a half no man did more than he to enthuse the common man and inspire and raise his dignity.

II

WINSTON CHURCHILL

THE PERSONALITY of Mr. Winston Churchill evokes among his biographers either adulation (stretching almost to idolatry) or vituperation and execra-tion. He has crossed the boundaries of partisan politics so frequently and—at times Liberal, Independent, or Conservative—spoken so many perorations that it really would be surprising were there not pegs upon which critics could hang him; and you get two equally capable journalists, Mr. Guy

Eden of the *Daily Express*, and Mr. Emrys Hughes, M.P., of the *Forward*, writing at such a variance about Mr. Churchill as one would write of a saint and another of a devil; while even Mr. Hughes' maledictions become gross flatteries when contrasted with the efforts of the late unlamented Lord Haw Haw from the German radio stations.

When many present day supporters of Mr. Attlee were in their cradles Mr. Churchill, in May 1908, was telling a Dundee audience that he had " no hesitation " in declaring for " a greater collective element being introduced into the State and municipalities. . . . I should like to see the State undertaking new functions, stepping forward into new spheres of activity, particularly in services which are in the nature of monopolies. There I can see a wide field for State enterprise." In 1918 he specifically declared for railway nationalisation and in January 1919 he got the length of saying:

> " I have not been quite convinced by my experience at the Ministry of Munitions that Socialism is possible, but I have been very nearly convinced. I am bound to say I consider on the whole the achievements of the Ministry of Munitions constitute the greatest argument for State Socialism that has ever been produced."

Churchill's speeches during the war tend to blanket from the public mind some of his earlier, and quite as distinctive, efforts. There was, for example, the time, in February 1912, during the intensity of the Irish Home Rule struggle, when he, then First Lord of the Admiralty, volunteered to go over to Belfast and address a public demonstration under the auspices of the Ulster Liberal Association, in support of Home Rule. The Belfast Unionists were outraged and announced their intention of preventing the meeting; they booked the Ulster Hall for the night previous to the Churchill meeting, and threatened to pack it with thousands of resolute men who would refuse to leave in time to permit the Churchill audience to enter.

Finally the Churchill meeting had to be held in a specially erected marquee in the nationalist quarter of the city, but held it was, Mr. Churchill driving to it through hostile streets.

" But he never flinched," says Mr. Ian Colvin in his *Life of Lord Carson*. He got

> " safely away. . . . That he escaped with his life that day seemed to those who saw the crowd which surged about him no less than a miracle."[1]

---

[1] The animosities of the time may be gauged from an anecdote retailed by Mr. Ian Colvin, evidently with approval (p. 405): " Sir Edward! " (Carson), shouted a man in his ear after one of his Belfast meetings, " Are ye a good hater? " " I am," said Carson, looking him in the eye. " Then gie me a grip o' your han', man."

And there is upon record an amazing speech by Churchill which well merits long memory. It is reported in the *Dundee Advertiser* for 15th November 1922, and not its least amazing feature is the fact that it was published at all, and published in one of the Dundee organs owned by Mr. D. C. Thomson, the man whom Mr. Churchill was lambasting. Moreover—so report went in journalist circles at the time—it was Thomson who had the ' copy ' specially submitted to him prior to publication, and it says something for Thomson's courage and journalistic *nous* that he authorised its appearance:

At Broughty Ferry Parish Church Hall Tuesday, 14th November, Mr. Winston Churchill referred to disturbances at recent public meetings and after declaring that advertisements on behalf of his candidature had been refused by the Dundee papers he said: " I am very glad to see the press here because I have no doubt that Mr. Thomson's papers will boycott every word I have said, and dare not print every word I have to say. I am sure it will only be in keeping with their conduct. Yet it is still a free country, and words which are spoken by persons speaking in a responsible position are not suffered to be stifled by any organised boycott by the representatives of the Press. That brings me to examine, if you will permit me, what are matters of great importance to our social life and social civil liberties. This brings me to examine the very curious position of the Dundee newspapers. Here you have a spectacle, I think, unique in British journalism. You have the Liberal and Conservative newspapers owned by the same man and issued from the same office on the same day. Here is one man, Mr. Thomson, selling Liberal news with his left hand and Conservative news with his right hand at the same moment. That is an extraordinary spectacle. I say, that if such conduct were developed in private life or by politicians in public life, every man and woman in the country would say, ' That is very double-faced. You cannot believe the two.' What would be said, I would like to know, of a preacher who preached Roman Catholicism in the morning, Presbyterianism in the afternoon, and then took a turn at Mohammedanism in the evening? He would be regarded as coming perilously near a rogue. It would be said of a politician who made Socialist speeches in Scotland, Conservative speeches in England, and Radical speeches in Wales—you would say he was downright dishonest, and I am bound to say I think the press of this country have a tradition to serve and obey.

A man who owns a newspaper is not simply selling apples off a stall or peddling goods across a counter. He has got a responsibility. The journals he owns and organises are supposed, in accordance with some definite scheme of political thought, to pay some attention to these traditions. In this case, the reporters, the editors, the staff, the sub-editors, all who are concerned in the bringing out of these journals—are absolutely at the mercy of the orders which they receive from this single individual.

Here we get in the morning the Liberal Mr. Thomson through the columns of the Liberal *Dundee Advertiser* advising the Liberals of Dundee to be very careful not to give a vote to Mr. Churchill because his Liberalism is not quite orthodox. This is the Mr. Thomson, the same Mr. Thomson, who failed to get elected as Chairman of the Conservative Party, telling the Liberals to be very careful of the company they keep, warning the Liberal Association that they have strayed from the true fold, and that by any attempt to stretch a friendly hand to progressive Conservatives they are running perilously in danger of jeopardising their political soul.

At the same time, the same moment, you have the Conservative, the ' Die-hard ' Mr. Thomson, through the columns of the Conservative *Dundee Courier* advising the Conservative electors of Dundee to be careful lest in giving a vote to Mr. Churchill they should not run the risk of building up opposition to the new Conservative Government; and you get the same man behind these two absolutely different served up dishes, hot or cold, roast or boiled, seasoned or unseasoned, according to taste, and both brought out by the same cook from the same kitchen. Behind these two, I say, you get the one single individual, a narrow, bitter, unreasonable being eaten up with his own conceit, consumed with his own petty arrogance, and pursued from day to day and from year to year by an unrelenting bee in his bonnet.

Addressing the reporters present: " Now put that down for the *Dundee Advertiser* and the *Dundee Courier*." (Laughter.)

Comment from me would spoil that effort.

Whatever may be said of Winston Churchill as a party politician, so long as history has a tale to tell he will be remembered, and with gratitude, for the outstanding services he rendered to his country during the war. His speeches, vibrant with courage and determination, enthused us and carried us along dark valleys; and sometimes not even a speech, but a phrase, or an ejaculation it was that enthused us! Once he was speaking in Canada, and was being relayed over most of the radio services in the world; he told how a Vichy French General had prophesied that the Germans would wring Britain's neck as if she were a chicken; then a pause followed by the derisive comment: " Some chicken! . . . Some neck! " That was all, but the English speaking world at its listening sets was thrilled to its marrows.

His Cabinet colleagues at sub-committees during the war—but only when he was absent—used to chuckle over the anecdotes which were fathered upon him, although in many the parentage was dubious. There was, for example, the one sponsored by Odette Keun, the Dutch journalist, in her book *And Hell Followed*. It was during the back-to-the-wall speech after Dunkirk, when Churchill stood in the House of Commons, with a united Cabinet seated around him, and declared that Britain would never surrender; the nation would fight on the beaches, on landing grounds, in fields, in streets, and on the hills; the House broke into prolonged applause; the Prime Minister stooped over his notes and muttered to those around him:

" and beat the b——s about the head with bottles: that's all we've got."

The version given by Mr. Guy Eden in his *Portrait of Churchill* (and it has an appreciative preface by Mr. Brendan Brackan, M.P., First Lord of the Admiralty and a close friend of Mr. Churchill's) is that the Prime Minister had said *sotto voce*:

" I don't know what we shall do it with—choppers, I suppose."

But I like the bottles version the better. It is more in character.

When he flew over to France in her hour of agony to offer every Frenchman common citizenship with us, a real incorporating union, and to urge that the French fleet should be transferred to our waters, or at anyrate, outside the possibility of German capture, he took with him a heavy-loaded pistol, vowing:

" If anything happens, and if I fall into the hands of the Huns, I want to account for at least one before they get me."

And there is a story of how he would insist upon going up to the roof-tops in Whitehall to watch an air raid. Somebody wanted him to put on an overcoat. " No," he was perfectly warm, and when it was again politely pressed upon him he got exasperated. " For heaven's sake, don't mollycoddle me! "

Then another official arrived on the rooftop.

" Well, what do *you* want? " asked the P.M.

" If . . . if you'll kindly excuse me, sir—— "

" Yes, yes, what is it? "

" You're sitting on the roof vent, sir, and the building's full of smoke."

It is recorded of him that on an occasion when he was not exactly *en rapport* with Sir Stafford Cripps, he had commented after Sir Stafford had left a meeting in a dudgeon:

" There but for the grace of God, goes God! " And there was a minister who shall be nameless, who sent him a long rather stiltedly phrased report. After reading it the P.M. commented:

"Here is every known *cliché* in the English language, except two: ' God is Love ' and ' Please adjust your dress before leaving.' "

For some reason completely unknown to me I found favour in his eyes, and on occasion, on less weighty matters, to my great embarrassment, he would defer to my opinion outside my Scottish domain, and against the views of experienced and weighty seniors, and once I was astonished when a prominent member of the Cabinet came to me with a request that I should sponsor a proposal in which I had only the most remote interest, on the ground that the Old Man (as he called the P.M.) would let it pass were I to promote the matter.

And once when the P.M. was in bed recovering from a dose of (I think) influenza, along to the Scottish Office came Lord Moran, his doctor, with the plea that I would urge the P.M. not to go off on a projected visit to Scotland, as the original purpose of the visit had now disappeared! Off I went, and in due course was ushered into the chief's bedroom, to find him propped up with pillows, a cigar and a siphon beside him, and signing papers. I got a friendly welcome, and after a while began to edge forward into the conversation my plea for a cancellation of his Scottish visit, whereupon came the immediate comment:

"Oho, so Moran's been at you, has he?"

And two days afterwards the old gentleman was off to Scotland in defiance of his doctors.

There was an even better Moran story than that. When Churchill was slowly recovering from a bout of pneumonia, Lord Moran thought that his recovery was being retarded by his constant attention to papers and despatches, so he begged certain ministers to interfere. One and all politely declined, and finally Brendan Brackan was brought in. He breezed into the P.M.'s bedroom with the blunt announcement:

"Sorry, P.M., you're going to die! "

The P.M. looked at Brackan with astonishment.

"Yes," continued Brackan, "if you go on like that you're going to die, a martyr to your red boxes."

Seeing the point the P.M. said gruffly: "You go to hell! "

But he was more amenable to doctor's orders after that—for a time.

In pre-war days he did not always succeed in overwhelming his opponents with his resonant and polished rhetoric. Snowden, for example, would listen to a great Churchillian piece of oratory, and then acidly invite an interpretation of " that rigmarole "; and George Lansbury, who was compelled to listen to a description of himself from Mr. Churchill, as " one who held up to us always that dim Utopia which would reduce our civilisation to one vast national soup kitchen, surrounded by innumerable municipal bathing pools," once lashed out at his tormentor: " He usurps," cried Lansbury, " a position in this House as if he had a right to walk in, make his speech, walk out, and leave the whole place as if God Almighty had spoken."

But Churchill at his best was assuredly a compelling gentleman. At one of the transatlantic conferences with President Roosevelt, the President's advisers humorously warned him before the meeting to insist at least upon Dominion status for America; and Sir Robert Bruce Lockhart tells[1] (with a little embroidery) how he found me once in Edinburgh having bolted out of Mr. Churchill's way in London. I had been scared out of London lest he exercise his powers of persuasion upon me to shift from the Scottish Office to another post. There had been rumblings in the press (after indirect leakage) that I was fated for a high jump, and when I was actually sounded by an emissary about a post for which I knew I was ill-equipped, and in which I would have eaten my heart out, I judged it was time to get off to the north on urgent business and remain out of harm's way until some other victim was secured.

During the war, I do not think Churchill slept much at night, or during the day either, for that matter of it. When Cabinets were summoned for 10 p.m. in an underground shelter facing St. James's Park, he would arrive as fresh as paint with a huge cigar and—with a siphon beside him—he could go on for hours while most of the rest of us who had been hard at it for twelve hours were almost toppling over for want of sleep. And when we would be feeling our way back to our lodgings through the blackout and the bomb crashings, our old gentleman would be with his chiefs of staff poring over maps, in the war map room.

And he who took so little care of himself once had the nerve to summon seven or eight of us to hear a lecture from him upon the inconsiderate folly and stupidity of us all sleeping in the same block of flats at Whitehall Court. The lecture was delivered with great solemnity, and the occasion the day after a bomb had hit the War Office across the road from our sleeping quarters. I remember sitting mum while Pa Woolton and Stafford Cripps took the lambasting for us all. The indignant P.M. asked us to consider at least the inconvenience to the administration of the country that would be caused if half the Cabinet were wiped out at once.

But we had nowhere else to go and his homily was soon forgotten.

[1] *Comes The Reckoning*, p. 186.

III

DAVID KIRKWOOD

SOME OF David Kirkwood's quips and jests ought to be preserved. What made David in the 1920s one of the most popular of the Labour Party's platform ' draws ' was not his wit—he had that—nor his sense of humour —he had that too; it was his vivid imagery. Sometimes his imagery would be completely irrelevant and extravagant, but then his audiences would enjoy it the more; and it would be interspersed and hotch-spotched with old Scots saws, and snatches from Scots history, and Biblical quotations, and all of it delivered with manifest sincerity and considerable vehemence. He was an artist and could flash into the minds of working class audiences mosaic pictures of social injustice and inequity in a way that the other more text-booky speakers among us found impossible.

He could be pungent and devastating too, as upon the night he embarrassed Mr. Churchill with:

" If ye couldna' get a regular war, ye'd gae doon tae Shoreditch tae fight Peter the Painter."

And one all night sitting, I remember, when a dignified officer of Parliament, who had obviously been solacing himself for his weary attendance upon the equally wearied legislators, by paying frequent visits to the lobby bar, was advancing towards the Speaker's chair, and bowing ceremoniously at every third step, as he was enjoined by the rules of the House to do, David, after one of the obeisances, suddenly shot out:

" Dinna bend doon ony faurer, Mister, or the beer'll fa' oot! "

The look of sheer malignity that escaped the victim of the sally only added to the general laughter.

After the Sankey Commission report, and on the eve of the General Strike, there was intense propaganda activity in placing the miners' case before the public, and four of us M.P.s, Messrs. Ernest Thurtle, Neil Maclean, David Kirkwood and I were despatched one night to Shoreditch Town Hall. The audience was Cockney, and it only absorbed in patches David Kirkwood's strong Glasgow accent, but what he got across about the Sankey Commission acted as an amazing rabble rouser. There was first his picture of the King's robing room at the House of Lords, where the Commission had held its sittings. Mr. Justice Sankey, with a wig, was in the chair, and Bob Smillie was beside him " knockin' oot the mineowners and royalty owners yin at a time as they came in." And then how the royalty owners had held a private meeting and decided to train up a champion to go for Bob Smillie. The champion they selected was the Duke of Northumberland—" drawin' £75,000 a year in royalties." And they had all the leading lawyers coaching him and teaching him how to answer Smillie.

Then the day for the great encounter came. Back to the robing room.

" A chap comes tae the door.

" ' Wha's there? ' asks Justice Sankey.

" ' It's me, the Duke o' Northumberland,' says the Duke.

" ' Come in,' says Justice Sankey, ' and tak' a seat, but tak' aff yer tile hat. . . . Ony questions at the Duke? '

" ' Ay,' says Bob Smillie, ' I have some questions to ask him.' (To the Duke): ' Whit dae ye dae for a leevin'? '

" No answer.

" ' Come on,' says Justice Sankey. ' Naebody gets aff withoot answerin' questions here, except Royalty, an' you're no Royalty. Answer Boab Smillie's question! '

" The Duke: ' I don't know what I do for a living.'

" Then says Bob: ' An' what dae ye get for it? '

" But the Duke he answered never a word for a frozen corpse was he."

The sudden *dénouement* was straight out of Mrs. Hemans; it was obviously unpremeditated, and it was received with rapturous cheering.

Mr. McNeill Weir in his book on Ramsay MacDonald quotes David Kirkwood as thus " leatherin' " the Tories in the House of Commons:

> " Look at them. There they sit the noo, but the day is comin' when we shall chase them ower the border an' awa'. We shall smite them hip and thigh and pursue them from Dan even to Beer-sheba unto the going down of the sun. The Minister of Health may get awa' wi' it the noo, but he shall not ultimately escape. He will have to pay hereafter for the deeds done in the body. ' Vengeance is mine; I will repay,' saith the Lord."

And David went about with a tremendous oration upon the British Empire and what the Scots had done to the building of it. Once in the House of Commons he was conducting us by speech on a tour round the Empire, but owing to English Tory interruptions he got stuck at the barren rocks of Aden and couldn't for the life of him remember where to go next. Maxton, sitting a few benches away, offered bets that he would be at Bannockburn inside five minutes if these English Tory interruptions continued. And as it happened Sir William Lane Mitchell ejaculated: " You've told us about Aden twice. Get on with it."

To which at once came David's rejoinder: " Oh, ye English. We've leatherit you at Bannockburn before, and we'll leather you again."

Mr. Speaker interrupted: " The Hon. Member must surely recognise that we are not discussing leather. That is covered by the Board of Trade vote."

David Kirkwood: " Correct, Mr. Speaker. I was only usin' leatherit in its classical meanin'. However, we'll now proceed from Aden to Burma." And so on we went round the Empire.

Kirkwood was splendidly equipped with old Scots proverbial wisdom. Of Mr. Baldwin, whom he estimated to be a " fly " man, he said: " He doesna' sell his hen on a wat day." And his description of receiving history lessons at his grandfather's knee was good for any Scots audience—how his grandfather would tell him of the English King Edward being called the Hammer of the Scots, and of his gathering a great army against the Scots. But how he died at Burgh on Sands before his army could get up at us. " He wanted," said the old man, " to conquer the Scots, that proud imperial race whom the might of Rome could never deface. But Davuck, he never was fed fur the job."

We Scots M.P.s used to make indignant protest whenever an Englishman was sent by the Chairman's Panel to take the chair at our Scots Grand Committee meetings. And once when an English squire, Sir Richard Barnet, arrived it was David Kirkwood's turn to protest. He was sailing beautifully into his piece when Sir Richard arose with a pained expression on his face. He was amazed, he said, that these epithets should be offered against him, as he was a direct descendant of Robert the Bruce. Whether this was fiction or not, it worked. David Kirkwood bowed respectfully and yielded him all the honours. It would be a sin and a crime to torment a descendant of the victor at Bannockburn.

One of David's best efforts was during a parliamentary speech upon the poverty of Clydebank. " If the Prime Minister kent aboot it he widna tolerate it. If the King kent aboot it——" (Cries of ' Order! ' for you must not mention the King in debate!)

David tried again. " If the Prime Minister kent aboot it he widna' tolerate it. If the King——" (Louder shouts of ' Order! ' during which a colleague whispers to David that the name of the King is barred!)

For a third time David essayed: " If the Prime Minister kent aboot it, he widna' tolerate it. If "—(a pause during which the House was ready to shout the speaker down)—" the Prince o' Wales's faither kent aboot it, he widna' tolerate it."

Decorum disappeared and it is said that when King George heard the story, he slapped his knees with glee and added it to his ample repertoire.

Near a town called Renishaw David got himself into serious trouble for an alleged seditious speech. At his trial, where some of his friends were spectators, the chief witness for the Crown was an English policeman, who deponed that he heard the seditious speech.

" Could you understand him? " asked David's lawyer.

" Easy," said the constable.

Then David was called upon to give the constable another test, and he began by reciting lines from the ritual of the Independent Order of Good Templars. Quickly and in the broadest accent said David:

". . . in naturre we find no strong drrink, nothing thatt caan intoxicate. The Almighty and all wise prreparred but one drrink purre waterr. This he furrnished bounteefully and sent it courrsing thrrough the airrth, rrushing down the hillside, glancing in the sunbeam, bounding thrrough the valley, distilling in the dew and trreasurred in the mighty deep. Placed at the head of all animate crreation, man is the only crreature that sinks below his level and yiellds to a strrange and acqqirred appetite."

The constable had, after the first few words, stopped pretending to take this rigmarole down in his notebook.

" What has Mr. Kirkwood said? " asked the lawyer.

" I dunno," said the constable, " but when I heard him before he spoke English."

And once I remember in the Scots Grand Committee Mr. Fred McQuisten interrupting Kirkwood, rather snobbishly by saying that surely he was aware of the adjuration " *Toujours la politesse mais rien de plus.*"

Kirkwood stopped. " The member for Argyll is no the only yin that kens Latin here. I reply with the Latin poet—and you'll be able to confirm this, Mr. Chairman " (who smirked unhappily), " Eeenty-tweenty haligolum. San frosensko nux vomica—pipe cley up the luma."

For the benefit of the official reporters I obliged later by repeating some dog Latin I knew, pretending it to be what Mr. Kirkwood had said, for the which I was later summoned to Mr. Speaker Whiteley's room and rebuked. It was, he said, a grave disservice to our great parliamentary institutions to make a mockery of the machinery of recording what transpired in the House!

There was another occasion when David's dialect was rather derided. It was during a debate on Emigration which Sir Alfred Mond had urged as a remedy for unemployment. This infuriated David.

" For brass face, Mr. Speaker, did ever ye hear the like? Aboot his nose I'll say naethin', for that wid pit me oot o' order. But look at him.

A man that's just so newly over frae Germany that his hair's haurdly dry.
He canna speak the English language——"

Upon which the Speaker broke in: "If any M.P. has a right to complain about the pronunciation of English, it is the M.P. for Dunbarton
Burghs."

Were I to write for a week of David Kirkwood, the Scots Presbyterian
elder, workman engineer, in politics, I could not make the man more
manifest than is done in his own words, quoted by Mr. J. L. Hodson in his
Through the Dark Night:

> " *I take no orders from Rome or Moscow.*
> *To the world I give my hand, but my heart*
> *I give to my native land.*"

IV

JAMES MAXTON

WHEN JIMMY MAXTON, stormy petrel in Scottish Socialist politics for
nearly 30 years, departed this life in 1946, he left behind him no personal
enemies; from no quarter came an unkind word about him; his smile,
his charm, his gaiety, were remembered; much friendly anecdotage about
him there was around the firesides of thousands of working class homes;
the tears and the laughter with which he could sweep his audiences were
already a legend.

My first recollection of Jimmy is of an occasion during a students'
'wild night' at a Glasgow variety theatre. It was the Pavilion. The doors
had been rushed and the artistes were bravely seeking to carry on with
their turns amid chorusing and trumpet blowing, and the throwing of light
missiles to and fro among the unruly audience. Then during a Japanese
wrestling act, Maxton and one or two cronies who had somehow got
round to the stage door, appeared from one of the wings, dancing with
arms akimbo to the footlights.

In those days he was no Socialist: only a harum scarum rooting for
his M.A. degree so that he could make a living teaching children in a public
school. In fact at his first Rectorial election he had voted for George
Wyndham, the Conservative candidate, against the Liberal John Morley.

Later in 1904 someone persuaded him to attend a lecture by Philip Snowden in Paisley. Snowden shook him and he began to read all the Socialist literature upon which he could lay his hands; then he took to orange boxes and chairs at city street corners and village greens expounding the faith.

He had none of the heavy, forbidding economic and philosophical jargon about dialectical materialism and the like then the fashion, and considered the hallmark of the third degree Marxian. His was the merry jest and the quip, well mixed with the stuff for pathos and tears, and sauced with apt Biblical quotation and graphic description of social wrongs and injustices. His long black hair was bunched at the back *à la* Henry Irving. He not only preached the revolution; he looked it. Once—he told me the story himself—he had been induced to go to Inverness and act as best man at a friend's wedding; he had, he said, got for the first and last time a tall hat, and he was seated gloomily hunched up in a corner of the tearoom in Buchanan Street Station with his tall hat, and his long hair, awaiting the early morning train for the north. Enter an effusive, garishly dressed gentleman, and addressed Maxton:

" Hallo, chum, waitin' on the train? "

" Yes."

" Where are you playing? "

" Playing? "

" Yes, old man. I see you're one of us. I'm on the halls myself! "

Came the first world war, and Maxton, like all the other members of the I.L.P., found extreme difficulty in accepting the story that the Tsar of Russia was our ally in a war for freedom and democracy. Maxton was a political objector to the war; he was no absolute pacifist, and he would, as he later declared, have volunteered for service in the international brigade in the Spanish Civil War, had he been able to get a doctor to pass him.

But in the first world war his anti-war opinions succeeded in getting him discharged from his teaching employment in a Glasgow school and transferred—he, physically of all men!—to employment for the duration of the war as a plater's helper in a shipyard. His dog, too, was cruelly stoned to death as a reprisal for its master's opinions; and then he, the plater's helper, was sentenced to imprisonment in Calton gaol, Edinburgh, for " sedition."

The war over, and turning the scales at a lighter weight than ever, he was back at his career of evening agitator, and now by day, full time organiser for the I.L.P., his diet being chiefly cigarettes and black coffee. In due course he was swept into Parliament for the Bridgeton division of Glasgow. At Westminster his patent sincerity, his friendliness, his wit and his eloquence, made him hosts of friends even among his political opponents —Messrs. Winston Churchill and Baldwin included.

At one time Ramsay MacDonald cultivated him, and there is a story told of a week-end when MacDonald, a vigorous hiker, persuaded Maxton to accompany him on a walking tour. Towards the end of the first day Maxton, bone tired and with blistering feet, gave it up and sat doggedly at a wayside station waiting on a train to take him anywhere. On the Monday he reported to his friends that the next walking tour he was going upon it was to accompany a cripple like Philip Snowden.

His suspension from Parliament in June 1923 is well told by Mr. Gilbert McAllister, M.P., in his *The Portrait of a Rebel*. It was a Scottish Estimates day at Westminster and a Conservative M.P. had ' hear heared ' in approval a reference to a reduction in the Scottish Health Services Grant by £89,000, although there had been a serious rise in tuberculosis. When Maxton began to speak he was calm enough. He pointed out that semi-skilled labourers in his constituency were earning 32s. 6d. per week, but that the maintenance costs at Barnhill Poorshouse for a man, his wife, and four children, without counting medical and maintenance charges, was 58s. 7½d. per week; that the emergency supplies of milk and food for nursing mothers and infants had been cut; and that hospital accommodation was now refused by Government order for children suffering from whooping cough and measles. He called the men who were responsible " murderers," and declared that Sir Frederick Banbury was " one of the worst in the whole House."

Then the storm broke. From the chair Maxton was asked to withdraw the word ' murderer ' as applied to any particular member of the House.

" Maxton folded his arms and stood his ground resolutely. ' I can never withdraw, I did it deliberately. . . . I should never dream of withdrawing for one moment.' "

Pressure, abuse, points of order!

" After forty minutes' continuous strain, keyed up to a terrible pitch of emotional intensity, Maxton appeared on the point of physical collapse. He turned to Wheatley who sat beside him, and said, ' You take my place, John, I refuse to withdraw. I cannot apologise.' Wheatley responded immediately. He repeated the epithet ' Murderers ' and refused to withdraw."

Then followed the suspension of Maxton, Wheatley, and Campbell Stephen. Shinwell, who next took the floor, adroitly stopped the continuance of suspensions, by refraining from the use of the word ' murderer ' and keeping his remarks within the bounds of parliamentary language, although in the midst of his speech, George Buchanan managed to get himself suspended for questioning the impartiality of the chair when somebody had shouted 'Jew' at Shinwell. But of all who participated in the 'scene,' the man whom it most affected, and from whom it took the largest toll in nervous energy was James Maxton.

He became chairman of the I.L.P., but the emotional qualities that endeared him to public audiences were not at all suited to the administrative hazards and encounters in a great organisation like the I.L.P., with its 30,000 members. These members were the mainstay of the Labour Party throughout the country, and when from headquarters of the I.L.P. under the new Maxton *régime* there came directions for voting against the Labour Government, and the issue of Cook-Maxton manifestos without first consulting even the executive of the I.L.P., there was first perplexity, then resentment, and finally wholesale resignations. Today the I.L.P. is only a poor relic of what was once a powerful organisation; it has now no members in the House of Commons where once it had 197, nearly one-third of the total membership in the House of Commons.

But Jimmy to the end was Jimmy, gay, lovable, unique, incomparable. He played a for ever memorable part in changing a public opinion which was complacent and acquiescent in face of needless suffering in the midst of plenty, to one that was resolutely determined upon fairer shares for all.

I am thankful to have known him.

V

ROLAND MUIRHEAD

ALMOST AS far back as spans the memory of living man Roland Muirhead has been a notable standard bearer for Self Government in Scotland, and now (1951) he is the G.O.M. of it. Half a century ago he packed his bag and walked out of the family tannery business in Renfrewshire to live the free life, first in an Owenite colony in the State of Washington (U.S.A.) and then in a non-violent anarchist colony in the same State.

I never rightly got the hang of what happened during his brief sojourn in these oases in the wicked world, but he was soon back in London organising a Co-operative Tannery, and shortly thereafter he was engaged managing the old family business in Renfrewshire, which—lest you think he is simply a starry-eyed dreamer!—he has managed for many years, and still does, with conspicuous success.

The Young Scots Society was founded in 1900, and shortly after its formation, began an intensive propaganda for Scottish Home Rule, and here Roland Muirhead got the set of his life, from which there never has been any deviation. He goes about today with quotations showing how near the Young Scots were to securing a Federal Home Rule. One is from a speech delivered at the King's Theatre, Edinburgh, on 8th September 1913 where Mr. McKinnon Wood, then Secretary for Scotland, made the following pronouncement:

> " When they began to draft a Home Rule Bill for Scotland as the Government had determined to do (cheers) they would have two of the best brains in Scotland to work on it."

The reference here is to the then Lord Advocate, Mr. Robert Munro (later Lord Alness) and the then Solicitor General for Scotland, Mr. T. B. Morrison. And in the literature calling the meeting it was categorically stated that the Prime Minister (then Mr. Asquith) had deputed the Secretary for Scotland to make a statement of the Government's intentions on Scottish Home Rule.

Mr. Muirhead stores other pledges and pronouncements on the same subject from Keir Hardie and Clement Attlee, and one from Winston Churchill, made at Dundee on 3rd October 1911 of which more may yet be heard:

> ". . . as to the future, we have to secure for Scotland a much more direct and convenient method of bringing her influence to bear upon her own purely domestic affairs. There is nothing which conflicts with the integrity of the United Kingdom in the setting up of a Scottish Parliament for the discharge of Scottish business. There is nothing which conflicts with the integrity of the United Kingdom in securing to Scotsmen in that or in some other way an effective means of shaping the special legislation which affects them and only them. Certainly I am of opinion that if such a scheme can be brought into existence it will mean a great enrichment not only of the national life of Scotland, but of the politics and public life of the United Kingdom."

Roland Muirhead became first chairman of the National Party of Scotland in 1927, and when the last great war broke out there was an energetic police round-up of the few—if any—subversive pro-Nazi and Mosleyite elements. At the time somebody took it upon himself to hint to the police that Roland might be a sympathiser with Hitler, or at anyrate was sufficiently anti-English to warrant a raid upon his house. A raid duly took place and after some locks had been forced there was borne off in triumph a sporting rifle of last century vintage which had belonged to an uncle or a brother, plus a few rounds of revolver ammunition, but no revolver.

Fortunately there existed at that time in the offices of the Crown Prosecutor and the Lord Advocate a sense of humour, and the engines of war referred to were hurriedly ordered to be returned, so that Roland Muirhead was deprived of a martyr's crown. But he complains that he has never yet been compensated for the damage to his locks.

He maintains an office in Glasgow which he calls the Scottish Secretariat, where there is stored many thousands of Home Rule cuttings, pamphlets and books, and to that office there wends daily this pioneer, still rosy cheeked, but now, alas, ageing and bent under the weight of years, all the pockets of his homespun tweed suit stuffed and bulging with memoranda— this voluntary, this anti-compulsionist, this resolute and determined opponent of all bureaucracy and centralised government, with his eyes fixed upon the, to him, essential condition precedent to any beneficent or worth-while change, a Home Rule Parliament for Scotland.

VI

SIR DUFF COOPER

I HAVE felt in recent years that our ambassador in Paris, Sir Alfred Duff Cooper, has never been given his justly merited place in contemporary history. Possibly the disregard is due somewhat to his aristocrat origins and connections, coupled with an apparently studied aloofness and unapproachability, as if he were some grand seigneur of the *ancien régime* moving graciously among his serfs.

But beyond doubt here was a man of notable personal courage, and there were political opponents of his who had never spoken to him when he was in Parliament but who fain would have paid a tribute to his quality even at the risk of being misunderstood.

When Mr. Baldwin in 1931 was having his notorious quarrel with the press Lords, Beaverbrook and Rothermere, a Parliamentary vacancy occurred in the safe Conservative division of St. George's, Westminster. The Lords ran a candidate of their own, one Sir Ernest Petter, and Mr.

Baldwin had to scrounge around for some capable platform representative possessed of courage, prepared to hazard his future, and act as shock absorber in a stormy contest. At that time Mr. Baldwin was supposed to be scuttling the Empire and in particular plotting to 'sell out' India to Mr. Gandhi. Mr. Duff Cooper was induced to leave the safe Conservative stance at Winchester to fight the press Lords' nominee at St. George's from the disruptions which they were organising from Fleet Street.

The contest was a savage one—nothing barred except libel, and even there the limits were stretched—placards everywhere, and streamers across the streets announcing that "Gandhi is watching St. George's," while half-naked life sized effigies of the Mahatma were trundled around the constituency to drive the message home!

Duff Cooper during the contest gave as good or as bad as he got, telling for example one of the press Lords by name that he did not possess the entrails of a grey insect found on unclean bodies (a sad departure that from grand seigneury!); he dealt faithfully and courageously with the squads of imported hecklers, and won the contest with a comfortable margin to spare.

And some years later, when the stresses with the German and Italian dictators culminated in Mr. Neville Chamberlain, the Prime Minister, returning from Munich bearing as he thought Peace In Our Time, but at the price of a betrayed Czecho-Slovakia, one of the few public figures who abstained from rejoicing was Mr. Duff Cooper, then his First Lord of the Admiralty. Mr. Chamberlain was received with widespread relief and cheering, but Duff Cooper refused to bow during the mass hysteria, and when as he told the House of Commons

"in the Cabinet room all his other colleagues were able to present bouquets to the Prime Minister, it was an extremely painful and bitter moment for me that all that I could offer him was my resignation."

In the light of Hitler's already broken pledges he could not accept another, and especially when that was at the shameful price of the betrayal of the Czechs.

"... I should never be able to hold up my head again. . . . I have ruined perhaps my political career. But that is a little matter; I have retained something which is to me of greater value—I can still walk about the world with my head erect."

Some moral courage was required to stand up in the midst of a House of Commons which believed it had just been rescued from the jaws of war, and say what Duff Cooper said in his resignation speech that day, but his attitude was not long in being justified by events, and when war broke out in 1939, no man in all Britain was more entitled than he to say " I told you so!"

One other memory! After the heroic and successful defence of Stalingrad by the Russians it was decided to have a Stalingrad Thanksgiving Sunday, and members of the British Cabinet were sent to various large centres as speakers. At Glasgow, where Russian speakers as well as Duff Cooper and myself had been allocated, there was great enthusiasm and, somewhat to my amazement, Duff Cooper, worked into nervous excitement, gave the audience the Soviet upraised arm and clenched fist salute!

VII

JOHN G. WINANT

DURING THE war it was my practice to bring north to Scotland knowledgeable and distinguished men to meet the editors of Scottish newspapers in private conference; and once I brought the late John G. Winant, then United States ambassador in London.

It was arranged between us that after a brief informal address to the editors Winant was to answer questions, but I, as chairman, was to rule out at a signal from him, any questions which might prove of serious embarrassment. The first question, plump and direct, came from Dr. Waters, then Editor of the *Scotsman*.

" Is or is not the United States coming into the war?"

I glanced at Winant to see if he wanted this question ruled out, but he kept silent, gazing fixedly at his finger tips from beneath his great dark eyebrows. A moment passed. Dead Silence. Another moment. Then slowly Winant looked at Waters and asked:

" May I put a question to you, sir?"

" Certainly," answered Waters.

" Do you think my President is an honest man?"

" I do!"

" Then, sir," said Winant, " you have answered your own question!"

How neatly by that retort was conveyed the suggestion that the United States *was* coming into the struggle, and yet how impossible it was for any isolationist in the States, if ever he had heard of it, to make political difficulties for Roosevelt out of the phraseology.

The English speaking world lost a powerful and incisive mind when John Winant died. The Friday night before his death I spent with him at his flat in New York. He was then full of a project for paying a personal visit to Stalin in the interests of world peace; he was bright, cheery and hopeful. Alas, on the Monday while at sea we got the news that John Winant was dead.

VIII

ROBERT SMILLIE

PERHAPS SOME day the British Miners Federation will issue a cheap, subsidised volume containing the evidence led by, and the cross-examination of, the coal owners and the royalty owners, before the Royal Commission on the Coal Industry, presided over by Mr. Justice Sankey in the year 1919.

Such a volume would be a fitting memorial to the greatest leader the miners ever had—Robert Smillie. It is characteristic of Smillie's modesty that in his book *My Life for Labour* published in 1924, he glossed over, in a short paragraph of five lines, all reference to his electrifying exposures of how the coal mining industry was conducted.

Day after day Smillie had filled the centre of the Sankey Commission stage at the King's robing room at Westminster, while a steady procession of wealthy and powerful men were subjected to a public grilling such as never before had occurred in our history; and non-mining readers of the press would sit aghast and astonished in railway trains at accounts of how Dukes and Plutocrats had made sorry exhibitions of themselves in the witness box.[1]

Smillie had earned for himself such a reputation for administrative ability, and for vision and courage, that Mr. Lloyd George in 1917 begged of him to come into the Government as Food Controller. But Smillie

---

[1] He worried the royalty owners and coal masters considerably when he produced the Scottish Act of 1592 wherein it was decreed that all mines and minerals belonged to the Crown and that minerals were only to be farmed out to operators provided they paid one-tenth of the produce to the Crown. The Act was designed to secure increased production and for the " entertainment and sustentation of a great number of lieges." That the Act was still in force was undeniable. It was included in the " Revised Edition of the Acts of the Parliament of Scotland 1424-1707 " published officially in 1908, and it was equally undeniable that the tenths of the produce had never been paid to the State. But it was held that the Act only applied to metals —silver and gold.

refused, as at a later date he refused a post in the first Labour Government, on the ground that he felt he could serve the mining communities better outside than inside any State Office.

He used to come to Stirlingshire on my election platforms and boast that he was the world's champion defeated candidate for Parliament, having lost seven consecutive contests. Nevertheless when he did at last get into Parliament he was promptly installed as chairman of the Labour Party there, but he tells us in his autobiography that looking back upon his struggles in life nothing had given him greater pride than his success as a member of the Larkhall School Board in securing the provision of free school books for all the children.

He had a fund of good stories. One of how he had once gone, accompanied by a commercial friend, to the House of Commons. The friend was wearing a top hat, and for a joke, when espying Keir Hardie coming in the distance, he hurriedly swopped hats with Smillie. When Hardie saw Smillie in the chimney pot he was greatly distressed, and cried: " Good heavens! You tae, Bob! "

Another story, and he could tell it most effectively upon a public platform, was of a deputation sent by miners to the late Duke of Hamilton to assure him that they were going to strike a pit unless they received an extra 6*d.* per day and free wicks and oil for their lamps. According to Smillie the spokesman for the deputation began:

" My duke, my lord, my man, sir,"

and then proceeded to state why the deputation had come.

The Duke in reply said that the colliery was losing money, but that he was prepared to hand it over to a committee of the men, the condition being that they would keep the colliery going and pay him a royalty of threepence or fourpence per ton. When the deputation had promised to report the offer to the men and had gone down the avenue it suddenly struck them that they had forgotten to ask the Duke about the free wicks and the free oil for the lamps, and back they went to complete their mission. What happened at the second interview I cannot recollect, but nothing further developed about the syndicalist colliery proposal.

Smillie's best platform effort I think was his narrative of how he had induced the President of the Board of Trade and Sir Guy Calthorpe and Sir Richard Redmayne to accompany him on a tour of miners' housing in Lanarkshire.. He had got them to Holytown and had picked some ' rows ' of single roomed houses with a front door only and the ashpits, large open brick built affairs, only 10 feet away from the front door. The stench was fearful and the party became obviously desirous of a hurried and fleeting inspection, and making their stay short. Smillie, however, kept talking to the inhabitants in the secret hope that one of the gentlemen accompanying him would have a mild fainting fit, preferably the President of the Board of Trade. If that personage had to be carried out to a less contaminated atmosphere, what a propaganda for improved miners' housing!

The President and the party escaped the fainting fit, but there were no dissentients among them afterwards that life was not worth living under the horrible conditions they had just witnessed.

IX

JAMES CONNOLLY

JAMES CONNOLLY was the son of an Irish dustman immigrant to Edinburgh. In the brief 46 years of his life which was ended by a firing squad at Dublin Castle after the abortive rising of Easter week in 1916, he had become a research scholar whose work on behalf of the working class in Ireland had become widely known in two continents. He had, declares Mr. W. P. Ryan, " powerfully affected " Lenin; and he along with Jim Larkin, had set agoing an intensive effort at rallying " the unconquered Irish working class, orange and green, into a common party struggling for economic freedom."

Larkin himself was a character, daring, reckless, defiant, dramatic (he is the only instance known to me of a man who elected to be discharged from his employment rather than take part in a Grand National Sweep-stake!) He had a considerable power of artistry in words, and could fashion nicknames for opponents which adhered to them like burrs; one instance I recall; there was a man in Dublin called Murphy who, when young, had owned a landed property in the centre of the city; this young Murphy had to take to his bed with an incurable but long lasting disease. While Murphy lay abed his property became more and ever more valuable until he was reckoned to be a millionaire. Larkin christened him " Cosy Murphy " and as ' Cosy ' he was always thereafter known.

But Connolly was a different type from Larkin; he, Connolly, was a cool level-headed analyst, precise, careful, and accustomed to weighing evidence and words, and to this hour it is a puzzle to me how he ever came to be a leader in an armed rebellion against the British Government, when his Citizen Army insurgents could only muster 118 rifles.

Down to 1913 Connolly wrote regularly for the *Forward*, mostly strictures on the Irish Home Rule Party; but nowhere did he ever give hint that he was developing into a military insurrectionist Sinn Feiner, and subsequent to his execution—he, though wounded, was taken from an hospital bed, and shot after drum-head court martial!—newspapers in America quoted lavishly from some of his writings in the U.S.A. where he had rather derided sentimental Irishism, and had stressed instead the need for economic change.

Once he sat in the *Forward* office, a thick-set man with a bulky black moustache, a soft musical voice, and shy retiring mannerisms, and elaborated his contention that it was necessary to upset the traditional adherences of both Catholic and Protestant workers in Ireland before any united labour effort was possible in that distracted country.

He had collected instances where, during the previous half century, the Catholic hierarchy had sided with landlordism and the English Government, and these he had produced in a pamphlet controversy with a learned Jesuit Father in Dublin.[1] His researches into the origins of the Battle of the Boyne must have been something of a shock to such Orangemen as saw the pamphlet. The Battle of the Boyne, he wrote,

" was the result of an alliance formed by Pope Innocent XI with William, Prince of Orange against Louis King of France. King James of England joined with King Louis to obtain help to save his own throne, and the Pope joined in the league with William to curb the power of France. When the news of the defeat of the Irish at the Boyne reached Rome the Vatican was illuminated by order of the new Pope, Alexander VIII and special masses offered up in thanksgiving. See Von Ranke's History of the Popes and Murray's Irish Revolutionary History."

In his volume *Labour in Ireland* he says that part of King William's expenses at the Boyne

" was paid for by His Holiness the Pope. Moreover when news of King William's victory reached Rome a *Te Deum* was sung in celebration of his victory over the Irish adherents of King James and King Louis. Similar celebrations were also held at the great catholic capitals of Madrid and Brussels."[2]

[1] *Labour Nationality and Religion*: 1910.

[2] My edition of Ranke's *History of the Popes* (1850 Translation by E. Foster) says that Count Cassoni, the Pope's minister, was "implicated," but that the Pope himself had engaged to contribute considerable subsidies to William of Orange. Vol. II, pp. 423-4.

Guizot, *Hist. Civilization* (Hazlett's translation I, 246) simply says: "The emperor of Germany and Pope Innocent XI supported William III." But neither authority refers to the illumination of the Vatican or to the singing of the *Te Deum* after the Battle of the Boyne.

The Rev. Dr. Murray in his *Revolutionary Ireland and its Settlement*, says (p. 36): "The

To Connolly the Irish question was a social question and to making it so he had devoted his adult life.

X

THE REVEREND JAMES BARR

ONE DAY in the nineteen-twenties, when most part of the British press was baying at the wild red M.P.s from the Clyde, a tall brawny man, a farmer to all appearance, but garbed as a clergyman, with the appropriate coat, collar, and hat, was leading a string of these Clyde M.P.s across the bare, bleak moor of Fenwick—leading them to the old farm of Loch Goin which had been in possession of a single farming family, the Howies, for seven centuries. Here a Howie had written *Scots Worthies*, and here were still housed great covenanting relics of the days when poor Scots folk were hunted and harried over the moss hags for refusing to have their Kirk dominated by the State.

It was a dripping wet day and the mist was well down and around the party, but the big brawny man in the clerical garb was in high fettle, for Fenwick was his native parish; he had been reared among the whaups on the moor and in the traditions of the conventiclers; and he visioned the inspiration that would surely come to the M.P.s if they could but be touched with the spirit of the men who had died for the Covenant. Hence the reason why the Reverend James Barr was shepherding and deploying his group across the Moor to Loch Goin and the flag

PHINIK FOR GOD, COUNTRY AND COVENANTED
WORK OF REFORMATIONS

James Barr had played many parts in his day—scholar, preacher, church moderator, home ruler, pacifist, educationist, temperance and Robert Burns orator, and Member of Parliament, but above all, and always, he was a fighter for spiritual and political freedom, one who lived in the traditions

---

Austrian Court ordered public prayers to be offered for the success of William's expedition to England," and quotes Klopp as saying " The Battle (of the Boyne) had nothing to do with the Catholic faith " (p. 161) and that the Pope " rejoiced to hear the good news from Ireland " and that the victory of the Boyne was " acclaimed in Vienna and Madrid " (p. 162).

of the minority men of the moors and hillsides, and who, for conscience' sake, had defied Princes, prelates and captains of horse.

Perhaps it was a mistake that he should ever have left a settled church and entered Parliament. There they had made him chairman of the Parliamentary Labour Party; but in that position I do not think he was in his element; too many compromises had to be made with the mammon of unrighteousness, and he could be seen almost any evening sitting in the Library of the House of Commons engaged at laborious administrative and political correspondence, when he might have served his generation more usefully and had greater joy in his activities had he been on the public platform telling rapt audiences about Richard Cameron, James Renwick, and Robert Burns, and Thomas Muir of Huntershill, his narratives interspersed with quotations from Abraham Lincoln, and Sir Walter Scott, and the Biblical prophets!

In the days when all Glasgow voted in one bloc for educational administration, James Barr on three occasions topped the poll, and he used to relate with gusto how his little grandson told him that popular as he was he still had to take second place to Jimmy Quin, the centre forward for the Celtic.

But why the Senatus of the University of Glasgow, his old *Alma Mater*, never conferred upon one of her most distinguished and erudite sons, an honorary degree of LL.D. or D.D., was always a question to which one could find no solution.

James Barr had taken prizes in each of the seven classes in the Arts course in his day, and beyond doubt he was one of the first half dozen public exhorters and spiritual uplifters and moral educationists of his time; he was the best regarded and most notable cleric of any denomination in Scotland; he was a great Social Democrat, a great Scotsman, a great citizen, an earnest Christian.

It has been said of his speeches that they often tended to be too meticulously exact and precise, his quotations too elaborate, his main purposes overlain with crusts of unnecessary detail. Maybe so. But he also possessed the spiritual power and passion to rouse audiences. What, for example, could be more compelling than the way he once touched a huge crowd in Vienna. The occasion was an international one; at least two Prime Ministers spoke, M. Vandervelde (Belgium) and M. Blum (France); the stewards had presented the speakers with bouquets of flowers. Barr in returning thanks held up his bouquet and said:

" Tomorrow morning I am going to get a box and put your bloom in it, and send it home to my wife in Glasgow, and ask her to undertake

a journey of 20 miles to our native cemetery and lay it on the grave of
our boy who fell in the Great War in order that as I have always said in
my opposition to war, that I had no ill-will to you, the people of Vienna,
so that those who see that bloom and know its story will realise that you,
the people of Vienna, have no ill-will to my little country of Scotland."

And when that was translated the audience broke into tears!

XI

OSBORNE MAVOR (JAMES BRIDIE)

AMONG THOSE who knew Osborne Mavor (alias James Bridie, alias Mary
Henderson) not at all, there used to exist an impression that he was a notorious
playboy, a dilettante, an irresponsible, a poseur, a farceur, clever perhaps at
light comedy dialogue, but lacking serious purpose or belief in life. Truly
enough he had earned for himself while a student at Glasgow University
the reputation of being a lightweight, pirouetting about as a sort of self-
advertised no-good: as an awful warning of where indolence and frivolity
leads the young.

Faced once with an examination paper on anatomy, the answers to
which were beyond him, he had flippantly written across the page:

" I should be wasting my own time and the time of my examiners
if I attempted to answer any of these questions."

And at his oral the professor said to him discouragingly:

" Well, Mr. Mavor, I suppose it is no secret to you that you know
nothing about Anatomy? You'll never be a doctor. Run away and be
an artist."

He was not the author or discoverer of the Gilmorehill war song
" Ygorra "—that was Arthur Wallace, who later landed in a sub-editorial
chair at the *Manchester Guardian* where he operated with great competence—
But Mavor churned out other popular nonsense rhymes of the period.
" Fairies in the West End Park " was his, and so too I think was the jingle
of which I recollect four lines:

" *Open your window the night is very derk*
The phantoms are dancing in the West End perk.

Thumbnails

Open your window, your lonely love to see
I'm here all alone and there's no-one here but me."

He developed, too, a considerable talent for cartoon drawing in the *G.U.M.* and which he was wont to sign: " Oh Did This."

But when he did take his degree in medicine he comported himself earnestly and efficiently in the art of healing, in hospital work, in army medical service for four years during the First World War, in general practice, as a consultant, and as a college lecturer. He took an almost passionate interest in the salaries of hospital nurses, and in the maintenance of the great voluntary hospitals, and one of the most persuasive and forceful pleas ever printed on their behalf was his *The Victoria Infirmary*.

But always he hankered after the writing of plays; there he knew his chief talent lay, but he was well aware that his reputation as a medical doctor suffered among his patients wherever his playwriting propensities became known. Hence his adoption of *noms de plume* for the stage, and when " James Bridie " the playwright had achieved an international reputation and Osborne Mavor had retired altogether from the practice of medicine —well, it was as James Bridie he was known to the end.

Of plays and books he had published some fifty-six—no hint of indolence there; he carried on a voluminous private correspondence, was always active in promoting causes, from Home Rule for Scotland and Citizens' Theatres, to the initiation of subscriptions and testimonials to artistic friends who had fallen by the wayside.

I think it was his Arts Council experience that excited him into Scottish Home Rule. He had been chairman of the Scottish Arts Council and chafed continuously along with his friend Dr. Tom Honeyman and his other Scottish Art Council colleagues, against the meticulous controls imposed from the London headquarters. Upon that subject he was declamant, and he used to discuss with me at the Art Club in Glasgow the prospect of our being able to induce a dozen or twenty prominent Anglo-Scots to cut their London ties and returning to their motherland, fight their battles out north of the Tweed, where their country needed them.

Mavor's head was sunk in his shoulders; his humorous eyes peered through his glasses and saw much—perhaps a little out of focus—of the whimsical and the absurd in contemporary life; he had a large mouth, a friendly smile, and could always light up a discussion with some quaint caprice or fancy. He would delight to tell of a Free Church clergyman of his acquaintance who, on becoming the subject of an abdominal operation, insisted upon being opened with prayer. Mavor would supply a note of his address to the reference books, as being c/o his banker. He declared that women smoking or drinking reminded him of " angels strapping their wings with electroplast to make themselves fit to associate with an income tax collector " (which analogy to me made a puzzlement, but no sense). He could describe a man as one who had " a face like the petticoat of Beelzebub's wife " (which was another mystery). He could make Mary Queen of Scots in a play, act the part of an hereditary secretary general of the Soviet Republic in Southern Russia. He could make Darnley a Communist Grand Duke and John Knox a Commissar.

Yet over and through his whimsies he could write the wittiest and most brilliant dialogue, and not only dialogue, but essays and vignettes too.[1] He could debunk any firmly held belief you chose; he could unleash himself in biting satire, for example his playlet " The Fat Women ", where he lashed out at the selfish scandalmongers who had sought the safe hotels during the First World War. He had some affinity with Dunbar's

" . . . Fyn Mackowel
That dang the Devill and gart him yowll."

But he did not set out to use the stage, as George Bernard Shaw did, as a vehicle for propaganda. Osborne Mavor's message was to amuse, and to the amusement of the public he devoted his great artistry and his lambent wit. He is beyond compare our most considerable Scottish playwright, and the Scottish Citizens' Theatre which he did so much to create is his enduring monument.

XII

SIR HUGH "ORPHEUS" ROBERTON

WHEN SIR HUGH ROBERTON, " the perfect choirmaster," whose economic bread and butter stand-by was a prosperous family business of funeral undertaking, announced at the age of 77 that he was going to lay down his *bâton* and disband the Glasgow Orpheus Choir, and that moreover all the members of the choir had agreed to disband, there was some amazed protest in Scotland.

The Orpheus under Sir Hugh's guidance had been singing in public for 45 years; it had staged 1300 concerts and 56 of them in London; it

---

[1] For example his *Some Talk of Alexander*, a collection of charming and amusing pen pictures of his war-time experiences on the Mespot and South Russian Fronts.

had sung in America and Germany, had achieved an international reputation and had put Scotland on the musical map; its disappearance therefore, declared the protestors, would leave a void; surely, surely there was some other conductor who could step into Sir Hugh's shoes and swing his baton!

But Sir Hugh's decision was the right one. Is not the world of journalism strewn with examples of what happens when the impress of the personality of a great editor is withdrawn? Garvin of the *Observer*, Blatchford of the *Clarion*, C. P. Scott of the *Manchester Guardian*, Delane of *The Times*! When the moving finger has written and moved on the successor has either to create his own ingenium and artistry, or the paper sags and withers. And so too with the Orpheus, the child of Roberton's flair and genius. Better there should arise new choirs and new efforts and leave intact and undisturbed the memory of the choir which has made Glasgow musically famous in two continents.

Upon me the fairies never bestowed the gift of sweet song, but I can respond to Sir Hugh's " Westering Home! " and I can still hear, after twenty years, the ringing tones of William Smith of Falkirk leading off as the Lettergae—the old precentor—in " Oh thou, my soul, bless God the Lord! " to the tune of French: and the choir's rendering of 23rd Psalm to Crimond. And Hugh Roberton once described to me and gave it as one of the major thrills of his life how a negro audience of 2000 in South Africa burst into " The Lord's My Shepherd " to the tune that the Orpheus had made popular over the world.

Hugh Roberton had a big family of sons, all of them dour, strong minded fellows like their father—from a Tory farmer M.P. in Australia to an extreme left winger in Canada—but all rallied to the support of their parent when he had his quarrel with the B.B.C. and refused to wind up his concerts with the National Anthem but insisted upon " Auld Lang Syne."

XIII

KEIR HARDIE

ONCE IT was a cloth cap: then a deerstalker: latterly a broad sombrero. When I knew him he was in the sombrero period: smoked a huge bent contraption of a pipe in the shape used by Bavarian peasants upon festive occasions: wore a Highland mackintosh cape coat, had a flowing artist's bow tie of some clan tartan design, and sported a huge watch chain, which ran diagonally down half one side his waistcoat. Philip Snowden reports that only once did he see him in a starched collar, and that there were apologies going for that lapse to convention—he explained he had been to his brother's wedding! Hardie's watch was a massive silver affair which bore marks of a favourite pit pony's teeth.

Philip Snowden tells of the one occasion when Hardie was induced to wear dress clothes. It was in Paris and Jaures had given him a ticket to the opera. Hardie had only his usual tweeds and flannel shirt and assumed that evening dress was essential, so recourse had to be made to a waiter who obliged with a spare evening coat and trousers, but no vest. Finally Hardie overcame that vest difficulty by wearing a broad silk sash, and so regaliaed he went to the opera. Judge his emotions when he and one other were the only two men in the theatre in evening dress.

Hardie when I knew him had a white beard, a well polished bald head, with fringes of white bushy hair; he had deep set rather sombre eyes; was of short sturdy build; an old evangelical from the Ayrshire moors. David Lowe[1] in describing the first meeting Hardie ever addressed—it was in 1879, and the occasion a presentation to Alexander Macdonald, the miners' leader—recalls how Hardie had prepared a long eulogium comparing Macdonald favourably with all the great men of history, beginning with Moses, but he never got farther down than Martin Luther because his description of Luther upset the predominantly Roman Catholic section of his audience, and the eulogist was actually threatened with physical violence.

Hardie was a collier, a journalist, an agitator who held fast to his faiths in all the storms and tempests of an agitator's life; an incorruptible if ever there was one. He had started out in adult life as a Good Templar, and there he remained to the end. He refused to speak for Labour Clubs which were licensed to retail alcohol, and was told: " You'll drive out many good men from the Labour Party." " I know," he replied, " and if I speak there I'll drive out many good women."

The snippet writers of the chit-chat columns called him Queer Hardie, and declared he had little sense of humour. That perhaps was true; he lived always on the edge of trouble and mass sorrow and hunger. But his face could light up with laughter, and he was filled to the brim with the old Scots ballads and with lore from the chap books. If you were interested in the politics of the left you were either a Hardie fan or you derided him as a sentimentalist. I was a Hardie fan.

Hardie was a prophet: a seer: a visionary. He told his friend Bruce Glasier that when he was in Parliament he felt like a bird with its wings

[1] *From Pit to Parliament.*

clipped. And much he suffered in his day from the animosities and bickerings apparently inevitable among splinter groups in all great causes.

Forgotten today may be his royal baby speech, when he broke through the House of Commons congratulations and monetary grants to another addition to the Royal Family with an impassioned plea for some note of condolence with and money grant to hundreds of widows and orphans who had lost their breadwinners in a Welsh pit disaster; forgotten today may be his pamphlets upon the Overtoun Horrors. But his struggles to build an independent workers' political party with Socialist ideals; and the insistence and ability with which he brought to public attention the principle of the Right to Work, have written his name indelibly upon the records of the working folk of these islands.

EPILOGUE

I LIKE well that story of the British naval interpreter with our supply expedition to Murmansk in the darkest days of the Great War when he became involved in angry altercation over some stores with his opposite number on the Russian side; the dispute raged furiously, and the Russian interpreter in conclusion pointed a derisory finger at the Britisher, yelling:

"I say, you know damn nothing, but I know damn all!"

That, however, I would hasten to dismiss as an inappropriate note upon which to close these selected reminiscences.

Nor, I am afraid, would I care to borrow for an epilogue from the triumphant eloquence of the late Sir William Mulock, Chief Justice of the Province of Ontario, who at the age of ninety-something could write:

"I am still at work with my hand to the plough and my face to the future. The shadows of evening lengthen about me, but morning is in my heart. I have lived from the forties of one century to the thirties of the next. I have had varied fields of labour and full contact with men and things, and I have warmed both hands before the fire of life. The testimony I bear is this; that the Castle of Enchantment is not yet behind me, it is before me still, and daily I catch glimpses of its battlefields and towers. The rich spoils of memory are mine. Mine too are the precious things of today—books, flowers, pictures, nature, and sport. The first of May is still an enchanted day to me; the best thing of all is friends. The best of life is always farther on. Its real lure is hidden from our eyes somewhere beyond the hills of time."

But although Sir William Mulock's epilogue is perhaps too Methuselah-Ancient of Ways, too much like cheer-leading and encouragement for a wearied runner on a last lap, still has he not a message for his juniors and for those who are still playing in the first half of life? Is not his eloquent survey one of essential gratitude and thankfulness that opportunities were allowed him to serve his fellows in some affairs of importance, and that he seized his opportunities as they came, and clung to them ere they passed? And what indeed can any one of us ask more than just that?

Epilogue

And there was old Lucius Cincinnatus too, a great character, whose renunciation of pomp and power and the rewards offered by the Senate rings down the ages as a great epilogue. He had saved Rome from the Volsci; all he asked was to be allowed to return to his farm by the banks of the Tiber, and be swallowed up in the obscurity of common citizenship.

Bertrand Russell says somewhere: " The past does not change or strive. Like Duncan in Macbeth, ' After Life's fitful fever it sleeps well.' What was eager and grasping, what was petty and transitory has faded away. The things that were beautiful and eternal shine out like stars in the night." Well, one would fain hope that is true and that our shortcomings and weaknesses and fumblings will be forgotten. And in the comparative obscurity and quietude of common citizenship in this realm, may it be counted to me for something of wisdom, and in expiation of my manifold follies and ineptitudes, that the message I was able to give my countrymen was that in co-operation and mutual aid and not in fratricidal strife can we win through to material plenty for all, and to a spiritual and cultural development and greatness for each of us.

Index

Index

Index

Simon, Sir John, 84
Sinclair, Sir Archibald, 149n, 190
Sinclair, Upton, 33
Singh, Sir Partarb, 70
Slimman, James, 15
Smart, Professor William, 41
Smillie, Robert, 236-8
Smith, Lees, 84
Smith, William, 245
Snowden, Lady, 217
Snowden, Philip, 58, 59, 102, 109, 222, 229, 246
Sokolinkoff, Mr., 98
Sorn Committee, 28
Stanley, Oliver, 50
Stephen, Campbell, 230
Stewart, William, 33
Strathclyde, Lord, 23
Streicher, Herr, 127
Sudan cotton estates, 48, 49
Suez canal, 68
Sullivan, Joe, 34, 35, 47, 48
Sutherland, Sir John, 187n
Swan, A. D., 143
Sweated imports, 53-5

Tchin, Andrei, 117
Tennant, Mr., 38
Tennessee Valley Authority, 150, 184, 210
Thomas, J. H., 35, 58, 103, 105, 106, 108
Thompson, Sir Basil, 128
Thomson, D. C., 136, 219, 220
Thomson, Sir William, 191
Tummel-Garry hydro-electric projects, 174, 176, 177

Turkey, ex-Sultan of, 49
Tweedmouth, Lord, 126

Unemployment, 93-8, 103-7

Vishinsky, Mr., 110, 119

Walker, Ryan, 33
Wallace, Arthur, 242
Wallas, Professor Graham, 199n
Wallhead, R. C., 58, 59
Ward, William C., 32
Warnings and Predictions, Rothermere, 125r.
Washington, 206
Waters, Dr., 235
Watson, Sir Duncan, 178
Webb, Sidney, 54
Weir, Sir Cecil, 139
Weir, McNeil, 47
Wells, H. G., 33, 117, 118, 120
Welsh, Major, 200
Westwood, Joe, 139
Wheatley, John, 33, 54, 230
Whiteley, Mr., 227
Wicksteed, Alexander, 121, 122
Wilson, Allan, 32
Winant, John G., 144, 235, 236
Wood, Sir Kingsley, 150
Wood, McKinnon, 232
Woodburn, Arthur, 154
Wotherspoon, Mr., 192

Yagoda, Mr., 123

Zinovieff Letter, the, 58, 59